# 109 WALKS

## IN BRITISH COLUMBIA'S LOWER MAINLAND

MARY & DAVID MACAREE

WITH **WENDY HUTCHEON**

# 109 WALKS

## in British Columbia's
## Lower Mainland

GREYSTONE BOOKS

D&M PUBLISHERS INC.

*Vancouver/Toronto/Berkeley*

Greystone Books
A division of D&M Publishers Inc.
2323 Quebec Street, Suite 201
Vancouver BC Canada V5T 4S7
www.greystonebooks.com

*Library and Archives Canada Cataloguing in Publication Data*
Macaree, Mary
109 walks in British Columbia's Lower Mainland/
Mary & David Macaree—6th rev. ed.

Includes index.
ISBN 978-1-55365-443-8

1. Walking—British Columbia—Lower Mainland—Guidebooks.
2. Trails—British Columbia—Lower Mainland—Guidebooks.
3. Lower Mainland (B.C.)—Guidebooks. I. Macaree, David II. Title.
III. Title: One hundred and nine walks in British Columbia's Lower Mainland.

GV199.44.C22B746 2009   917.11'3045   C2008-907725-3

Editing by Lucy Kenward (sixth edition)
Cover design by Jessica Sullivan
Cover photograph © Rich Wheater/Getty Images
Text design by Naomi MacDougall
Interior photographs by Mary Macaree and Wendy Hutcheon
Maps by Mary Macaree and Gray Mouse Graphics
Printed and bound in Canada by Friesens
Distributed in the U.S. by Publishers Group West

Printed on acid-free paper that is forest friendly (100% post-consumer recycled paper) and has been processed chlorine free.

We gratefully acknowledge the financial support of the Canada Council for the Arts, the British Columbia Arts Council, the Province of British Columbia through the Book Publishing Tax Credit and the Government of Canada through the Book Publishing Industry Development Program (BPIDP) for our publishing activities.

# Contents

. . . . .

Key to Map Symbols *xiii*

Index Map *xiv–xv*

Foreword *xvii*

Introduction *1*

### VANCOUVER

1 UBC Gardens (North) *6*

2 UBC Botanical Garden *8*

3 Pacific Spirit Regional Park *10*

4 Chancellor Woods *12*

5 Point Grey *14*

6 Musqueam/Fraser River *16*

7 Jericho Park/Spanish Banks *18*

8 English Bay *20*

9 False Creek *22*

10 Stanley Park *24*

11 Renfrew Triangle *26*

12 Champlain Heights *28*

### EAST OF VANCOUVER

13 Burnaby Heights/Trans Canada Trail *30*

14 Capitol Hill *32*

15 Burnaby Mountain West/SFU *34*

16 Burnaby Mountain *36*

17 Barnet Trails *38*

18 Burnaby Mountainside Trails *40*

19 SFU/Stoney Creek 42

20 Burnaby Lake 44

21 Brunette River 46

22 Deer Lake Park West 48

23 Deer Lake 50

24 Molson Way (Central) 52

25 Molson Way (South) 54

26 Burnaby Fraser Foreshore Park 56

27 Mundy Park 58

28 Shoreline Trail (Port Moody) 60

29 Sasamat Lake/Woodhaven Swamp 62

30 Buntzen Ridge 64

31 Belcarra Regional Park 66

32 Buntzen Lake 68

33 Colony Farm Regional Park 70

34 Ridge Park Loop 72

35 Coquitlam River/Town Centre Park 74

36 PoCo Trail 76

37 Woodland Walks (Lower Burke Ridge) 78

38 Minnekhada Regional Park 80

**WEST VANCOUVER**

39 Whytecliff 82

40 Seaview/Larsen Bay 84

41 Trans Canada Trail/Nelson Creek Loop 86

42 Lighthouse Park 88

43 Sahalee/Caulfeild Loop 90

44 Caulfeild Trail/Klootchman Park 92

45 Whyte Lake Loop 94

46 Cypress Falls Park 96

47 Hollyburn Mountain *98*

48 Lower Hollyburn *100*

49 McDonald Creek/Larson Creek Loop *102*

50 Brothers Creek Trails *104*

51 Hollyburn Heritage Trails *106*

52 Ballantree *108*


## WEST / NORTH VANCOUVER

53 Capilano Canyon *110*


## NORTH VANCOUVER

54 Bowser Trail *112*

55 Baden-Powell Trail (Grouse Mountain) *114*

56 Mosquito Creek *116*

57 Mahon Park *118*

58 Lynn Headwaters Loop *120*

59 Rice Lake *122*

60 Two-Canyon Loop *124*

61 Fisherman's Trail *126*

62 Maplewood Flats Wildlife Sanctuary *128*

63 Northlands Bridle Path *130*

64 Historic Mushroom Loop *132*

65 Three Chop/Old Buck Loop *134*

66 Goldie Lake *136*

67 Dog Mountain *138*

68 Mystery Lake and Peak *140*

69 Baden-Powell Trail (Deep Cove) *142*

70 Indian Arm Parks *144*

## SOUTH OF VANCOUVER

71 Lulu Island Dykes *146*

72 Richmond South Dyke Trail *148*

73 Richmond Nature Park *150*

74 Deas Island *152*

75 Boundary Bay Regional Park *154*

76 Elgin Heritage Park *156*

77 Redwood Park *158*

78 South Surrey Urban Forests *160*

79 Green Timbers Urban Forest *162*


## FRASER VALLEY SOUTH

80 Tynehead Regional Park *164*

81 Derby Reach Regional Park *166*

82 Campbell Valley *168*

83 Aldergrove Lake Regional Park *170*

84 Matsqui Trail *172*

85 Seven Sisters Trail *174*

86 Teapot Hill *176*


## FRASER VALLEY NORTH

87 Chatham Reach *178*

88 Alouette River Dykes *180*

89 Grant Narrows Regional Park *182*

90 UBC Malcolm Knapp Research Forest *184*

91 Mike Lake *186*

92 Alouette Nature Loop *188*

93 Gold Creek Trails *190*

94 Kanaka Creek *192*

95  Hayward Lake  *194*

96  Bear Mountain Trails  *196*

97  Mission Trail  *198*


**HOWE SOUND**

98  Killarney Lake  *200*

99  Shannon Falls  *202*

100 Squamish Estuary  *204*


**SQUAMISH / WHISTLER**

101  Four Lakes Trail  *206*

102  DeBeck Hill  *208*

103  Evans Lake Forest  *210*

104  Brohm Lake Interpretive Forest  *212*

105  Brohm Lake  *214*

106  Brandywine/Cal-Cheak  *216*

107  Crater Rim Loop  *218*

108  Cheakamus Lake  *220*

109  Shadow Lake Interpretive Forest  *222*


Useful Books  *224*

Web Sites  *224*

Walking Times  *225*

Round-trip Distances  *228*

Acknowledgements  *232*

Index  *233*

Your hiking days are over, but your memory lives on long after in the walks and hikes in the mountains you have left behind in your books. One has no idea of the pleasure there is in hiking and climbing; to reach one's goal—high or low—is a wonderful, all-embracing feeling. You have opened up this avenue to so many to gain so much pleasure. We are proud to have had you for family, and we shall miss you.

{ THE CLAN ALEXANDER }

# KEY TO MAP SYMBOLS

| | | | | | | |
|---|---|---|---|---|---|---|
| ════════ | highway, freeway | ⓟ | parking and starting point | ∩ | monument | |
| ────── | paved road | ❶ | information station | ∩ | corral | |
| ──── | street | ☀ | navigational light | ▲ | campground | |
| ========== | unpaved road | ⌐ | microwave tower | ◠ | informal campsite | |
| +++++++ | railroad | | viewing tower or other tower | ⅂ | picnic area | |
| ------------ | described trail | | | | boat launch ramp | |
| ▬▬▬▬▬ | trail is parallel to road | ▯ | tank, water tower | ) ( | bridge, boardwalk, trestle | |
| ············· | walk on road | ⊗ | lookout | | | |
| ·············· | other trail | 🖾 | viewpoint | ❀ ❀ | marsh | |
| ║║║║║║║ | stairway | 🏠 | large building | | | |
| ···················· | route | ⬈ | school | ⌒ | river or stream | |
| ─ ─ · · ─ | park boundary or other boundary | ⌂ | church | ╫ | waterfall | |
| ⋀ ⋀ ⋀ | power line | ⬛ | small building, cabin or lodge | ⬅ | direction of stream flow | |
| ✕ ✕ ✕ ✕ | fence | 🏭 | factory | | | |
| •──•──• | ski lift | ▭ | reservoir | ⬅ | direction of river flow | |
| ♣ | Trans-Canada highway | ▭ | sports field | | | |
| 99 | provincial highway | ⊟ | cemetery | ⬭ | body of water | |
| •─• | gate | | | | | |
| ▬ | parking area | | | | | |
| ▭ | large parking lot | | | | | |

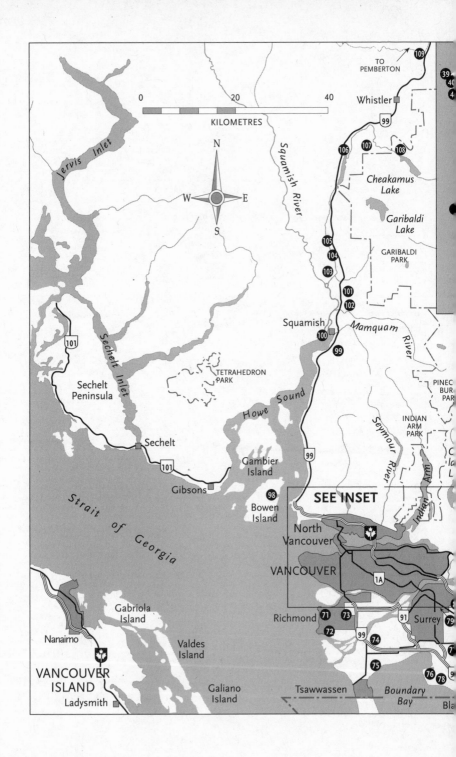

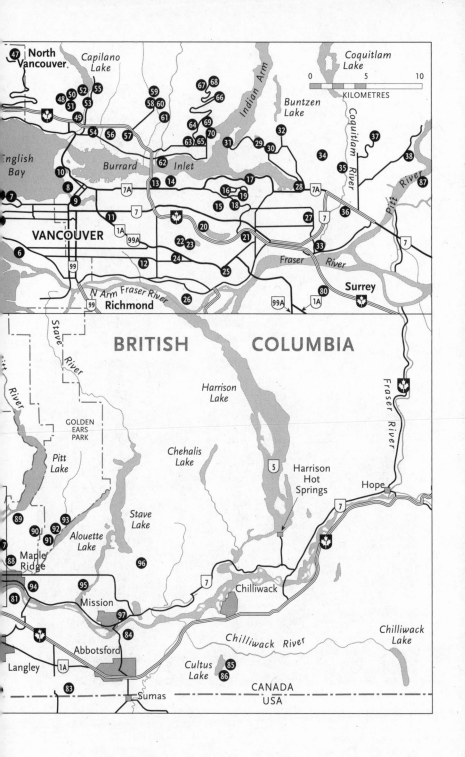

# FOREWORD

MARY MACAREE always said that she liked to have a project on the go, and *109 Walks in British Columbia's Lower Mainland* was a project that lasted more than 30 years. Along with its companion volume, *103 Hikes in Southwestern British Columbia*, these guides have made the wilderness spaces in and around Vancouver accessible to several generations of walkers and hikers. Before she passed away in July 2008, Mary and her late husband, David, had between them written, illustrated and updated nearly ten editions of these books.

In 1955 when the Macarees immigrated to Canada from Scotland, they could hardly have imagined what would lie ahead. Both of them were keen on the outdoors, Mary having grown up on a farm and David having spent many years serving with the Royal Marines during the Second World War, and soon they had joined two local clubs, the North Shore Hikers and the British Columbia Mountaineering Club (BCMC). With other club members—many of them also new immigrants from Europe curious to explore their adopted country—they spent many weekends exploring peaks in the area and establishing and clearing little-used trails on the North Shore Mountains.

A like-minded group of hikers and mountaineers based in Seattle had banded together as The Mountaineers, founding a book publishing company in 1960 and successfully printing several guidebooks of trails in northern Washington. No trail guides existed for the areas north of the border, however, and The Mountaineers approached the executive of the BCMC in 1966 to see whether any of its members would be interested in putting one together. A committee of BCMC members was struck, and following criteria set by The Mountaineers, the group was charged with assembling 103 hikes, all four hours or longer and with a trail or a discernible route.

As The Mountaineers had already published three previous volumes, *100, 101* and *102 Hikes*, this fourth book was meant to follow the same format, which is to say, concise instructions accompanied by one or more photos and a map. Progress, however, was slow. By the early 1970s, the members had come up with only forty-seven hikes. However, the committee chair, John Harris, submitted fifty more, and the club had the makings of book. Still, the scribbles had to be turned into readable prose, and David—who was a faculty member in the English Department at UBC—was asked to help write the text.

As the book started to take shape, The Mountaineers were able to secure a favourable rate with a local Vancouver printer as long as the printing took place by a certain date. The Labour Day deadline loomed, and Mary and David stepped in to help fill in missing gaps in the text and to supply additional photographs. Working evenings and weekends around her full-time job as the head librarian at MacMillan Library, Mary also hand-drew all of the maps, and she spent the entire long weekend doing the layout, essentially pasting all of the pieces onto boards so they could be printed the following week. The first printing of that first book—6¾ × 8½ inches with two columns per page and the statistics at the end of the hike—came out in November 1973 and was so successful that it was reprinted in April 1974 even before the snow had melted enough to begin hiking!

*109 Walks*, a guide to walks four hours and shorter, was published for the first time in 1976. Just three years later, a second edition of *103 Hikes*—in a smaller 5½ × 8½-inch size—was due to be published by The Mountaineers. The BCMC had given Mary and David Macaree approval to become sole authors of the books, without having to involve an entire committee. However, with more than 100 trails to walk, they spent countless evenings and weekends hiking and researching so they could update the text and maps as old trails changed and new ones were added. Just as the second edition was due to be published, a small recession hit the United States and the company was persuaded to turn over distribution rights to this title, and *109 Walks*, to Douglas & McIntyre, then a small Canadian publishing company based in Vancouver.

Having gathered an enormous amount of knowledge about local hikes and walks, Mary and David were favourite tour leaders. After they retired in 1985, David originated and led the Ramblers, a hiking group based out of the West Vancouver Seniors' Centre, and Mary led many hikes with the Vancouver Natural History Society and two groups—loosely made up of friends and friends-of-friends—known as the Wednesday and Sunday groups. Throughout this time they continued to update their guidebooks and ultimately produced four editions of *103 Hikes* (the two subsequent editions have been written by Jack Bryceland) and five editions of *109 Walks*.

In essence, Mary and David devoted their lives to recording and mapping trails in the Lower Mainland. They were helped by many BCMC and North Shore Hikers members (and many friends who were members of neither club)—but they were the prime movers. Clearly, these books have become of inestimable value for the hiking community of Vancouver and environs. The Macarees were devoted to making sure that others could enjoy this landscape, and they were working on these books long before the current craze for hiking and walking existed. In this respect, they were real trailblazers.

The books certainly—but also this community they have created—are Mary and David's legacies, and they will continue to inspire new generations of hikers and walkers and work to protect the natural areas these two so enjoyed. All royalties from the sale of this sixth edition of the book will be donated to the British Columbia Mountaineering Club for conservation purposes.

# INTRODUCTION

THIS SIXTH edition of *109 Walks* retains, with a few exceptions, the principles established in its predecessors: the walks described are generally less than 4 hours; elevation gains, if any, are moderate, and routes are clearly established; and, with the exception of Vancouver itself and West Vancouver, in each area, walks nearer the city centre precede those farther afield. Descriptions, both verbal and graphic, record the state of affairs at the time of publication. However, you should be on the alert for possible changes due to human intervention, natural disasters or both. Houses, schools and shopping malls spring up where once was freedom to roam; flash floods and washouts are all too commonplace, given this area's climate and topography.

We focus on walks close to the region's population centres, Vancouver and its neighbouring municipalities, though we also provide for those of you who want to sample the trails in the vicinity of campgrounds or combine country excursions with walks. Many walks are accessible by public transport, especially within the metropolitan area, and study of the transit system (or a telephone call to TransLink's information line, 604-953-3333) will often suggest a one-way in preference to the out-and-back walk required of those captive to their cars. For all outings, we mention approaches, provide liberal time allotments and, in the case of the longer walks, suggest intermediate destinations. When distances of less than a kilometre are supplied in the text, they are given in metres only, as one yard is roughly equivalent to one metre. Please note that distance alone is not a sufficient guide: the state of a trail and its ups and downs are important factors in determining how long a walk will take, and thus we have included elevation gains of 150 m (490 ft) or more. Note also that the weather and seasonal variations may affect the "Best" period suggested for any walk, more particularly in rural areas. Be prepared, therefore, when hiking in forest or on mountain, to abandon any outing if you find conditions beyond your capabilities or the daylight hours too short to permit your safe return.

We are pleased to record the appearance of new walks as well as the refurbishing of some old favourites. Lately, the idea of the long-distance trail has sparked popular imagination; thus, the 1971 Baden-Powell Centennial Trail from Horseshoe Bay to Deep Cove has been succeeded more recently by the more ambitious Trans Canada Trail, and the distinctive TCT markers now appear along many familiar routes. Another fairly recent positive trend has been the increased involvement of public bodies in trail creation and maintenance, supplementing the activities of outdoor clubs and individuals. B.C. Parks, regional districts and the B.C. Forest Service are joined in their activities by municipal boards and even B.C. Hydro. An unexpected spin-off from SkyTrain a decade ago was the creation of B.C. Parkway, one element of which is John Molson Way, spanning the 21 km (13 mi) between Vancouver's Main Street and New Westminster Quay, with scenic features en route devised by the area's cultural communities. And the provincial government, the North Shore municipalities, First Nation leaders and other agencies and organizations are at work on the development of the North Shore Spirit Trail, a 35-km (22-mi) greenway that will connect existing paths with several new routes all the way from Horseshoe Bay to Deep Cove. At the short end of the distance scale, imaginative green strips and trail systems have been designed in new residential neighbourhoods and augment facilities in municipal parks, themselves expanding opportunities for the walker.

Should you seek company on the trail, the Federation of Mountain Clubs of B.C. (604-873-6096) will provide information about outdoor clubs, and many community centres sponsor walking groups. If you wish to go out informally with a few friends, you have many aids to assist you. Major provincial, regional and municipal parks often supply brochures at their entrances, as does B.C. Hydro at its recreation sites. A useful publication produced by TransLink is its *Getting Around: Transportation Map and Guide for the Metro Vancouver Area* (available from 7-Eleven and Safeway stores), as well as its many schedules for the various municipalities (available in public libraries or on its Web site). Tourist infocentres, too, and many municipalities now produce leaflets describing opportunities for walking within their boundaries. As well, most organizations today have Web sites with more or less up-to-date, more or less useful information.

In addition, you may wish to have a basic stock of maps, including the two City Series maps: *Greater Vancouver, British Columbia* (including Whistler) and *Fraser Valley, British Columbia,* (including Whistler) published by Rand McNally and free to members from the British Columbia Automobile Association (604-268-5000). A good selection of recreation maps, as well as the federal topographic map series, is available from International Travel Maps and Books, 12300 Bridgeport Road, Richmond, B.C. v6v 1J5 (604-273-1400).

Part of the pleasure of walking is combining it with other pursuits: bird and animal watching, the study of rocks, flowers, fungi, trees and other natural features, plus local history as represented in various restored buildings, old roads and abandoned rights-of-way. All these, along with the health-giving effects of exercise, are yours for a minimal expenditure on books or equipment. Necessary, of course, are stout boots or shoes, well broken in, and suitable clothing for this province's changeable weather. You will want food and liquid for all but the shorter walks, and sunscreen has become a constant necessity in these days of the thinning ozone layer. You will want sunglasses and, last but not least, a first-aid kit to take care of accidents, though these are no more likely on a woodland walk than on our downtown streets.

Outdoor etiquette requires that you do not damage trails by cutting corners, and you will, of course, leave gates as you find them. In fact, please leave all property, public and private, undisturbed, and carry out any garbage, leaving the surroundings unspoiled for others to enjoy. These few injunctions aside, the freedom of the trails is yours.

# 109 walks

# UBC GARDENS (NORTH)

**Round trip** 4 km (2.5 mi)         **Allow** 1.5 hours

**Paths and roads**         **Good all year**

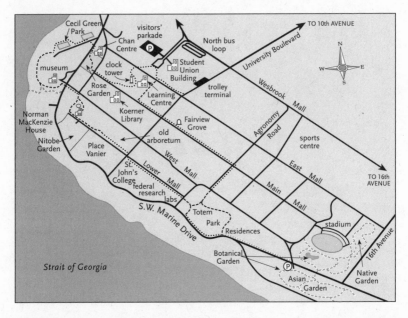

THE UNIVERSITY OF British Columbia, despite its superb setting, provides little inspiring architecture. For this reason a campus walk is best fashioned through its gardens and along treed avenues, where, especially in spring and summer, art and nature are in harmony. In fact, you may enjoy a world tour—a European-style rose garden, a Japanese landscape in miniature, and a park with totem poles and related West Coast Indian artifacts.

With public transport, you begin at the North bus loop on Wesbrook Mall just west of University Boulevard, while visitors' parking is available nearby. From either arrival point, walk right of the Student Union Building (SUB), cross East Mall and with the new Irving K. Barber Learning Centre on your left enter the old Main Library Gardens. From here continue to Main Mall, the plate-glass Koerner Library now before you a striking contrast to the old buildings of the original university core. Turn right along the tree-shaded avenue towards the flagpole, with its magnificent marine and mountain view in front, and below the glories of a formal rose garden.

From the viewpoint, descend through the garden, veering right by the

Gardens at the Asian Centre.

Chan Centre for the Performing Arts before crossing NW Marine Drive and going left past Green College and then right into Cecil Green Park, with its attractive grounds and fine view. Next make your way west and south along the cliff top opposite the Museum of Anthropology, finally going left past Haida House and its totems to arrive in front of the museum. Cross NW Marine Drive here onto West Mall and take a path between the C.K. Choi Building and International House that leads you through tall trees to the templelike Asian Centre with the Pacific Bell in its courtyard. A few steps more bring you to the Japanese Nitobe Memorial Garden (admission fee in season) with its ornamental gate and its miniscule rendering of a whole landscape: a river system from mountain stream to deltaic marshland, complete with a lake surrounded by cherry trees, which make a rare show of blossoms in spring. There is even a Japanese teahouse, expertly reconstructed.

When you emerge, go south along Lower Mall, passing on your left the old arboretum with the First Nations House of Learning in its midst, and on your right more trees surrounding the Place Vanier complex. Continuing thus, cross the end of University Boulevard, pass St. John's College and the Marine Residences. Next cross Agronomy Road and make your way towards Totem Park Residences with the little wooded Totem Park itself on your right. Now, leaving the Botanical Garden with its outstanding collections for another day, go left, cutting through on residence pathways to West Mall and Agronomy Road and thus to Main Mall, on which you turn north for the last lap of your trip. Presently, on your left, you pass the Barn, rescued and restored for its role as a coffee shop when the farm moved to the south campus; and, on the right, the remnants of another piece of university history, Fairview Grove, a commemoration of UBC's first home, now in danger of being overwhelmed by new construction.

Continuing northwards you come to the intersection with University Boulevard, beyond which you continue along Main Mall, passing the university's simple War Memorial before going right, perhaps to linger in the Library Gardens before heading back across East Mall to bus or car.

# UBC BOTANICAL GARDEN

**Round trip** 4 km (2.5 mi)

**Paths**

**Allow** 2 hours or more

**Good all year**

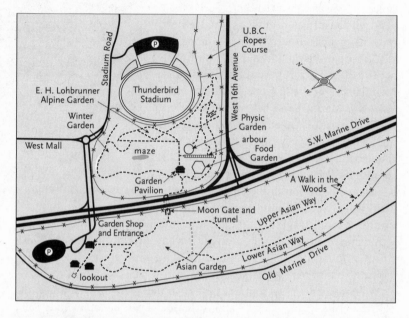

IF YOU ENJOYED your tour of the gardens at the north end of the university campus, you will delight in the variety offered by those at the south end. Armed with the map available at the entrance, you can stroll "through 44 ha (110 acres) of gardens to see alpine and Asian treasures, medicinal and culinary plants and the towering trees of a B.C. coastal native forest." So reads the brochure, which goes on to look at the history of the UBC Botanical Garden and to describe its role as a resource for teaching and research.

The garden is located on SW Marine Drive, across from Stadium Road, itself just west of the traffic lights at West 16th Avenue and Marine. Once through the entrance formalities (payment of your admission fee), a pathway leads into the David C. Lam Asian Garden. Here you are in a world of tall trees, massed rhododendrons and magnolias, plus a variety of exotic shrubs and climbing vines. It is a wonderful place for hot-day walking, its shady paths abloom with a profusion of primulas, Himalayan blue poppies and Asiatic dogwood. But each season has its beauty and you will want to experience every one.

E.H. Lohbrunner Alpine Garden.

To progress through the maze of trails, try going right on Straley or Stearn to Lower Asian Way, then stay with it as it heads south making little forays aside to points of interest. Finally, after passing a wide meadow with a large rock, an erratic left by the receding glaciers, you come to "A Walk in the Woods" trail, a 20-minute loop through relatively undisturbed second-growth forest, with explanatory signs along the way. At the end of the "Walk" you find yourself on the Upper Asian Way, heading north. Eventually, you are back on a paved pathway with, on your right, the Chinese Moon Gate guarding the tunnel under sw Marine Drive and the path to the North Gardens.

On the other side of the tunnel an imposing Garden Pavilion lies athwart several paths, so you may wish to explore its facilities and study the garden layout from its balcony. Along the path to the north, various areas on the left have been named for noteworthy botanists and plant explorers while in the midst of the meadow, to the right, a unicursal maze has been fashioned. Above, the slope has been landscaped to make the E.H. Lohbrunner Alpine Garden (named for the collection's donor), the garden containing representative plants from the world's mountain regions. As you travel east, various trails lead into and around the B.C. Native Garden, which contains indigenous plants, shrubs and trees. Stepping stones ease the way across the boggy lands around a small pond and bring you back to the main trail south into the utilitarian gardens. The first of these is the Physic Garden, a re-creation of a medieval garden of medicinal plants, and separating these from the Food Garden is a large wooden arbour with a fine display of climbing plants and vines. Finally, on the outer perimeter of the Food Garden itself, an amazing array of espalier-trained apple trees line the path, while in the centre, fruit and vegetable cultivation for private homes is demonstrated.

This brings to an end your circumambulation of the North Gardens. To return, descend into the tunnel to the west and, back at the Moon Gate, turn right to end an inspiring and instructive outing.

# PACIFIC SPIRIT REGIONAL PARK

**NORTH TO SOUTH: Round trip** 8 km (5 mi)     **Allow** 3 hours

**EAST TO WEST: Round trip** 5.5 km (3.4 mi)     **Allow** 2.5 hours

**Trails**     **Good all year**

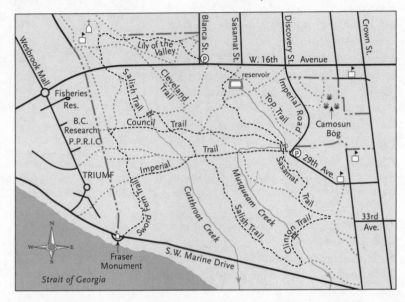

THIS REGIONAL PARK encompassing the former University Endowment Lands has a surprising drawback for the uninitiated walker: too many trails rather than too few. At first glance, even the map provided at the information office off West 16th Avenue is somewhat overwhelming. To help you get started, here are two walks, one from north to south, the other from east to west, each described by naming the trails used, names celebrating the history and natural history of the area.

For the former, a good parking spot is on Blanca Street just north of 16th (with a bus stop nearby), where Vine Maple Trail takes you into the forest, meeting Newt Loop shortly after. Then Newt is taken over in its turn by Lily of the Valley after crossing Salal. Finally, you reach your major trail, Salish, after one more path crossing. Turn left (south). On Salish, you first intersect a power line (Heron Trail) and, beyond one more fork, must cross busy West 16th Avenue prior to continuing on Salish.

On this part of your walk, you follow Salish (now briefly joined with Hemlock Trail) over Zeke's Bridge and after crossing Council Trail arrive at

Imperial Trail in winter.

the wide clearing of Imperial, once a road but now reverting nicely to lane condition, the illusion of rusticity spoiled only by the power line that runs along it. Here you must go left for a short distance before picking up Salish again. Turn right onto it, plunging once more into the forest. At last, however, the sound of traffic disturbs your sylvan idyll, the signal that you are reaching sw Marine Drive, and here you leave the trail that you have followed so long, going left to pick up Clinton, then, on the verge of a wide clearing by the West 33rd Avenue entrance, forking left again on Sasamat, your main return route. On it, you recross Imperial, reach a covered reservoir and, having skirted its edge, go briefly left on Top Trail before emerging on 16th again, a short distance from where you started.

For the other outing, drive south off 16th on Imperial Road until, at a divider, it breaks back sharply to become West 29th Avenue. Park here and set off along the one-time road beyond the barrier, gently descending, and perhaps noting the two segments of Salish Trail as you pass them. Where the power line you have been following goes straight ahead, you veer off left, the forest deepening around you. The disembodied voice that you may hear need not disturb you; it is merely the public-address system of TRIUMF, tri-university meson facility. But before that installation has come into sight, you have turned left on Sword Fern, to emerge unexpectedly on sw Marine Drive just opposite Simon Fraser's monument.

Here, at the top of the sheer drop to the North Arm of the river that bears Fraser's name, you have a view of the deltaic lowlands and the southern Gulf Islands. Now, recross sw Marine Drive and return on Sword Fern as the start of your way back. This time, however, stay with the trail when it crosses Imperial and stay with it as it intersects two more routes, Long and Powerline, before you turn right onto Council Trail, which, most accommodatingly, takes you back to your starting point.

# CHANCELLOR WOODS

**SHORT CIRCUIT: Round trip** 3.9 km (2.4 mi)  **Allow** 1 hour
**LONG CIRCUIT: Round trip** 6 km (3.7 mi)  **Allow** 2 hours
**Trails**  **Good all year**

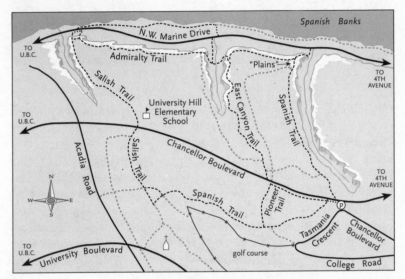

THE NORTHERN SEGMENT of Pacific Spirit Regional Park—extending from Chancellor Boulevard to Spanish Banks—contains a number of trails, mostly in forest. There is, however, considerable variety of tree cover, some quite deep ravines, and the beach if you want an alternative route for part of the way.

The trail system lends itself to circular walks; so, described here are two of them, starting from the same point and in part covering the same ground. Your point of departure, at the break in Chancellor Boulevard, allows you to park off a main thoroughfare; it is convenient for buses also, being only a short distance west of Blanca Loop. If driving, turn west off Blanca Street onto Chancellor Boulevard and drive to road's end at a small grove of young trees. Just beyond, Chancellor is reborn, connecting with West 4th Avenue on a considerable bend. Cross here to the north side.

Now, take Spanish Trail into the forest, travelling north among tall trees, second-growth though they are, as the great stumps of the original forest show. Thus, you proceed in the midst of fine cedar, Douglas-fir and hemlock, the trail dropping gently as you advance until, after some 20 minutes,

Sunshine-dappled forest path.

you find yourself at a three-way junction. The little track beyond the stile takes you into an overgrown field, the remains of a pioneer homestead on the "Plains of Abraham." Cross to the seaward side and, if you do not wish to drop to the beach here, turn left to head west close to the edge of the bluffs on Admiralty Trail. Next comes a deep ravine, and here is the parting of the ways: the left-hand trail gives a short outing of 3.9 km (2.4 mi) that takes about an hour, while the right-hand branch descends into the depths.

The shorter route follows the ravine's eastern edge fairly closely, though it is forced away from the main canyon by washouts here and there. As you head inland, you begin to hear traffic and you find yourself back on the boulevard some distance west of where you started. To return, you may use the pedestrian sidewalk on the south side; however, an attractive alternative presents itself if you take the forest trail (Pioneer) into the woods opposite. Follow this for some 300 m to a cross trail and go left. At the next fork, go left again and you are back near your point of departure.

On the longer loop, you drop into the ravine, necessitating a climb out of it again if you wish to continue on the bluffs. You may, however, avoid this by crossing NW Marine Drive and walking along the beach until the road starts uphill. A little above the Acadia Beach parking lot, recross to the landward side and pick up Salish Trail heading inland past the west end of Admiralty Trail. Now you proceed above another deep gully until you emerge by University Hill Elementary School, with Chancellor Boulevard just ahead of you.

Use the pedestrian crossing and stay with Salish south to its intersection with Spanish Trail, then go left. This track goes through scrub timber and crosses a creek before entering nice open forest. Here, you are joined by the short route on Pioneer Trail and henceforth the two routes coincide, with the next fork left bringing you back to houses and transportation.

# POINT GREY

**Round trip** 13 km (8 mi)

Beach, paths, roads and trails

Allow 4.5 hours

Good all year

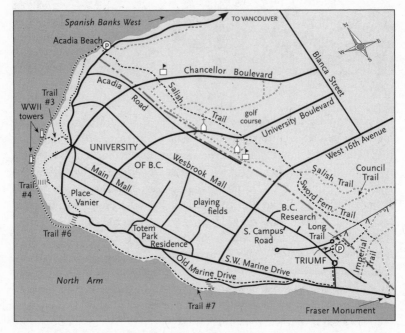

HERE IS A circuit that you may shorten or lengthen according to your inclination, thanks to various trails connecting the beach with the cliff top near UBC. Your starting point is at Acadia Beach parking lot west of Spanish Banks, where NW Marine Drive begins its rise towards the university. (The Spanish Banks bus stop is some 20 minutes' walk to the east.)

First, you wander west along the beach, then, after about 25 minutes, by an old searchlight tower, comes Trail 3, the ascent of which, with a turn left at the top onto the path downhill alongside Marine Drive, gives you a short circular tour with views of mountain and city on the return leg. If you stay on the beach, you see evidence of the sometimes spectacular effects of erosion as you make for a second wartime installation like the first tower, then round the point for the first sight of the Fraser River's North Arm breakwater. Here, you have a second flight of steps, Trail 4, this one giving access to a point just south of UBC's Museum of Anthropology.

To complete this circuit of 5 km (3.1 mi), go left along the track behind

Steps on Trail #3.

the museum and proceed past Cecil Green House and Green College via a one-time section of Marine Drive to its intersection with the present thoroughfare near the top of Trail 3, whence you take the same route as the shorter walk. Yet a third option is to continue farther along the beach to Trail 6, which brings you up opposite the Place Vanier Residences. This time you turn back left on Marine Drive until, just beyond Norman Mackenzie House, you go left again to join the earlier trail behind the museum.

If you are really ambitious and are not deterred by numerous downed trees and other obstacles, make for Wreck Beach itself, working along the bottom of the treed slope on a rough route that skirts the mud flats and salt marshes to reach the next access point, Trail 7, the original Wreck Beach Trail. Here you must choose. The one-time pleasant trail that continued along the shore (providing access to the Fraser Monument and thus to the Sword Fern Trail at its Marine Drive terminus) has been rendered well-nigh impassable by several landslides and is no longer recommended. One alternative is, of course, to return to Trail 6 and complete the loop as described from there. Otherwise, ascend the steps of Trail 7 emerging on Old Marine Drive, follow it to the right until it merges with the new sw Marine, then head right alongside the busy thoroughfare to its junction with Wesbrook Mall. Turn left here and walk north past a traffic circle, working to the left of the greatly expanded TRIUMF buildings and across the parking lot towards the forest, where you veer first slightly right on a well-made trail then left on Long Trail finally to enjoy peace amid the majestic trees.

Very soon you come to Sword Fern Trail, which, with a few interruptions, goes clear across Pacific Spirit Regional Park. Turn left, then, on Sword Fern and stay with it as it crosses Powerline and Council Trails and then is absorbed temporarily by Salish, which you follow to West 16th Avenue. Now, though you might jog left here to regain Sword Fern, which continues along the margin of the forest, your best plan is to stay with Salish as it winds its way towards University Boulevard, on the far side of which it continues, to be reunited with Sword Fern a little short of Chancellor Boulevard. Cross this thoroughfare and enter the trees again beyond the elementary school, a verdant ravine on your left as you near NW Marine Drive and the parking lot.

# MUSQUEAM / FRASER RIVER

**Round trip** 9 km (5.6 mi)

**Trails**

**Allow** 3 hours

**Good all year**

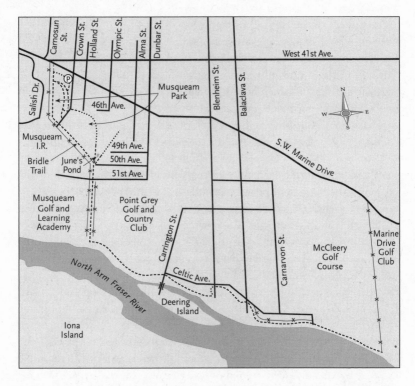

**DESPITE ITS NEARNESS** to the city, this area includes woodland, a marsh with ditches, the Fraser River's North Arm, sloughs and mud flats and the vegetation endemic to the different environments. To begin, park on Crown Street just south of sw Marine Drive and a little east of its junction with West 41st Avenue, buses also being conveniently nearby.

Here you are beside Musqueam Park and you walk across the grass towards its treed western edge, where you turn roughly south on a bridle trail. Quite soon a foot trail heads into the forest on the left along a shallow, lush ravine. Then you come to a T-junction at which it is immaterial whether you go left or right. Both routes lead to Crown Street where you go right for a short distance, then left once more, this time back on the bridle trail.

Next you cross a large covered water main at ground level, and here you

Shelter on Deering Island.

fork half right, continuing more or less southwards. Stay with the bridle trail as it crosses West 51st Avenue, now with a deep drainage ditch on your right separating you from the Musqueam Golf and Learning Academy while the Point Grey Golf and Country Club is to your left. Then comes the river, with views up, down and across to Iona Island. Still on the bridle trail, you turn upstream, the golf course on your left separated by a fringe of trees, and an impenetrable wall of shrubs and blackberries. Then comes the access road and bridge to Deering Island, part of which had been preserved as park, at the end of which is a shelter with four panels in its roof spelling out the history of Deering and Celtic Islands.

Back on the mainland the route now continues eastwards on a path between some stables and a slough across which lie the houses of Deering Island and the mooring ramps for their pleasure craft. At the next street end you encounter the "Booming Grounds Rock" inscribed with the story of the booming grounds that once were here. Then you are forced out onto the Celtic Avenue, but only temporarily if you follow a little track heading right into the scrub and providing an off-road alternative. At your next emergence onto Celtic Avenue follow the trail bounded by a white rail fence to separate it from the large properties planned for an area once occupied by the B.C. Forest Service Marine Station and "the last wooden ship-building facility in the Lower Mainland"; a maintenance depot existed here from 1941–81. Still heading upstream, you come to a stretch with views over the pleasant public McCleery Golf Course until you are brought to a halt at the approach to the less-welcoming Marine Drive Golf Club grounds.

So you retrace your steps, until, having turned north at the Musqueam Golf Academy, you go half right on the water-main path just beyond June's Pond, a plaque commemorating her work to protect the Musqueam Park wetlands. This route takes you to the south end of a wide grassy sward where you bear right to West 46th Avenue, and, when it ends at Holland Street, go straight ahead on the little lane to Crown, just where it changes direction. A little to the right, a track goes off into this most northerly part of Musqueam Park and takes you back to your transport.

# JERICHO PARK / SPANISH BANKS

**Round trip** 6 km (3.7 mi)

**Trails and streets**

**Allow** 2 hours

**Good all year**

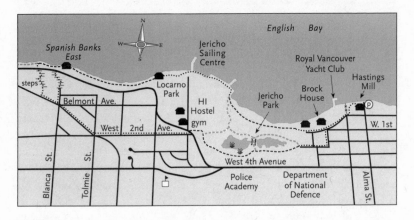

SPARED FROM RESIDENTIAL development, Jericho Park, a pocket wilderness north of West 4th Avenue between Wallace Street and NW Marine Drive, was opened to the public when the Department of National Defence relinquished it several decades ago. At that time, a whole stretch of parkland fronting English Bay became available to walkers. Nor are you confined to one route: walks of varying length are possible; even round trips along streets of stately Point Grey dwellings are feasible.

To make the most of what this area has to offer, begin not in Jericho Park proper but at the Hastings Mill Store Museum at the end of Alma just north of where it meets Point Grey Road. (The nearest bus stop is at 4th and Alma.) The unpretentious wooden building is a relic of Vancouver's earliest days: built in 1865 by Capt. Edward Stamp, it served as the first post office, community library and recreation centre on Burrard Inlet.

Starting here, cross little Pioneer Park and head west past the Royal Vancouver Yacht Club and Jericho Tennis Club before swinging past Brock House Senior Centre (once the Brock family home) towards the beach and a small Park Board pavilion. From now on, you have the North Shore mountains across the bay on your right and Bowen Island more or less ahead as you step, on the seaward side of a small lagoon, towards what is left of the old Jericho army base, now the Jericho Sailing Centre. Once past it, continue

Lagoon in Jericho Park.

half left towards a grove of trees, and you come to a second pavilion, at Locarno Beach.

This landmark may serve as the destination of a short walk (round trip about one hour); however, if you wish to go farther, there is nothing to stop you. Make your way, then, to Spanish Banks East, with its refreshment counter and changing rooms. Here, too, you may turn around. An interesting alternative presents itself, though, if you do not wish to return by your outward route.

Across NW Marine Drive, you will note a flight of steps ascending the steep bank on the landward side. These bring you out at the foot of Blanca Street, and a short walk uphill leads to a five-way intersection. This point you may also reach by a slightly longer route if, from Spanish Banks East, you continue westwards on the waterfront to about halfway along the parking lot, where another set of stairs ascends to emerge on Belmont Avenue. Turning left along this street of majestic homes takes you to the five-way crossing where you go half right onto Bellevue and down West 2nd, passing Aberthau, a one-time gracious home, now a community centre. From here, recross NW Marine Drive and return across Jericho Park, this time taking the track south of the lagoon, perhaps pausing a little to watch the wildlife in its vicinity, before heading back towards Pioneer Park and the end of your excursion.

# ENGLISH BAY

**Round trip** 13 km (8 mi) or less

**Paths and ferry**

**Allow** 4 hours

**Good all year**

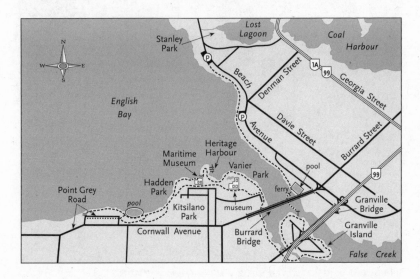

HERE, IN ONE of Vancouver's most attractive areas, you have a walk that may be as long as a 13-km (8-mi) lung-expander or, if you elect to do only the West End part and do not cross the ferry to Granville Island, a gentle stroll of less than half that distance. You may even make it a leisurely one-way walk by using the public bus service for your return. And to enhance your enjoyment, Vancouver Park Board has provided information at strategic points about the natural environment and the wildlife to watch for.

Walking from north to south, you begin in Stanley Park at the end of Beach Avenue, along which there are several parking lots or bus stops that you could use to shorten the walk. Once on foot, your route is along the seawall towards Burrard Street Bridge, passing the tall inukshuk, legacy of Expo 86, occupying its own little green space on your right. Then, near the Vancouver Aquatic Centre is the ferry terminal with boats to Granville Island and to the Maritime Museum close to Kitsilano Point.

Embark for Granville Island, and once there, head past Bridges Restaurant, following the south shore round to the causeway, which you cross under the shadow of Granville Street Bridge. Now proceed west, townhouses

View from Kitsilano Point towards Point Grey.

and gardens on one side, a marina on the other, to Burrard Street Bridge and Vanier Park, a spot favoured by kite enthusiasts. Here you continue along the shoreline, the mountains of the North Shore before you and, closer to hand on your right, the Heritage Harbour, with the Vancouver Museum and the Maritime Museum successively on your left.

As you move round the point and through Hadden Park, Kitsilano Pool appears, and you may note the parking area (or beyond it Cornwall Avenue and its bus route) if you wish to do this walk in reverse from another of its intermediate points. If you want to go farther, you continue round the bay, now on a narrow path below houses and above the beach with its interesting geological features, until a flight of steps takes you up to the level of Point Grey Road, here a quiet residential street.

Now, head back, first through Kitsilano Park, then Hadden and Vanier back to Granville Island, with its market to distract you as you make for the return ferry. This you may reach either directly or by a counterclockwise detour over Lookout Hill to East Point and round by Sea Village, with its colourful assortment of houseboats. Of course, you will miss all these and more if you choose to use the alternative ferry service from the Maritime Museum or take the bus back across Burrard Street Bridge.

# FALSE CREEK

**Round trip** 10 km (6.2 mi)　　　　**Allow** 3 hours

**Paths and ferry**　　　　　　　　　　**Good all year**

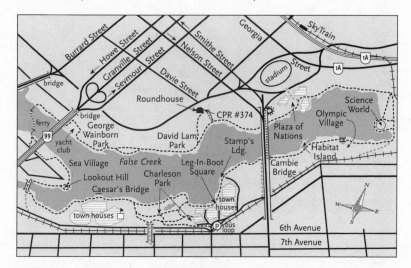

BEGINNING IN THE 1970S, urban redevelopment has rescued this core-city area from the blight that had settled on it during its industrial age. Thus, it has become of renewed interest to walkers, indeed to all people pursuing outdoor activities in an urban environment, providing as it does something for almost everyone—from a children's adventure playground to theatres, from markets to marinas and parks, with a fine stretch of seawall thrown in.

There are many ways to reach Granville Island from downtown Vancouver, one being by ferry from terminals near the Vancouver Aquatic Centre on Beach Avenue and at the foot of both Hornby and Davie Streets. You may even vie for a parking spot with all the other visitors on the island itself, but for the walks described here, approach the area at its east end from West 6th Avenue by the Charleson Park entry, where there is a bus loop and visitors' parking.

For an overview of the whole neighbourhood, turn west from here along Sawyers Lane, then go left on a track that leads up to the development's highest point, the top of an attractive Japanese-style garden, with a waterfall at your feet flowing to a placid lake below. And the views beyond are

Marina on False Creek.

even more arresting, with the stark landscape of the inner city looming across False Creek set against a backdrop of the North Shore mountains.

Now, make your way to water's edge and follow the shore east past Stamp's Landing and a residential area until, east of Cambie Street you reach the most recent additions to the seawalk, those through the site of Olympic Village. On the seaward side you soon come to Habitat Island, a man-made island with information panels and the story of its creation and purpose nearby. Frequent lookouts along the way also provide views of activities on the creek until you cross a contemporary metal bridge and approach the Science World globe at the easternmost extremity of your walk.

Now, you turn west, making for the towering Concord Pacific developments via a casino and the Plaza of Nations to Coopers' Park, which rims the shore both east and west of the Cambie Street Bridge. From here, you remain at the water's edge until, at the head of a little bay, you may wish to make a detour by Heritage Yard on Davie Street to visit the Roundhouse, a historic building renovated to serve as a community centre. Here, too, you may pay your respects to old CPR Engine No. 374 before continuing westwards past David Lam Park to resume your walk along the shoreline and through George Wainborn Park, only briefly leaving it to skirt the False Creek Yacht Club property.

Next, cross False Creek by ferry from the foot of Hornby Street. On Granville Island, make your way east past the sights and sounds of the busy market, past the cluster of floating homes called Sea Village, round or over Lookout Hill to the little footbridge and the final stretch along the south shore to your transport.

# STANLEY PARK

**Round trip** 7 km (4.3 mi)

**Trails and paths**

**Allow** 2 hours

**Good all year**

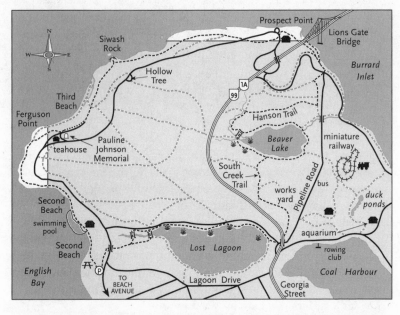

HERE IS A circuit that takes in many features of Stanley Park in the aftermath of the devastating storms of winter 2006–07 while leaving some trails for further exploration on your own. For this, start at Ceperley Park parking lot near the west entrance off Beach Avenue, a spot easily accessible by bus or car. Note that parking fees are in effect throughout the park.

Make for the seawall to sample one of its most picturesque sections, running north along the shore of English Bay past Second Beach. At the same time, you surely do not wish to plod mechanically round the whole length of the seawall, crowded as it is. Instead, ascend the steps at Ferguson Point to emerge on top of the low cliff opposite the Sequoia Grill at the Teahouse restaurant. Stay close to the cliff's edge, keeping the sea on your left as far as possible, a rule to follow on this stretch to Prospect Point.

The first point of interest is the roughly hewn stone monument to Pauline Johnson, a poet who loved the park, gave Lost Lagoon its name and was thus commemorated following her death in 1913. Having paid your respects, continue along the sidewalk to the Third Beach parking lot, remaining on

West End beyond Lost Lagoon.

the landward side of the pavilion in order to pick up Merilees Trail then Siwash Rock Trail, which runs along the top of the cliffs. From these trails, you enjoy views through the trees over the bay to Point Atkinson and Bowen Island. Particularly spectacular is Siwash Rock, seen from the old coastal defence platform that now serves as a lookout point; you may even see a cormorant or some other seabird perched on the rock.

Past the rock, stay with the trail as it works its way round to the northeast in a regenerating forest of Douglas-fir, cedar and hemlock, finally rising via a flight of steps to a higher level and eventually coming out on Stanley Park Drive a little south of Prospect Point. Even now, you have no need to pound the sidewalk; cross the road and follow a trail north to emerge opposite the café. Here you may pause for refreshments, look down at First Narrows, examine the walking beam of the old ss *Beaver* or contemplate the basalt dyke that helped to create the headland by resisting erosion.

To resume, take Eldon Trail downhill from the west side of the café, going under the Lions Gate Bridge and, after dropping to the seawall, approaching the park road near its junction with Pipeline Road. Leave the seawall again, cross the main road and start on the path to the right of Pipeline Road, then go left at the first opportunity onto Eagle Trail paralleling that road. Next take Hanson, the second trail on the right, which plunges you into some satisfactorily dark forest, with yet one more left onto North Creek Trail taking you to Beaver Lake, with its profusion of marsh plants and bird life.

It is immaterial whether you go round the lake to left or right, though right is shorter; the trails rejoin on the lake's south side. There, turn south onto South Creek Trail, which leads through a fine stretch of forest. Now, approaching the settled part of the park, go first left, then right, with one more dog-leg left to take you past the rose garden and on towards the underpass of Stanley Park Causeway. Now you may go along either shore of Lost Lagoon, home of myriad waterfowl, crossing the meadow on its west side to reach the park road and your starting point.

# RENFREW TRIANGLE

**Round trip** 5 km (3.1 mi)          **Allow** 2 hours

**Trails and sidewalks**                **Good all year**

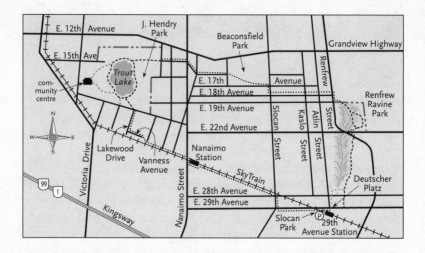

NO, THIS IS not a tale of illicit passion! The title simply indicates that this is a walk with three clearly identifiable points of reference, any one of which may serve as a start: 29th Avenue Station, John Hendry Park and Renfrew Ravine Park. Farthest south is the station, which you may reach by SkyTrain or by bus, though you may drive to its vicinity just as easily, a small park lying just to the west of it. Should you start from here, you first follow John Molson Way north, gradually descending and in the process enjoying the wide sweep from Bowen Island in the west to the twin peaks of Golden Ears in the east.

Molson Way is a walking trail, part of B.C. Parkway, that follows SkyTrain for much of its length, its route punctuated by parkway features, many of which represent the local community's ethnic mixture and give an excuse to pause along the way. On your way to John Hendry Park, with its centrepiece, Trout Lake, you must cross Nanaimo Street, after which comes one such feature, the Filipino Garden, a charming little piazza with a traditional arched entrance. Thereafter, your route changes to the east side of the elevated tracks, then parts company with the transit line at Lakewood Drive as you head for John Hendry Park. There, you may choose the slightly

Tai chi in Ravine Park.

longer track round the west side of Trout Lake, perhaps dropping in at the community centre en route.

From the northeast corner of the lake, walk eastwards out of the park onto East 15th Avenue, on which you recross Nanaimo to the second park of your outing, Beaconsfield. Head diagonally across the park to its southeast corner and another short stretch of residential street, with East 18th Avenue bringing you to a crossing of Renfrew Street and the north end of Ravine Park. Your direction now is upstream (south), until, after passing yet another community centre, you must rise to a busy intersection, which you cross to the diagonal southwest corner of East 22nd Avenue and Renfrew Diversion.

From here you continue upstream, but at road level, the ravine below on your right, first on a lane, then on a short stretch of trail and natural plantings with a unicursal maze to meditate on. This brings you to a crossing of upper Still Creek, a name that is hardly appropriate for it on this part of its journey to Burnaby Lake. Stay on the east side, however, on the last part of what you discover is the Renfrew Ravine Sanctuary Park when you arrive at its attractive entrance on East 29th Avenue, a short distance east of your start. One block west and there is another parkway feature, the plaza created by Vancouver's German community, with its touch of nostalgia for veterans of the Second World War: a lamp standard reminiscent of the one Lili Marlene stood under by the barrack gate waiting in vain for her lover. Maybe this walk has its touch of passion after all.

# CHAMPLAIN HEIGHTS

**Round trip** 8 km (5 mi)

**Paths and trails**

**Allow** 2 hours

**Good all year**

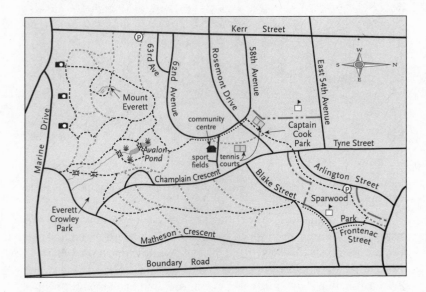

THE EAST SIDE of Vancouver is not very well endowed with parks. For this reason, it is pleasant to discover in the city's southeast sector a little urban wilderness, Everett Crowley Park, the name commemorating a pioneer Vancouver dairyman and supporter of the area. Nor need you confine your walk to the park alone. The neighbourhood has been laid out for walking, with paths winding through wide grass pleasances and groves of trees.

One suggestion is to turn south off East 49th Avenue a short distance west of Boundary Road onto Arlington Street and to park alongside Sparwood Park, where a track heads off east between the Champlain Villas and a line of trees. Next, cut across the grass past Champlain Heights Elementary School, turn right briefly on Frontenac, then go right again on Hurst, a cul-de-sac to the south of the school. From here, a path veers left, crossing Matheson Crescent to the beginning of Red Alder Walk, your route through this little urban maze, the trail names telling you something of the present tree cover. At the first fork where left goes to White Birch Trail, stay right, then go left at the next three forks, then right, left, and right again,

Morning Glory blossoms.

continuing ever downhill until you pass a small playground and emerge on Champlain Crescent beside a convenience store just below Riel Place.

Cross Champlain to Grey Gum Trail and follow it to a fork where you turn down left to cross two footbridges. After the second footbridge, ascend a bark-mulch trail on the right into Everett Crowley Park and a choice of circuits. If you go right at the first T-junction, then right again, you may follow the ravine, with a side trip to investigate Avalon Pond before continuing your tour west along the northern perimeter, the backs of houses on East 62nd Avenue on your right. Then just after you turn south, you pass a road entrance coming from a parking lot on Kerr Street just south of East 63rd Avenue, the access point if you intend to confine your outing to the park itself.

Next, unless you want to make the short detour left to ascend Mount Everett, a man-made hill affording a view of the park, continue south to the escarpment above the Fraser lowlands and, turning east, enjoy three viewpoints from which you see the southern islands of the Strait of Georgia and Mount Baker, majestic in the southeast. Next, soon after the third viewpoint, go left, then left again to join the Champlain Loop, which circles Mount Everett. Go right here, never deviating until you reach the northern perimeter of the park once more. A final right turn brings you to a small open area where you go left on the path leading out of the park onto Butler, the continuation of East 62nd Avenue. This takes you past a sports field and a recreation centre to the edge of Captain Cook Park, into which your path leads just opposite Rosemont Drive. Finally, cross Champlain Crescent and follow the path along Arlington back to Sparwood Park and your vehicle.

Incidentally, the earlier mention of Kerr Street may evoke from older Vancouverites recollection of the city dump. Well, Everett Crowley Park was that very site, now risen phoenixlike from the waste. If you like blackberries, this park sports a prolific crop of them, which the Friends of the Park hope someday to replace with native species.

# BURNABY HEIGHTS /
# TRANS CANADA TRAIL

**Round trip** 5 km (3.1 mi)          **Allow** 2 hours

**Trails and roads**          **Good all year**

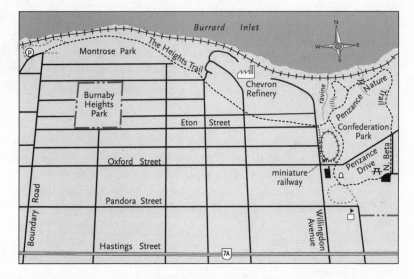

NORTH BURNABY IS blessed in its rolling topography, with numerous little eminences to provide vantage points over city, sea and mountain; it is doubly blessed in its many little parks and green spaces with their vistas of the distant North Shore mountains, from The Lions to Golden Ears and its neighbours.

To reach the beginning of this walk, you drive over one such hill going from Hastings Street north on Boundary Road, the whole of Burrard Inlet and its surroundings in front of you as you descend to road's end at little Bates Park. On foot, start your walk at the north end of Boundary Road. Facing east, you will see two green gates. Take the left-hand one and head downhill.

Soon joined by the Trans Canada Trail as it heads eastwards, your route runs north of the houses of Burnaby Heights, while on the left a narrow strip of deciduous forest grows down to water's edge and, in summer, permits only glimpses of the ridges and valleys across the inlet through the leafy screen. Still, as compensation, there are notice boards and photos to inform

McGill Park.

you about life on the waterfront in its early days. Then, your distant views improve but, replacing the forest on your seaward side, the foreground is now a Chevron "tank farm" as you make your way across two little parks to North Willingdon Avenue, busy with gasoline trucks. Ignoring the TCT signs and starting just south of Eton Street, head east on a rough track north of the miniature-railway compound to join the Penzance Nature Trail in the relatively untouched section of Confederation Park, not far from its western end beside the Rainbow Creek Station. Thus, going right offers you a quick escape from nature to the trim bowling lawns, picnic grounds and play areas of the urban precincts south of Penzance Drive.

The more rewarding choice, to the left, is about 1 km (0.6 mi) longer and winds through rich second-growth forest. It drops to just above the water's edge, unfortunately separated from the park by the CP Railway line, with only one or two viewpoints to reveal the beauties beyond. But there is plenty of interest by the path itself in the varied undergrowth and enormous cedar stumps, nurses to a new generation. Rising again, your trail emerges on Penzance Drive opposite a dead-end street (North Beta Avenue) on the margin of Confederation Park's more developed section, and at this point you may depart from the Burnaby Scenic Trail, leaving the eastern leg for another day (see Walk 14).

Accordingly, cross the road and make your way up North Beta in the direction of the picnic area to enjoy the fine views to the northwest, The Lions as centrepiece, before returning to Penzance Drive, there to decide whether to descend the Nature Trail briefly and retrace the unimproved track to Eton Street or to make straight for Willingdon and thus to Eton and a return by your outward route.

A point to note, however: if you travel by bus, your reward is freedom to make a one-way trip along the whole 5.5-km (3.4-mi) Burnaby Scenic Trail, with transport convenient to both ends (see Walk 14).

# CAPITOL HILL

**Round trip** 6.5 km (4 mi)

**Elevation gain** 150 m (490 ft)

**Trails and streets**

**Allow** 2.5 hours

**Good most of the year**

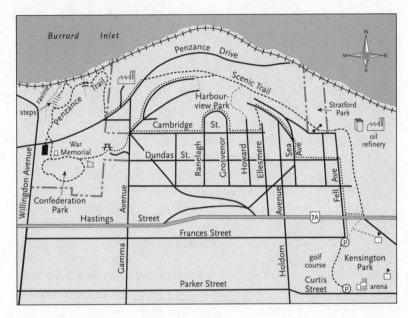

HASTINGS STREET, the face that North Burnaby presents to the casual passerby, does not rate high for attractiveness. No, the beauties of the area have to be sought away from that bustling thoroughfare. And what better destination than Capitol Hill via the Burnaby Scenic/Trans Canada Trail?

To reach this mecca, you may start from Kensington Park, from its north side at the corner of Fell Avenue and Frances Street, one block south of Hastings Street. Better still, drive along the more attractive Curtis (called Parker farther west), the next through street south of Hastings, and turn into the park's southern parking lot between the golf course and the ice rink. Buses are convenient for both approaches as well.

Starting from the south side, make your way along a path west of the playing fields to the north parking area, then continue on Fell Avenue to cross Hastings Street at the traffic light and go right along the north side to where the trail begins on the west side of an oil refinery, which is fortunately hidden from view by a line of trees. Next comes a stretch of dead-

Monument in Confederation Park.

end road, then, from the end of another street, you find yourself entering an area of second-growth forest. As you proceed, ignore successive trails coming from the left, before finally you step out on the quiet Penzance Drive. You are, however, not finished with forest yet. On your right, a short distance to the west, lies Confederation Park's Penzance Nature Trail, which takes you downhill, crosses a pipeline right-of-way and bottoms out a little above the CP Railway tracks. From here, you start rising again, meeting and crossing Penzance just east of the Rainbow Creek Station and entering the "civilized" section of Confederation Park.

For your return, you have at least two options: for the easier, make your way to the upper boundary of the park at Gamma Avenue, then north to a five-way intersection. Still bearing left, follow Bessborough briefly, then angle uphill on Brisbane Avenue to Scenic Highway, a road that, despite its grandiose title, is a peaceful dead end, soon becoming a trail. Go straight ahead here, until you slant gently downhill to join your outward route.

For a more strenuous but more scenic choice, from the five-way intersection on Gamma, head straight uphill on Cambridge Street. The beauty of this route, besides splendid views of Vancouver's inner harbour when you pause to take breath and look behind, is that a small substation in a grass plot splits it, inhibiting through traffic. Continue upwards to Ranelagh Avenue and turn left on it to reach Harbourview Park, your view of the harbour now obscured by houses.

After consoling yourself with the sight of mountains across the treetops to the north, resume your walk on Grosvenor, thence to Cambridge which does have spectacular views, this time of the head of the inlet and east as far as Golden Ears. Descend to Ellesmere, go left on it to its end, then down a forested track to Bessborough, where you go right as far as Dundas Street. A left turn takes you to Fell and thus back to bus or car, your expedition to the hidden face of North Burnaby over.

# BURNABY MOUNTAIN WEST / SFU

**SHORT CIRCUIT: Round trip** 5 km (3.1 mi)  **Allow** 2 hours

**LONG CIRCUIT: Round trip** 8.5 km (5.3 mi)  **Allow** 3.5 hours

**Elevation gain** 180 m (590 ft)  **High point** 340 m (1115 ft)

**Paths and trails**  **Good most of the year**

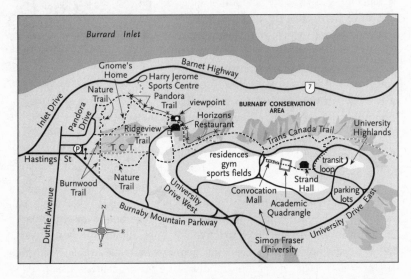

THE SPECTACULAR VIEWS attract many people, locals and visitors alike, to Burnaby Mountain and Simon Fraser University. Then the visitors find that the university is set in the midst of the Burnaby Mountain Conservation Area, with its mixed second-growth forest and streams that provide diverse habitats for a variety of wildlife. As well, they find that a network of trails allows them to enjoy these attractions. The following walk, the first of three in the area, is an introduction to the west side of the mountain and culminates with an incursion into the university's centre.

For a start, drive or take the bus east along Hastings Street, then, just past the traffic light at Duthie Avenue, keep left on Hastings when the Burnaby Mountain Parkway swings off to the right. There is no parking area, so you must leave your car on the street near a gate barring further vehicular progress. Continue up Hastings Street on foot to a crossing of the ways, where you are greeted by a Trans Canada Trail (TCT) sign. Rather than taking the direct, multi-purpose pathway, head to its right on the Nature Trail that winds

Kamui Mintara, the Ainu totems.

uphill through mixed forest before rejoining the main trail just short of Centennial Way. Cross this road and stay with the TCT as it rises in a wide sweep before arriving at its Burnaby Mountain Pavilion.

Here, if you opt for a short walk, you head north towards the Horizons Restaurant, noting en route the fine rose garden on its right, the magnificent views up Indian Arm and down Burrard Inlet to the city, and finally to the Kamui Mintara, the Ainu totems commemorating Burnaby's friendship with its sister city in Japan. Below the totems, close to the boundary fence, your trail resumes, descending close to the paling and adorned with warnings about the steep drop-off. The next point of decision comes when Gnome's Home goes off to the left, angling over to join the Ridgeview Trail and the Burnwood Trail, but you may leave those for another day. Continue a few more steps then, to peer over the edge of the steep slope at the ruins of a one-time trail from the Harry Jerome Sports Centre below. Not much farther, you arrive at the junction with your route back on the unmarked Nature Trail, a sometimes muddy track meandering through the lush undergrowth to meet Ridgeview just above its junction with Burnwood, which takes you back in short order to Hastings Street and your transport.

For the longer walk and to savour the architecture of Arthur Erickson's campus, head east on the TCT from its pavilion, ignoring two trails striking off right, then at the next, furnished with an information kiosk, turn uphill, cross University Drive and enter the university by a dark stairway on the left that brings you up into the light just west of Convocation Mall. Beyond, steps lead up to the Academic Quadrangle. Then, after Strand Hall and a square with a fountain in its midst, you veer left past a bus loop to East Campus Road and downhill to University Drive. Just below the road junction you find your return trail heading off left and dropping steeply enough for students to have called it Cardiac Hill. At its meeting with the TCT, turn left and follow this trail as it undulates through the forest back to the Burnaby Mountain Conservation Area, where you proceed as for the shorter outing.

# BURNABY MOUNTAIN

**Round trip** 8 km (5 mi)

**Allow** 3 hours

**Roads and trails**

**Good most of the year**

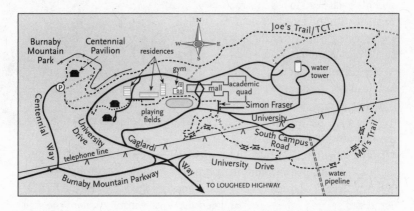

EVERYONE KNOWS THAT Simon Fraser University is situated on top of Burnaby Mountain; not so many are aware, perhaps, that the mountain is also the site of Burnaby's Centennial Park, which lies about 800 m to the west of its illustrious neighbour. It is in the park that this walk has its beginning and end, the two separated by a circuit of about 8 km (5 mi).

One way to reach Centennial Park is to drive east on Hastings Street. After it curves into Burnaby Mountain Parkway and houses are left behind, go left up the steep Centennial Way to a parking lot by the pavilion. Alternatively, you may approach via Gaglardi Way from Highway 1 or Highway 7 (Lougheed Highway), turning left on Burnaby Mountain Parkway and right up Centennial Way. Here on a commanding spur overlooking Burrard Inlet, you may enjoy views of city, sea and mountain.

After paying homage to your surroundings, set off past the Ainu totems, Kamui Mintara, around the perimeter of the park, keeping the wire fence on your left. Pass the rose garden and the children's playground and arrive at a meeting of the ways to the left of the one-way road leading from Simon Fraser University. Here, a well-defined trail (Joe's, now also the Trans Canada) strikes off to the left in the second-growth forest on the north side of the mountain, below the crest and out of sight of the university, though linked with it by two trails on the uphill side. Your trail travels eastwards, dropping a little as it progresses until, after about 3.2 km (2 mi), by a small

View of Mount Seymour and the mouth of Indian Arm.

spring, a foot trail—Mel's—strikes off uphill to the right. Turn right on this trail.

The trail rises and descends as it rounds the east flank of the mountain, intersects a power line, then crosses several small streams on wooden footbridges, followed by an old access road where you drop a little to get over a larger creek. Next, you rise to cross a major approach to the university, your route continuing up a bank a little to your left. Stay with the more travelled route, now somewhat degraded by bikes, until you come to a trail crossing under a power line. Go straight ahead here to the next crossing, then turn left to a fork with bridges on both branches, the two arms encircling what used to be Naheeno Park. The right fork is slightly shorter, so why not go left? Then, after yet another bridge, turn right through a derelict adventure playground after which either the first or second left brings you out onto South Campus Road opposite Science Road. Proceed along Science Road briefly before turning west in front of the university buildings.

Now, cross Gaglardi Way, then walk diagonally left across the running track in front of the gym to the next sports field, at the end of which a track takes you right to join Residence Lane. There, you go left to West Campus Road, where you veer left, passing Chilcotin, Kitimat and Penticton Houses on their south sides. Next, head for the northwest corner of Quesnel House to find your trail running gently downhill on the bank above University Drive West. Finally, cross this road and turn back into the park from which you set out, passing a Trans Canada Trail pavilion on your way to the parking lot.

# BARNET TRAILS

**BARNET AND COUGAR CREEK:**
**Round trip** 4 km (2.5 mi)                    **Allow** 1.5 hours

**WITH INLET TRAIL:**
**Round trip** 10 km (6.2 mi)                   **Allow** 3.5 hours

**WITH BURNABY MOUNTAIN:**
**Round trip** 14 km (8.7 mi)                   **Allow** 5 hours

**Elevation gain** 256 m (840 ft)              **High point** 300 m (985 ft)

**Trails and paths**                            **Good most of the year**

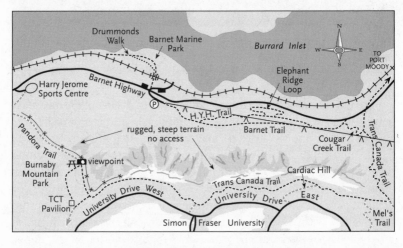

THE BARNET TRAIL has unlimited possibilities as the precursor to more
ambitious outings, but the most attractive of all—a complete circuit on this
north side of Burnaby Mountain—lies in the future pending the restoration
of some and the creation of other connecting trails. In the meantime, however, you may combine existing trails while you visualize what may be to
come. The approach to the parking lot for this area is opposite the entrance
to the Barnet Marine Park, which is reached by driving east on Highway 7A
(Barnet Highway) and turning right at the traffic light.

The true beginning of the trail lies in the hollow beyond the new Bike
Skills Facility, and there you turn your back on the busy road and rise to share
your route with a power line in the usual wide clearing, a productive habitat
for salmonberry bushes and the hummingbirds attracted by their bright
flowers in spring. Away from the sight and sound of traffic, you make your
way along the hydro road until, just ahead of some elderly swings—legacy

Uphill on the Barnet Trail.

of a vanished settlement—you come to a sign on the left for Hang Your Hat (HYH) Trail. Turn onto this very attractive walking and biking trail and wind your way through the forest and across several small creeks that are conveniently bridged. The wide, bushy valley sloping down from your left gives way to a little ridge, and the Elephant Ridge Loop invites you to explore. Wander upwards for a short distance to reach the top of the trail, which provides a view of Burrard Inlet through the trees, before you descend to rejoin HYH and continue to the main trail. Then, at the crest of a minor bump, you reach a sign announcing the end of Barnet Trail and the beginning of Cougar Creek Trail. Leaving the power line, which heads uphill, you drop sharply, losing the little height you had gained, before you approach the road briefly and swing away and up again, finally meeting the Trans Canada Trail about 2 km (1.2 mi) from your start.

If you wish to continue you have several options. You may go left and east on the TCT, descending to and crossing the highway at the pedestrian crosswalk at the Petro-Canada Refinery, then continuing on the Inlet Trail towards Port Moody. After its start at the highway, the trail is remarkably peaceful as it undulates among trees with many glimpses of the inlet and with some panels interpreting the area's natural and human history. You may even return by bus if you fancy a one-way outing.

Going right and uphill on the Trans Canada Trail is more strenuous, for you start with the better part of 145 m (475 ft) of fairly steep trail to ascend to the information kiosk at the junction of TCT and Powerline Trail. Staying with the Trans Canada here is a good choice, though a little farther on you could elect to go left on Mel's Trail, described in Walk 16, following the directions therein as far as the Burnaby Mountain Conservation Area.

There, after admiring the nearly panoramic views of lowlands, city, water and mountains, as well as the gardens and totems close to hand, you may return to the Trans Canada Trail to finish the loop round the mountaintop. Finally, from the information kiosk at the power line, you drop downhill to rejoin Cougar Mountain Trail with its sharp little ascent to Barnet Trail and thus back to your transport.

# BURNABY MOUNTAINSIDE TRAILS

**SHORT LOOP: Round trip** 5.5 km (3.4 mi)  **Allow** 2 hours

**LONG LOOP: Round trip** 9.8 km (6.1 mi)  **Allow** 3.5 hours

**Elevation gain** 238 m (780 ft)  **High point** 280 m (920 ft)

**Paths and trails**  **Good all year**

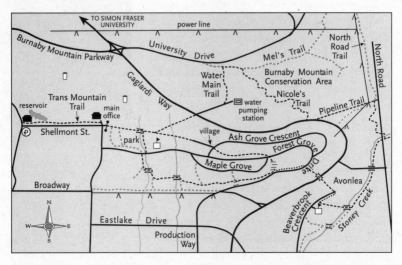

THIS LOOP INCORPORATES the Trans Mountain Trail, a delicious little path of less than 1 km (0.6 mi), created along the margin of its property by the Trans Mountain Pipe Line Co. It may be treated as the prelude to a ramble through the residential clusters on Burnaby Mountain's south face.

To reach the start, drive or take the bus south on Arden Avenue, reached from Curtis or Hastings Streets by turning south on Duthie, then going left on Greystone Drive, which curves into Arden Avenue. Alternatively, you may come north from Highway 7 (Lougheed Highway) on Lake City Way and Arden. Turn east on Shellmont and park by the roadside just clear of the corner. The beautifully laid-out trail starts at the intersection on the north side of Shellmont and winds its way uphill among quite large trees, with here and there a picturesque little bridge. But it is only 750 m, and in no time you come to its end at Trans Mountain's main entry.

Straight ahead, beyond a gate, a trail continues eastwards to a fork beyond three tracks on the right that lead into various school and recreational areas. The route on the left runs along a power line to Gaglardi Way; the right, which you follow today, trends southeastwards into a residential

enclave at Mountainside Village. Maintaining your direction, cross Ash Grove Crescent onto a track running downhill between townhouses and Forest Grove Drive to end on that road at its junction with Maple Grove Crescent. Across Forest Grove, descend the stairways to a path just above the lower section of this same road.

Now, turn back west on this trail, which ascends gently along the face of the slope, joined by successive paths and stairs from the adjoining houses. Soon you come to a trail forking back left from your route, which crosses a pedestrian bridge high above a deep ravine and continues to a T-junction in front of another gorge. Ignoring the left branch, turn right alongside the ravine, the air in spring redolent with the sweet smell of cottonwood trees. A second high bridge takes you to the west side of the abyss, and there you remain until you emerge on Forest Grove Drive again. Opposite is a playground, east of which a path heads up beside a creek to join your outward route, where a left turn takes you back to the Trans Mountain Trail.

For a trip nearly twice as long with a significant altitude gain, you should take that left fork along the power line west of Mountainside Village and cross Gaglardi Way onto an access road to a water pumping station. Here you take the wide, gravelled Water Main Trail, which rises on the left of the tank and leads you upwards to join Mel's Trail, where you go right for a short distance until, shortly after an information board, you come to Nicole's Trail dropping steeply to the right. This trail winds back and forth and down the slope with some breathtaking biker "improvements" to its end, close to Gaglardi Way. Now you go left on the smooth Pipeline Trail, rising gently to meet and cross Powerline Trail, just beyond which you go right on the North Road Trail and descend to emerge on North Road at the beginning of the Stoney Creek Trail. Follow this route, travelling under Broadway in a pedestrian underpass until, at an interpretive kiosk, you cut in to your right, passing north of Stoney Creek Community School to Beaverbrook Crescent. Next go right to Avonlea, where a path leads you to an overpass of Gaglardi Way and thus to Production Way. Just over 100 m to your left you will rejoin the walk described in the shorter circuit for a gentle end to your outing.

# SFU / STONEY CREEK

**One-way trip** 8 km (5 mi)

**Trails, sidewalks and roads**

**Allow** 3 hours

**Good most of the year**

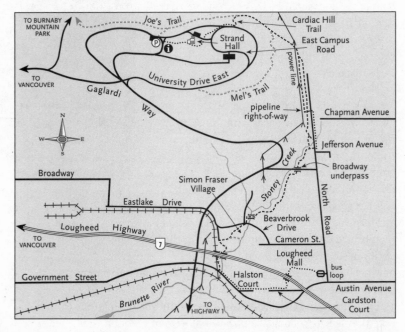

THIS WALK TAKES you downhill nearly all the way from Simon Fraser University on the summit of Burnaby Mountain to end at the bus loop at Lougheed Town Centre, the busy Burnaby shopping mall. Of some interest is the mountaintop location from which you set out, the start, incidentally, of the 1967 Centennial Trail, so that you retrace a part of the route as you go east from the campus centre. Savour, too, the architecture of Arthur Erickson's creation until, at Strand Hall, you veer left across a parking lot to East Campus Road, on which you continue downhill to University Drive.

Just below the road junction and its "No Entry" sign, you find the trail heading off left and dropping steeply down the evocatively named Cardiac Hill. This joins the trail system that takes you right, descending to the junction of the mountain trails, where you go straight ahead when Mel's Trail turns off to the right. Then, reaching the power line right-of-way, you head right on it, with the option of descending by North Road Trail in the line of forest to the east.

Steps up to Academic Quadrangle.

Next, you come to Pipeline Trail at a small installation beside which North Road Trail continues through the forest, finally emerging on North Road itself at the Stoney Creek Trail. Start to the right along the lane on the south bank and continue until a cross street (Broadway) appears and a pedestrian underpass takes you beneath it. Your route now gradually diverges from the stream until, at the second track right, you return to the waterway, choosing either bank as you head south for the next cross street, Beaverbrook. This time you must rise to road level at the pedestrian crossing that gives access to Simon Fraser Village. Here, instead of dropping at once to creekside again, cut clear across the subdivision to a little park on its south side, where, from the dead end of Eastlake Drive, your trail resumes. Bounded by a fine split-rail fence, it descends to cross a tributary stream near its confluence with the main creek and pass beneath SkyTrain and the Lougheed Highway in quick succession.

Your walk along Stoney Creek is now almost over, for on Government Street you must turn left, then go left again on the dead-end Halston Court before following the wide parkway that takes you over the hill, the townhouses along your route becoming high-rises as you descend, Keswick Park on your right. Here, you turn ninety degrees left and walk via Discovery Place Garden Apartments to an underpass of Highway 7 (Lougheed Highway), beyond which the mall appears.

To catch a bus back to the top of the mountain, work right of the Bay department store to the bus loop for a relaxed, mechanically assisted return to your mountaintop starting point.

# BURNABY LAKE

**Round trip** 11 km (6.8 mi)

**Trails**

**Allow** 3 hours

**Good all year**

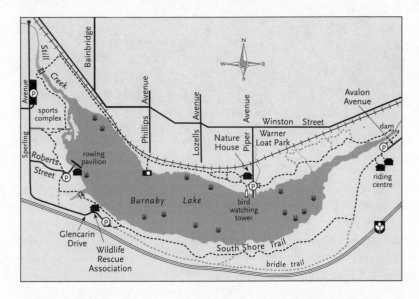

COMPLETION OF THE South Shore Trail makes possible a circumambulation of Burnaby Lake, with only the distant roar of traffic to remind you that you are walking in a peaceful oasis surrounded by highways and industrial and commercial endeavours. Numerous access points accommodate many variations to your hike around the lake and also allow you to tailor the length of the outing to time and ability.

One of the most convenient starts to a complete round of the lake is at the Burnaby Sports Complex, reached from the west by going off Highway 1 at Sprott Street (Exit 32), turning left on Sprott Street and crossing the highway before proceeding to the traffic lights on Kensington Avenue, just beyond which lies the sports complex and its parking. Approaching from the east, leave Highway 1 at Kensington Avenue (Exit 33), go north on Kensington Avenue to the Sprott Street intersection, then right to the sports complex. A second start may be made from the rowing pavilion, which you reach by turning right on Sperling Avenue after crossing Kensington, then left on Roberts Street to the pavilion parking lot. You may reach yet a third starting point by staying with Sperling as it curves round into Glencarin

Cariboo Dam.

Drive and following it to the end, where a trailhead kiosk provides maps and information.

If you choose to start at the Glencarin trailhead and go clockwise, you first pass close to the water behind the Wildlife Rescue Association and several other buildings through interesting marsh scenery, crossing a bridge from which you may gaze into the depths of Deer Lake Brook before arriving at the parking lot for the rowing pavilion. Across this and slightly to the left, Pavilion Trail continues through head-high vegetation to reach the sports field behind the complex and the crossing of Still Creek, some 3.2 km (2 mi) from your start. Now you change direction as you embark on the long straight Cottonwood Trail, paralleling a railway and with only a few fleeting glimpses of the lake, eventually coming to the main Piper Avenue entrance with its Nature House, viewing tower and picnic area. (To confine your outing to the short, self-contained walks near Nature House, you may reach this spot from Highway 7 (Lougheed Highway) by turning south onto Brighton Avenue, which lies between Gaglardi Way and Kensington Avenue, then driving west on Winston Street to Piper Avenue, where you go south again, passing the attractive little Warner Loat Park as you near the parking lot.)

Continuing your walk round the lake, follow the trail east of Nature House, emerging into the open just where the Brunette River debouches from the lake, the crossing at the dam a short distance ahead. From here, turn upstream on the south bank to the Avalon Avenue parking lot (for access, see Walk 21). Leave the water here and set off west on the riding and hiking trail before branching off to the right on the pedestrian-only South Shore Trail. This winds through groves of quite large conifers and deciduous trees and over boardwalks across marshy areas, with here and there a viewpoint and here and there a connecting route to the bridle trail beside the highway, until a final connector brings you back to the Glencarin trailhead.

# BRUNETTE RIVER

**Round trip** 8 km (5 mi)    **Allow** 3 hours

**Roads and trails**    **Good all year**

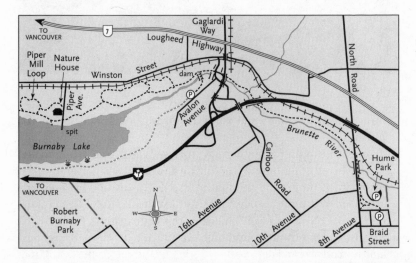

THIS WALK ALONG the Brunette River, so named for the brown colour derived from the peaty soil through which its headwaters flow, may be tackled from several access points: from the west at the Piper Avenue entrance to Burnaby Lake (see Walk 20) or from the Avalon Avenue trailhead, reached from Highway 1 by turning onto Gaglardi Way (Exit 37). Cross the overpass, stay right at the traffic lights, then go left on Cariboo Road North to descend into the valley of the Brunette beneath Gaglardi Way. Immediately after the underpass, cut back left on Avalon Avenue, passing an equestrian centre on your way to the parking area. From your vehicle, walk north to cross at the Cariboo Dam and join the trail downstream to Hume Park for a return walk of some 6 km (3.7 mi).

The walk also lends itself to an upstream approach from Hume Park, with an incursion into Burnaby Lake Regional Park as far as its Nature House as a bonus. For this, leave Highway 1 for Brunette Avenue South (Exit 40A), continue south on Brunette, then go right at the first traffic light onto Braid Street and right again on Fader Street, which leads you to parking above the sports fields at Hume Park. Now on foot, make your way westwards to find the nature path that winds along the side of an old riverbank,

gradually dropping to the valley floor
near a park entrance off the busy North
Road. Cross at the pedestrian light then
head right over the bridge to join the
service road, which starts you on your
route upstream.

Across the river, on your left, are tall
trees, and between you and them the
water flows, still and dark, until you
reach the little waterfall created by the
first of two weirs controlling the free
movement of the current. On your right,
hidden by a screen of trees, runs the CN
Burlington Northern Railway track,
bearing the occasional train to disturb
the peace. Eventually, though, another kind of traffic becomes audible as
you pass under the high arches of the highway bridge. Next, after crossing
Stoney Creek at its confluence with the Brunette, you meet the road into
a trailer park and pass under yet another main road, Gaglardi Way. Then
you arrive at Cariboo Road and, a few minutes beyond it, the Cariboo Dam,
where you may look down on the dark water with its scattering of lilies or
westwards, up the lake, to the tall buildings rising, somewhat incongru-
ously, above the rural scene.

Staying on the north side you may now head off on the Brunette Headwaters Trail. Three right turns at successive forks will allow you to sample
the outer limits of the Spruce Loop and Conifer Loop Trails on your way
to the Nature House at Piper Avenue, with its viewing tower and spit. Farther to the west, another short loop, the Piper Mill Trail, leads you round
the sawdust heaps and other signs of the area's industrial past, now disappearing under a healthy growth of blackberries and other vegetation. But,
inevitably, the time to return must come, and, back east of Piper Avenue,
you may again choose right forks on the Brunette Headwaters Trail for the
direct route back to the dam and your downstream walk.

# DEER LAKE PARK WEST

**Round trip** 5 km (3.1 mi)

**Allow** 1.5 hours

**Trails and roads**

**Good all year**

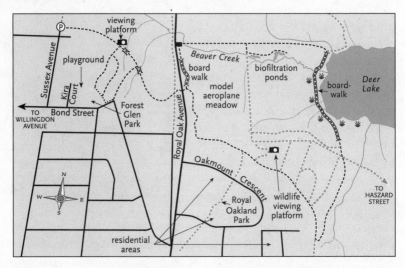

AFTER THE ORIGINAL forest was logged, this small block of land lay fallow, regenerating naturally over many years around some massive stumps that remain in testimony to the grandeur of the first growth. Mostly deciduous, the present forest cover shelters a small wetland at its heart and makes a home for a variety of plants and wildlife. Now a footpath has been constructed through this tiny wilderness, and several entry points provide convenient access to these natural surroundings. As well, this walk may serve as prelude to an exploration of its more illustrious neighbour to the east, Deer Lake proper (Walk 23), with its matchless variety of attractions.

The main trailhead for this outing is at the north end of Sussex Avenue, which you reach by going east from Willingdon Avenue on either Bond Street (accessible also by bus) or Grasmere Street, then north on Sussex to its end. Here you will find a kiosk with a map and some information. You begin by descending into the glen through which several tributaries flow on their way to Beaver Creek. Shortly after passing a trail entering on your right you come to a platform over one of these streams, where you are provided with facts about this wetland and the birds, fish and plants endemic to it. Armed with this information you proceed on the gently rolling path, passing yet another track from the right before arriving at what was the old

Boardwalk through the wetlands.

Royal Oak Avenue, its present incarnation rising on stilts ahead of you. If you want a short walk of rather less than 2 km (1.2 mi), this is where you turn around, though you may return by going left at the first junction and ascending to emerge at the foot of Bond Street. Continue uphill, veering right into the grassy expanse of Forest Glen Park, from which two trails go right into the trees, soon converging en route to the Main Trail, where a left takes you back to Sussex Avenue.

If you prefer a longer walk, the route to Deer Lake Park itself leads downhill for a few steps then turns right to pass under Royal Oak Avenue. At the T-junction beyond, you go right alongside the marsh grass–covered lowlands then wind uphill towards the townhouses that have replaced the former penitentiary, scattered conifers gracing the way as you ascend. Keep right and high, rising above a wildlife viewing platform, overlooking meadows and marsh and with splendid views across Deer Lake to the North Shore mountains and east as far as Golden Ears. You may choose any one of four trails down to the lake but the most attractive lies farthest east. You reach it by keeping right consistently until, just short of an exit to Oakland Street, you turn left and down a wooded ravine. Given that the two parks are contiguous, you may already have decided that a longer walk encompassing both is well within your limits. To do this, turn right (east) along the lake and proceed as suggested in Walk 23.

If you prefer to return to your starting point more directly, at the lake go left briefly then right on a trail with a long boardwalk protecting the wetland along the western shore of Deer Lake. Next, turn west on Beaver Creek Trail, the creek itself hidden by a screen of trees. Turn off at the T-junction on an access road going south to an information kiosk for the Beaver Creek Bio-Filtration Ponds, which you may investigate from a path along the north side of the project. Then, on your way back, you catch sight of model airplanes over the meadow to the west before rejoining the route to Royal Oak Avenue, where there is parking for this side of the park.

Still some distance from your own transport, turn south on the trail-cum-boardwalk paralleling Royal Oak to reach the underpass and so to return to Sussex Avenue by any of the routes previously described.

# DEER LAKE

**Round trip** 5.5 km (3.4 mi)  **Allow** 2 hours

**Trails and roads**  **Good all year**

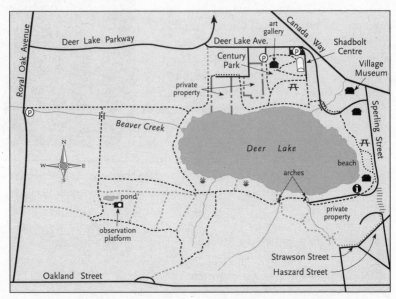

APART FROM THIS park in Burnaby, probably few other locations in the Lower Mainland allow you, from one parking spot, to visit an art gallery or an arts centre, explore a re-created village, stroll through formal gardens and enjoy a walk along a trail system by an enchanting little lake. Here, at Deer Lake, the city's art collection is housed in a one-time mansion, its carefully preserved gardens providing a fitting setting also for the magnificent architecture of the Shadbolt Centre for the Arts, Burnaby's 1992 Centennial Legacy Project. Downhill to the east is the Burnaby Village Museum. As well, you may swim or go boating from a separate small recreation area and beach off Sperling Avenue, reached from Canada Way via Burris Street. The other pleasures are approached by turning south off Canada Way onto Deer Lake Parkway, then left on Deer Lake Avenue, with parking by the art gallery or Shadbolt Centre. From either building, you may begin a walk round the lake by going due south to the lakeshore.

However, you have yet a third option, this one from the west side, where there is a small parking area off Royal Oak Avenue just south of Deer Lake Parkway (right turns only both in and out). From here, with Beaver Creek

Ducks on the frozen lake at Century Park.

through the trees on your right, you may walk east to pick up the lake trail, on which you turn right for a walk anticlockwise round the marshy west end on a boardwalk trail. However, some interesting developments besides the residential in the old Oakalla Prison lands have taken place, and to take advantage of these, you should take the first right after leaving your car. This route takes you across some low-lying meadows and up to an observation area overlooking meadows and marsh. Next, continue upwards and eastwards along the front of the new townhouses, enjoying wide views of the North Shore mountains east to Golden Ears, with Deer Lake as foreground. Resisting the temptation to drop too soon to the lake on the first descending tracks, stay high until you reach a fork just short of another entry, from Oakland Street. Now, turn left and make your way down beside a shallow, leafy ravine to the lake trail, then turn east again, heading towards the woods and a wooden arch. Go left onto the boardwalk, stopping just before the bridge and taking a small trail down to the lakeshore. Returning to the boardwalk, follow it through another arch, across a small park and then left onto a small paved road (Deer Lake Drive). Follow this route among the houses to an information board. Turn left and follow the trail to the beach.

From the beach, make a short jog to the north, and after passing Hart House, go left on Dale Avenue, with the Burnaby Village Museum to your right. Cross the creek and turn left again on the park trail to get back to the lake at the foot of Century Park, with its beautiful gardens.

Beyond here, you are once more forced away from the lake, past a large white house to another quiet road. Two more left turns take you back to the lakeshore, and soon after is a fork where right takes you straight back to Royal Oak. But if previously you missed the walk along the westerly boardwalks and the bog plants they protect, you may wish to continue to your left, going right only at the next junction to rejoin and retrace your outward route.

# MOLSON WAY (CENTRAL)

**One-way trip** 10 km (6.2 mi)          **Allow** 3 hours

**Paths and trails**          **Good all year**

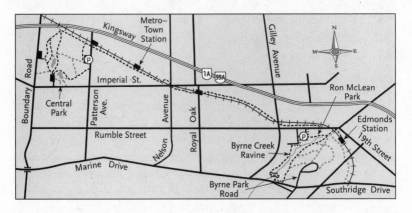

JOHN MOLSON WAY, the pedestrian portion of B.C. Parkway, follows
the SkyTrain route for 19 km (11.8 mi) from False Creek in Vancouver to New
Westminster. In its entirety and using transit for the return, it makes a comfortable one-way outing, its many parkway features, created by communities
along its route, a source of recurrent interest for the walker.

But for those who would prefer to sample a little at a time, here is a section of the parkway that links three of Burnaby's parks, one the well-known
Central Park, the other two little-known contiguous green spaces with distinctive names and functions—Ron McLean Park, a sports and picnic area,
and Byrne Creek Ravine Park, a tiny wilderness.

Your approach is by SkyTrain to Patterson Station in Central Park. (If
you drive, you may park and join the walk at the entrance by the tennis
courts on Patterson Avenue.) Leaving the station, follow the John Molson
Way markers towards the tall trees of Central Park. On entering the park,
however, turn left, away from Molson Way, to embark on a clockwise circuit along quiet forest trails amid giant Douglas-firs. Ignoring tracks to the
right, shortcuts across the heart of the park, pass the tennis courts entry
and veer right, following the split-rail fence that borders the pitch-and-putt
course occupying the southeast corner. Next comes the model-yacht pond,
home to various ducks and geese, its outlet at the east end crossed by a picturesque wooden bridge and, farther west, its inlet straddled by an equally

Peaceful scene in Central Park.

attractive bridge. Now, turn right (north), following the stream through a Japanese-style garden to another body of water south of the horseshoe-pitch, then continue through the forest to the picnic areas near Variety Park, an adventure play area for children.

Here, you rejoin Molson Way for your walk southeast, passing first the Rhododendron Garden, the bushes donated by the society of the same name. The next stretch of the B.C. Parkway is further enhanced by other community-inspired floral displays: the Dutch Mile, the Sears Garden and the Garden of the Province, to name a few. Peace, however, is notably lacking as you traverse this busy commercial and industrial section of Burnaby, and it may be with some relief that, shortly after the little garden at Gilley Avenue, you espy on your right the green fields of Ron McLean Park and head for the wooded area across the sward.

From the parking lot there, turn south on Hedley Avenue and proceed to its end, then, passing north of the tennis courts, you'll find the trail starting among trees along the western perimeter and descending into the attractive Byrne Creek Ravine. Soon you reach the low end at Marine Drive, with no apparent return trail on the other side of the creek; however, a search east reveals a steep track heading up the embankment and into the trees to join a braided trail system following the east side of the ravine and finally emerging on a paved path entering from the right. Go left on this until it meets B.C. Parkway once more, follow its markers left as the pathway curves round and under SkyTrain, then go right for Edmonds Station and your speedy return on the elevated railway.

# MOLSON WAY (SOUTH)

**One-way trip** 5.5 km (3.4 mi)          **Allow** 2 hours

**Paths and roads**                       **Good all year**

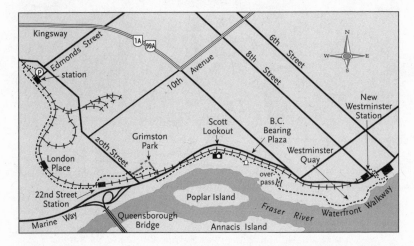

YOU MAY ALREADY have used a stretch of the John Molson Way feature of B.C. Parkway on one or both of Walks 11 and 24. This time your outing begins at Edmonds Station and ends with a walk along New Westminster's riverfront, culminating in a visit, perhaps, to the Westminster Quay Market, a short distance from the transit station, from which you may return whether you used SkyTrain to reach Edmonds or parked nearby.

Your first task is to find the route, hidden as the walkway is, in low ground west of the station. Begin, then, by going under the right-of-way to where the 7-Eleven trail markers greet your eyes. Then, the path veers to the east, and you begin to rise, the "City in the Park" on your right, B.C. Hydro headquarters on your left. Now, travelling more south than east, you enjoy the familiar sights of Mount Baker and the flatlands of the Fraser delta, with the southern Gulf Islands on the horizon. Then, starting your descent to river level, you note over to your right a sign of mortality, Schara Tzedeck Cemetery, with, beyond it, the soaring spires of the Alex Fraser Bridge, the twentieth-century equivalent of the Gothic cathedrals of the age of faith.

Still descending, you come to another of the parkway features, the Japanese Garden, now neglected and forlorn like so many other parkway gardens, before coming to 22nd Street Station. This you pass on its north side, watching the trail signs with extra care as you come to the crossing of

Busy waterfront on the Fraser River.

20th Street. Thereafter, Grimston Park provides a respite before your next street crossing, one that has to be undertaken in two stages. Once over, however, the noise of heavy traffic stays with you on your left for some time, a state not compensated in any way by the industrial plants and railway yards between you and the river.

Then, at the crossing of 14th Street, comes the B.C. Bearing Plaza, at its centre the brick foundation once housing a giant bearing. A few minutes later you turn right to cross an overpass spanning the railway yards, the riverside housing developments ahead replacing the industry of yester-year. Once over, leave the official Molson Way temporarily at Rialto Court and head for the waterfront to enjoy the full length of the esplanade, the river and its traffic on one hand, the multitude of architectural styles on the other; on the river, an old railway bridge, its spans open to permit passage for shipping, and nearby on land, the Quayside Children's Place, a playground with a nautical theme. Finally, SkyTrain's SkyBridge appears, itself an interesting contrast to the old Patullo Bridge, and, at the market, your walk ends, an overpass of Columbia Street taking you to the station for your return trip.

You might, of course, walk back, but if you want to lengthen without repeating your outing, you might begin or end with a visit to Byrne Creek Ravine Park, a delightful little remnant of wild British Columbia. To reach it from Edmonds Station, head for Molson Way going south (left) but go right almost immediately thereafter between the verge of a ravine and a row of townhouses. This leads you to Ron McLean Park, from which you follow the directions in the previous walk (Walk 24).

# BURNABY FRASER FORESHORE PARK

**FROM BOUNDARY ROAD:**
**Round trip** 8 km (5 mi) or less

**Allow** 2.5 hours

**Trails and roads**

**Good all year**

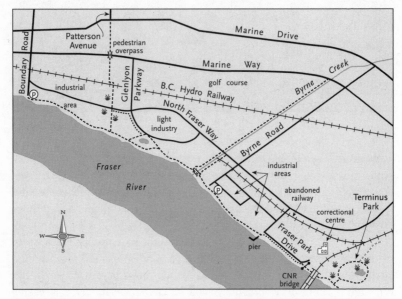

WITH DEVELOPMENT STILL going on, with new buildings and their linking parkways springing up where once was green space in Burnaby's Big Bend, the recreational picture is by no means complete. Even so, you have numerous possibilities at present.

To reach the central picnic area of Burnaby Fraser Foreshore Park, drive south from Marine Way on Byrne Road. Once parked, you must decide whether to go downstream towards Boundary Road for a return walk of 4.4 km (2.7 mi) or take the slightly shorter distance upstream to the eastern limits of the park, a possible destination being a pier with seats around a wooden structure reminiscent of a ship's masts.

A trailhead on Marine Drive is most easily reached by bus and starts opposite the foot of Patterson Avenue. Your trail takes you south from here towards Marine Drive's upstart successor, Marine Way, but a pedestrian overpass clears this hurdle. Continuing towards the river, you next cross a creek, followed by a Southern Railway of B.C. rail line and a roadway, North Fraser Way. Though most of the ground to the right has been industrialized,

Log booms on the Fraser River.

the trees on your left have been spared, as have the wet brushlands along the trail, which meets the riverside pathway 1.5 km (0.9 mi) from Marine Drive. Once more, you have the choice of going east or west, though you may simply pause to contemplate the river with its traffic.

From the western entrance at the foot of Boundary Road begins the complete walk to the east. Although industry is not far off, the riverbank is tree-clad, and from the end of the Patterson access onwards, stately cottonwoods grace either side, their perfume in springtime and their golden beauty in fall delighting the senses as you go east, once more a possible target being the pier just within the bounds of the park.

However, to add distance and interest to your outing, you should continue upstream alongside Fraser Park Drive to a gated road on the right of the Burnaby Correctional Centre for Women and thence to the CNR's bridge, with its centre span left open for the free passage of river traffic. Immediately beyond the railway, you come to the Fraser Foreshore Restoration Project with, as well as the wetland habitat surrounding it, Terminus Park, a wide meadow providing a hunting ground for raptors.

Another possible extension is to take the Byrne Creek Trail, which runs northwards from just west of the picnic area for 2.5 km (1.6 mi) alongside the still waters of that stream. Alternatively, you may walk along one side of Byrne Creek to cross at North Fraser Way and return down the other.

Farther west, your return to Boundary may be varied by swinging right around a pretty little pond and continuing along Glenlyon Parkway to a path going left opposite the Ballard Building back to the riverside trail. Or you may continue on the sidewalk as far as North Fraser Way, turning left there to the Patterson access trail, then left again towards the river, where you head west once more for Boundary Road.

Note that a new trail has been created along the riverside westwards from Boundary Road as far as Kerr Street, suggesting the inclusion of Waterfront and Gladstone Parks, still farther to the west, in a riverfront outing once the area development (in its initial stage in 2008) and landscaping are completed.

# MUNDY PARK

**Round trip** 7 km (4.3 mi)

**Trails**

**Allow** 2.5 hours

**Good all year**

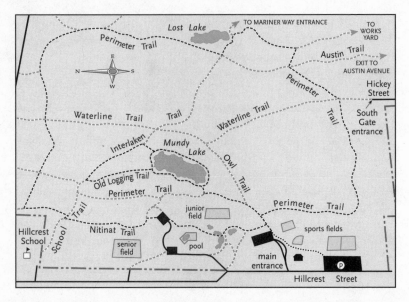

FOR A PLEASANT afternoon outing on well-laid-out forest trails with intriguing views of small lakes, try this delightful park located near the eastern boundary of the Municipality of Coquitlam. Whether you wish to circle the park on its perimeter trail or concentrate on the heartland round Mundy Lake itself, there is something to suit most desires. As well, trail plans at main intersections help to make route-finding easy, adding to the pleasure from this area of urban afforestation, Coquitlam's response to Stanley Park.

From Highway 1, turn off north on Gaglardi Way (Exit 37) to join Highway 7 (Lougheed Highway), on which you turn right. Next, go left under SkyTrain and uphill on Austin Avenue, with which you stay for some 4.5 km (2.8 mi) before going left on Hillcrest Street—and suddenly you are at your destination, the parking area just ahead of the park's main entrance. Here, you are close to sports fields with washrooms just to the north. Beyond them is yet another parking lot and, on its right, the Mundy Park Urban Forest Map, which provides an introduction to the park's environmental history as well as a map of its trails.

For a first visit's sampling of the many possibilities, walk north between

Reflections in Mundy Lake.

the small lakes and continue on the path through a disc-golf installation to yet another parking area. Cross this, making for its northwest corner, where going left on Nitinat Trail takes you north, forest on your right and a sports field on your left at first, but giving way to trees on either hand. Stay with Nitinat as it meets and leaves School Trail, then turn right at a point where going straight on would take you to Como Lake Avenue, the first of five such exits on this eastward leg of your trip. Soon, at the next trail crossing, you join Perimeter Trail (which, perversely enough, has avoided the perimeter so far), then, not long after, you cross Waterline Trail, which cuts across the whole width of the park from north to south and may suggest ideas for another walk.

Eventually, your trail turns south, and for a few paces your route coincides with the paved multi-use Community Trail that circles the park on its periphery. Soon you are treated to tantalizing glimpses of water in the forest, and where Interlaken Trail intersects Perimeter go left for a closer sight of Lost Lake. Keep going south to a T-junction, at which go right to rejoin Perimeter, now heading west through fine second-growth forest, its floor adorned with trilliums in spring.

Finally, with a sports field ahead, you meet the trail from the main entrance and you are ready for the climax to this trip: Mundy Lake itself. For it, stay with Perimeter going right, then, when Owl Trail goes straight on, keep left briefly before swinging right for Mundy Lake and its Lakeside Loop trail, which has viewing platforms at strategic spots. Towards the northwest end of the lake, you may be interested in making a short detour left to walk Old Logging Trail, built on one of the original routes used early in the century. At the top of the little hill, go right on Interlaken, with another right bringing you back to Mundy Lake to resume the loop, after which a left on Perimeter returns you to your starting point.

# SHORELINE TRAIL (PORT MOODY)

**Round trip** 5 km (3.1 mi)                    **Allow** 2 hours

**Trails**                                       **Good all year**

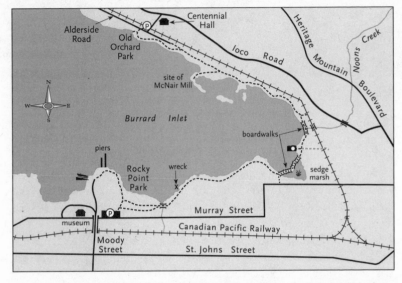

EVEN IF YOU are a regular user of St. Johns Street in Port Moody, here serving as Highway 7A (Barnet Highway), you may well be unaware that between you and the head of Burrard Inlet lies a trail, hidden from the road by a screen of trees. Giving a succession of views and points of historic interest, it follows the line of the original Ioco Road partway between Rocky Point Park and Old Orchard Park in the district of Pleasantside.

To reach Rocky Point Park from St. Johns Street, turn north at the Moody Street intersection. This road takes you over the CP Railway tracks before decanting you on Murray Street beside, appropriately enough, the Port Moody Station Museum, given that this city was intended as the western terminus of the transcontinental railway. On Murray Street, turn left, then left again for the parking lot, near the recreation area with its open-air pool, its jetty and its children's playground, built atop an ancient Native midden.

Starting on the trail at the east end of the park, you soon reach your first stream, picturesquely named Slaughterhouse Creek, beside which stands a large board with a map and information about the plants and animals you may see. On the shore, you may also note an old wreck, abandoned and forlorn, as you head north among groves of trees, fir and cedar being

Deteriorating wreck.

prominent. Along the way, steps, sturdy footbridges and boardwalks take care of obstacles, one stretch of walkway at the head of the inlet over the thick coarse sedge grass being particularly impressive. Here, a notice board tells something of the trail's creation, giving credit to those who helped bring it into existence as well as providing an overview of the area's history, natural and human. Just beyond, a short detour left takes you to a bird-watching platform, complete with seat, which offers fine views down Burrard Inlet even if you are not especially interested in the great blue herons and lesser birds of the tidal marshes. Then, cross the mouth of Noons Creek, on which a fish hatchery has been created upstream beyond the old railway bridge, and head west.

The next part of your trip is interesting historically as well. By your path, you may spot scraps left from an early steel mill, and fire bricks underfoot bear testimony to a one-time brickworks, Stanley's. On this stretch, too, you may want to diverge from the trail to visit the remains of one of the cedar mills that once dotted this part of the coast. At low tide, you may stand on the concrete foundations of the old McNair cedar mill and look around at the rotting stanchions, relics of old wharves, busy with shipping in the mill's heyday. Then, towards the end of your journey, you walk through a grove of poplars before the appearance of fruit trees indicates your approach to Old Orchard Park.

You may vary your return by choosing the multi-use paved route running above the meandering walking trail. It's slightly more direct, with fewer ups and downs, but infinitely less interesting than its pedestrian neighbour, which you should rejoin at the head of the inlet for the final leg of your trip.

# SASAMAT LAKE /
# WOODHAVEN SWAMP

**Round trip** 8 km (5 mi)

**Trails**

**Allow** 3 hours

**Good all year**

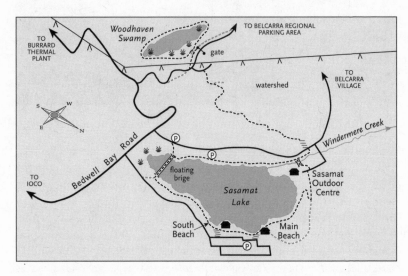

FOR THOSE WHO like to combine a short walk with some swimming, picnicking or fishing, all within comfortable distance of Vancouver by bus or car, Sasamat Lake is an ideal spot, for the lake is reputed to be the region's warmest and the trails are well treed, providing shade on hot summer days.

From Highway 7A (Barnet Highway), turn onto Ioco Road just east of Port Moody and drive west, following signs for Belcarra. Turn right on 1st Avenue in the historic community of Ioco, left at the next fork onto Bedwell Bay Road, then go right for White Pine Beach shortly thereafter. On foot, make your way down to the main beach and turn right past the building at its north end, where the trail starts off into the trees along the lake's edge. Quite soon you rise to an access road on which you turn left to meet the approach to the Sasamat Outdoor Centre, a private camp run by the Association of Neighbourhood Houses.

Across this road, the trail resumes, dropping to and crossing the lake's outlet, before coming to a T-junction. For a short walk of 3 km (1.9 mi) around the lake, go left along the shore, the noise of traffic from Bedwell

Looking across to Main Beach and Buntzen Ridge behind.

Bay Road above on your right. (Indeed, you might very well start from that thoroughfare, descending a rough track conveniently placed for small parking spaces on the verge. These are 200 m and 700 m beyond the junction of the Bedwell Bay and Burrard Thermal Plant Roads and may provide attractive alternatives on a busy summer weekend.) Next, you come to the floating bridge, with its fishing and swimming decks, which saves you a long trip on pavement round the marshy area at the south end of the lake. Take this direct route to the east side and continue on the final lap of your circumambulation, assisted here and there by little bridges over feeder streams. Soon you come to South Beach, with its picnic tables backing onto Pine Point, the natural separation from Main Beach and the end of your walk.

But what of Woodhaven Swamp? To make the connection, you must turn right after crossing the outlet by the Sasamat Outdoor Centre, follow the creek, Windermere Creek, downstream for about 200 m, then rise to road level at the Belcarra Village welcome sign, where a crosswalk takes you to a flight of steps. These start you on a trail ascending between private properties, beyond which the route veers briefly east of south, the lake visible below through the trees, then you swing away again, gaining height and crossing a long bridge en route over a damp hollow. Thereafter, still rising gently, the trail works its way round the side of a bluff before it levels and comes to a power line access road, which in turn is joined by a bike path and emerges on the park road to Belcarra picnic area directly across from the swamp. Cross the road and follow the bike path briefly until, just below a small parking lot, you drop to the walker's route round the margin of this little wetland, a long boardwalk at its north end, a strategic spot from which to survey the scene. Then, the circuit complete, retrace your steps to Sasamat Lake to resume your course round its shore.

# BUNTZEN RIDGE

**Round trip** 8 km (5 mi)

**Elevation gain** 275 m (900 ft)

**Trails**

**Allow** 3.5 hours

**High point** 335 m (1100 ft)

**Good most of the year**

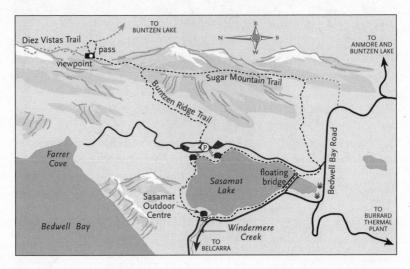

IF YOU ENJOY a swim and a picnic at the end of your hike, this may be the walk for you. However, it does start at Sasamat Lake, one of most popular lakes within easy reach of Metro Vancouver, and so, to avoid finding the park full and the gates closed on a hot summer's day, you should arrive early (or take the bus). In any case, your driving instructions are the same as for Walk 29 but, if you have a choice when you arrive, drive round to the far northeast parking lot where the Buntzen Ridge Trail begins just across from the steps down to the facilities at North Beach.

On foot, you head immediately into trees, emerging very soon to cross an access road and skirt another parking lot, before arriving back in the shade of the forest. Next you meet and turn uphill beside a little old power line, which brings you in short order to a newer one in a wide swath up the mountainside. At the clearing you go left slightly to regain the trail on the opposite side and ascend in wide zigzags through pleasant second-growth forest to meet the Sugar Mountain Trail, originally a forest-access road from Bedwell Bay Road.

Here, if you've had enough of climbing, you may opt to turn right and downhill on this multi-purpose trail, which is severely eroded in its steeper

Floating Bridge on Sasamat Lake.

segments by the water that pours down it in periods of heavy rainfall or runoff. After negotiating the rough places, you come to yet another power line, the most recent of all, one that sweeps from the east across the face of the mountains on its way to feed an energy-hungry Vancouver. Now you go right, staying with the power line to crest a little rise, then leaving it for a grassy road opposite, which leads you down to a gate on the White Pine Beach access road. Now you go left a few paces, then cross to descend some steps to the trail making its way north below the level of the road to meet the trail along the lake's edge at the floating bridge. If you return to North Beach along the shorter east-shore route, you would have a walk of about 4 km (2.5 mi) with an elevation gain of roughly 200 m (655 ft).

If, however, when you reach the point of decision, you are keen to reach the viewpoint, you go left and uphill on the old road. On this section, the route has fewer rough, eroded places and, for the most part, has matured into an agreeable walking trail undulating upwards towards the saddle through which the power line you crossed earlier passes on its way from Buntzen Lake. When the trees thin as you approach the pass, you have the finest view of the trip, down the length of Indian Arm to Burrard Inlet. But to fully explore the area, continue a little, going right at the fork to meet the Diez Vistas Trail coming up from the Buntzen Lake side of the ridge, go left on it to the col, then when Diez Vistas goes right on its way up and along the ridge, keep left again and thus complete the loop back to the viewpoint.

To return, retrace your steps to the junction of Buntzen Ridge and Sugar Mountain Trails, where you may return as you came. For variety, stay with Sugar Mountain as previously described as far as the floating bridge, but this time cross the bridge and make your way along the meandering, undulating lakeside trail until, just past the Sasamat Outdoor Centre, you reach and cross the bridge over Windermere Creek. Next you climb up to traverse the camp road onto a gravel road following the north shore of the lake. Quite soon you leave the road to descend some steps onto a more appealing lakeside trail, which brings you back to the North Beach picnic area for your pre-prandial swim.

# BELCARRA REGIONAL PARK

**TO JUG ISLAND BEACH:**
**Round trip** 5.5 km (3.4 mi)          **Allow** 2.5 hours

**TO BURNS POINT:**
**Round trip** 5.2 km (3.2 mi)          **Allow** 2 hours

**Trails**          **Good all year**

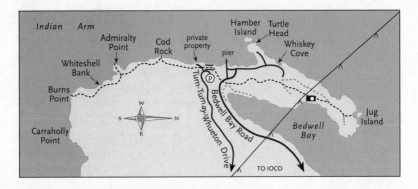

NOW THAT A fair amount of the point of land between Indian Arm and the head of Burrard Inlet is regional parkland, walking has been added to the more traditional activities of swimming, fishing and picnicking associated with Belcarra. Besides the walks at Sasamat Lake, you have the choice of a woodland walk along the spine of the peninsula to a delightful little beach at its north end or a ramble south along the shoreline above Burrard Inlet.

For a start, turn left onto Ioco Road from Highway 7A (Barnet Highway) at the eastern end of Port Moody and follow it to 1st Avenue, where you turn right for Belcarra. At the next fork, stay left on Bedwell Bay Road, until, just past the approach to White Pine Beach on Sasamat Lake, you leave it to go left again for Belcarra picnic area and Burrard Thermal Plant, then fork right for the former after 1 km (0.6 mi) of rising, twisting road. Your next concern comes at the gate, which closes when the park is filled to capacity, but once over that hurdle you are free to enjoy this novel approach to Belcarra as it winds up and down to the parking area.

For Jug Island Beach, head northwards from the picnic shelters through the trees and cross Bedwell Bay Road to an opening opposite, there ignoring the trail on your right to West Road. A few steps on, two trails have their beginnings: the Bedwell Bluffs trail on the right is a 35- to 40-minute round trip to a tidal flat; your route, an old logging road, continues

Jug Island with Raccoon Island beyond on right.

on the left, working its way north along the ridge. After some 30 minutes, you come to a fork with the original trail, now closed, going left beyond a barrier. Going right on its successor, you rise quite steeply on a rocky path alongside a mossy slab to a viewpoint just below and east of the ridge crest. Then, the track drops to rejoin the former route, levelling briefly before the final descent to the little secluded beach.

Contrasting with the inland northward walk is the gentler excursion that takes you south along the shore past Cod Rock, Periwinkle Notch, Maple Beach, Admiralty Point and Whiteshell Bank on the way to Burns Point. This time, you start from below the concession stand on the south side just above the shore.

Heading south, you first cross a footbridge, then a road leading to a piece of private property before beginning to rise in pleasant forest to continue a little above the waters of Indian Arm's southern reach. As you proceed, you will note small cleared areas with their garden flowers gone wild, the few relics of squatters' homes from the 1930s. Next comes Cod Rock, your first extended viewpoint, followed by the other features, with the trail descending to sea level at Maple Beach.

Five minutes more brings you to a major fork. Left takes you on towards your destination, right a few steps to Admiralty Point. There, where the waters of Indian Arm meet those of Burrard Inlet, you may enjoy the view down the inlet to the Ironworkers Memorial Bridge or lift up your eyes to Mount Seymour; in fact, this makes a satisfying destination for a short walk. If, on the other hand, you continue eastwards on the main trail, you first find yourself down at Whiteshell Bank before rising fairly steeply prior to your final descent to the present end of the trail at a bluff above Burns Point, with its sheer drop-off and its views up, down and across the inlet.

# BUNTZEN LAKE

**SHORT LOOP:**
**Round trip** 8 km (5 mi)                    **Allow** 4 hours

**LONG LOOP:**
**Round trip** 10 km (6.2 mi) or less         **Allow** 5 hours

**Roads and trails**                          **Good all year**

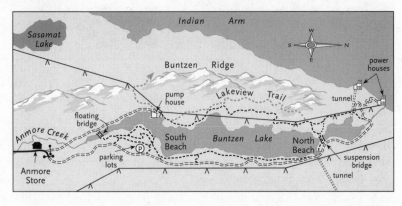

**WHERE DO YOU** have the choice of several delightful walks, ranging from a gentle stroll to a lung-opening circumambulation lasting several hours? The answer: Buntzen Lake, that attractive body of water, man-made though it is. Here, B.C. Hydro has done a superb job of creating recreational facilities: developed beach areas, launching sites for pleasure craft (no power boats) and trails for horse riders and hikers, the whole set in an impressive basin with tree-clad mountain slopes on either side.

To partake of what Buntzen Lake has to offer, turn left off Highway 7A (Barnet Highway) at Ioco Road and drive uphill on Heritage Mountain Boulevard, thereafter following signs for Buntzen Lake as you work through developments springing up apace on the mountain slope. Finally, from East Road, go right on Sunnyside Road to the entrance gate at Anmore (where you may also arrive by bus, in summer only), the parking lots lying 2 km (1.2 mi) beyond.

From here, to sample outings along the lake's east side, walk through the dog off-leash area or head away from the lake to pick up the trail behind the washrooms on the east side, cross a footbridge and embark on an exceedingly fine forest trail that undulates gently as you proceed north. Various lakeside viewpoints give you short there-and-back outings, but if you are

Looking west towards North Beach, Mounts Seymour and Elsay above.

more ambitious, you may reach North Beach, beyond the tunnel that carries water from Coquitlam Lake on the other side of Eagle Ridge.

Here, at 4 km (2.5 km) from your starting point, you may feel that honour is satisfied, but if you wish to complete the circuit, you have two options: for the shorter, cross the footbridge west of the picnic area and bear left to join the power-line trail, here designated for both hikers and riders; on the longer, the original Buntzen Lake Trail, you go north on the road by Trout Lake to the dam. Here, you fork left, then left again just after a bridge onto a forest track that winds south to emerge near a water intake building. Continuing south on the power-line trail, you soon meet the shorter route from the suspension bridge and part from the horse route (Lakeview Trail), which goes uphill to the right. Then you descend into a hollow and climb up again over the next bluff, with views of Swan Falls across the lake to raise the spirits.

In forest again, the track undulates along, crossing and recrossing the right-of-way, before eventually approaching the shore once more and bringing you back down to lake level beside a pumphouse. Now you walk south on the service road, then cross a long wooden floating bridge spanning the lake's southern extension and the surrounding wetlands to the final lap, through another attractive stretch of forest back to your starting point.

And the short outing at South Beach? For it, go left past the boat launch and follow Energy Trail to a knoll with a view along the whole length of the lake, once so appropriately called Lake Beautiful before it was renamed for a power company official.

# COLONY FARM REGIONAL PARK

**Farm loops** 7.2 km (4.5 mi)          **Allow** 2 hours

**Dykes and trails**                    **Good all year**

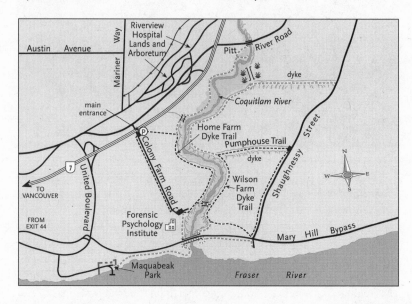

COLONY FARM WAS long known as one of the most productive farms
in B.C. Straddling the lower Coquitlam River, it was farmed intensively for
much of last century and provided food for Essondale (Riverview), Woodlands and the Forensic Psychiatric Institute as well as rehabilitative employ-
ment for the patients of these institutions. Despite its agricultural potential,
however, in the 1980s much of the land ceased to be farmed actively, and
now the Metro Vancouver Regional Parks Department manages it for wildlife, recreation and a little horticulture. Containing marshes, grass and trees
as well as streams, ditches and sloughs—and the wildlife attracted by these
habitats—the dykes are wonderful places for walking and nature study.

To sample some of the pleasures of the area, leave Highway 1 at Exit 44
following signs for Highway 7 (Lougheed Highway). Just east of the United
Boulevard overpass, turn south (right) onto Colony Farm Road then, immediately beyond the railway tracks, into the small parking area on the east
side of the road. On foot, take Colony Farm Road Trail which runs along
the west side of the road all the way past the "village green" to the Community Gardens with a picnic area and parking lot nearby. Pass to the east

In Riverview Arboretum.

side of the gardens and follow the trail there north alongside a ditch to a small bridge that takes you across to the Home Farm Dyke, on which you could make a speedy return to your transport by going left. But doing so would give you only a walk of about 4 km (2.5 mi), so instead go right and over the high, arching Millennium Bridge, then left and upstream with views to distant mountains over the flatlands. Continuing, you next pass a pumphouse and a rush of water debouching into the river and soon thereafter reach a transverse dyke, the Pumphouse Trail, heading across an area reserved for wildlife habitat. This dyke ends at Shaughnessy Street, where there is parking and information.

To complete this loop, walk right on the grassy verge of Shaughnessy for about 1 km (0.6 mi), to the southern margin of what was the Wilson Farm, and there connect with an attractive segment of the PoCo Trail winding westwards among trees with a wetland on one hand and the old farmlands on the other. Back on the dyke trail you soon reach and cross the Millennium Bridge again, this time to turn north along the Home Farm Dyke Trail, a ditch on your left and the river meandering to and fro on your right. At the next junction, you must leave the river, the area now closed until such time as the route on its bank is repaired and restored. In the meantime, go left on the Mundy Creek Trail on the last lap of an interesting walk.

Across Highway 7A (Lougheed Highway) from Colony Farm lie the Riverview Lands, home to the hospital and Western Canada's first arboretum, with its fine collection of native and exotic species. The future of the area is uncertain, but it is still possible to cross the highway to an approach road that embarks you on a tour of the grounds. As well as the extensive lawns with their rare trees you would surely enjoy a walk up Fern Crescent to The Backyard Trail and Finnie's garden, an ongoing restoration project courtesy of the Riverview Horticultural Society which also conducts tours on scheduled Sundays during the summer. (For details, call 604-290-9910.)

Note that in the event you may again walk the Sheep Paddocks Trail along the river to Pitt River Road, you might enter the arboretum at its north end by going left and crossing the Lougheed at the traffic lights to the approach road into the grounds. Then you may depart by the main entrance road.

# RIDGE PARK LOOP

**Round trip** 5 km (3.1 mi)   **Allow** 2 hours

**Elevation gain** 245 m (800 ft)   **High point** 400 m (1310 ft)

**Trails**   **Good most of the year**

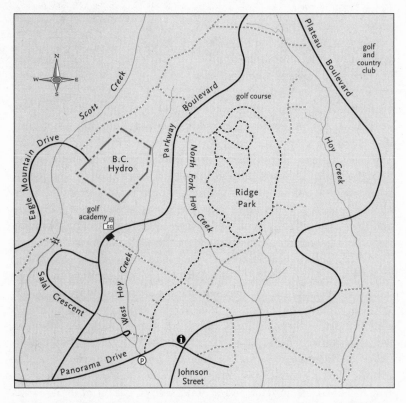

NOWHERE IS THE population expolsion in the lower Fraser Valley more visible than on the once-forested south slopes of Eagle Mountain, where residential development creeps relentlessly upwards from the town centres of Port Moody and Coquitlam. Fortunately, a few areas along streambeds and over rocky outcrops have been saved and provide an escape from pavement to some pleasant green oases. Such a haven in the Westwood Plateau area of Coquitlam is Ridge Park, with a loop trail and access points from several existing streets. Plans exist for other recreational routes as developments are completed, so that eventually it will be possible to make extended walks linking various green strips across the area.

Bunchberry with maidenhair fern.

One starting point is the West Hoy Creek trailhead on Panorama Drive, 300 m west of Johnson Street, which runs north from Highway 7A (Barnet Highway), just west of its junction with Highway 7 (Lougheed Highway) in Coquitlam. Here, the street is wide, with room for parking along the verge, convenient for the steps that start you on the trail. You rise with a thin fringe of trees separating you from nearby houses for a short distance. Then, you reach a power line and a crossing of trails, with left climbing quite steeply to another access point on Parkway Boulevard opposite the West-wood Plateau Golf Academy, and right dropping to Johnson Street.

Going straight ahead takes you into the forest that is Ridge Park, and quite soon you must ford another branch of Hoy Creek, the North Fork, a few metres beyond which begins the loop encircling the park. It is immaterial which way you go: left starts more steeply then eases, while right begins by losing height and saves its stiff section for later, but unless you bail out onto one of the adjacent streets, you will arrive back at this point.

Choosing to go counterclockwise takes you down to level just inside a thin margin of trees with views of Mount Baker, then you swing left and up, ignoring tracks from the right, which would take you out to residential streets east of the ridge. After some 20 minutes of climbing blissfully free of sights and sounds of human endeavours, you begin to get glimpses of a golf course with mountains beyond, and the less pleasant sight of another power line as your trail begins to curve left and south. Now approaching the high point on the main loop, you may be tempted to go still higher on a short loop to the top of the ridge, where a bench invites you to pause, though there is no view of distant scenes to beguile you.

Continuing, you soon come to a three-way fork, with a map giving you the choice of a quick plunge to meet the main trail at another exit point or a more leisurely zigzagging descent to join it a little farther south. Then, you walk roughly parallel to and above the golf fairways for a short time before turning away and dropping quickly to the end of the loop, thereafter retracing your steps to Panorama Drive.

# COQUITLAM RIVER / TOWN CENTRE PARK

**Round trip** 9 km (5.6 mi)

**Allow** 3 hours

Trails, paths and roads

Good all year

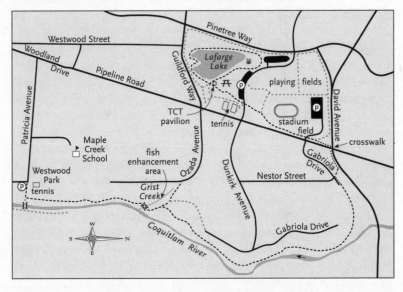

MOST OF THIS walk follows the route of the Trans Canada Trail (TCT), so despite a multitude of inviting side trails in Coquitlam River Park, the distinctive TCT markers keep you on the right track in moments of doubt. Indeed, access to the trailhead may be the most complicated piece of route-finding you will encounter on the outing. A short distance east of the junction of Highways 7 (Lougheed Highway) and 7A (Barnet Highway), turn north on Westwood Street and, at the first traffic light, jog right on Kitchener Avenue, then go left immediately onto Woodland Drive, which soon brings you to Patricia Avenue. Turn right onto this residential street, which ends near a tennis court not far from Coquitlam River, and park here.

Start along the path leading towards the pedestrian bridge over the river, but before you reach it go left on the TCT trail and continue through mostly deciduous then mixed forest with some large conifers and cottonwoods. In spring, the cottonwood's sweet smell (sometimes called Balm of Gilead) perfumes the air, and the lush undergrowth sports a variety of

Pleasant trail through the forest.

lesser plants for you to notice and admire. After about 10 minutes, you cross the bridge over Grist Creek and pause to learn about the restoration projects from the information board there before continuing briefly upstream along the tributary and then turning back towards the main river. Finally, however, you leave the riverside altogether and turn westwards on a lane to emerge on Gabriola Drive, across which a TCT sign beckons just opposite Nestor Street. A short track between houses leads to a main road (David Avenue), and you turn left along it to cross Pipeline Road at a traffic light and pedestrian crossing. A short walk to the left brings you to the protection of a band of trees between park and road as you approach the heart of the park, passing expansive sports grounds on your right.

Beyond the playing fields and their associated parking lots you become aware of the blue waters of a lake, Lafarge Lake, a former gravel pit site, which, along with the surrounding parkland, was gifted to the city at the cessation of the company's activities. Then as you descend to the TCT pavilion near the eastern shore of the lake, you espy the many fishers lining the banks and the waterfowl afloat on the surface. Turn north on the TCT, skirting the wetland environment at the north end, then turn back south along the western shore, taking your farewell of the TCT when it heads off west towards the David Lam Campus of Douglas College and forested Hoy Creek with its salmon hatchery. Rather, stay with the lakeside trail to the south end where you may choose between the paved multi-use path or the Lakeside Nature Trail, the nature trail winding up and down close to the water.

Both will bring you back to the TCT pavilion, from which you start your return walk, rising to meet and cross Pipeline Road and to find the right-of-way that leads you back to the Coquitlam River Trail and eventually your transport.

# POCO TRAIL

**FROM RED BRIDGE TO DOMINION AVENUE:**
One-way trip 12.5 km (7.8 mi)          Allow 4 hours

**ALONG THE COQUITLAM RIVER:**
Round trip 12.5 km (7.8 mi)          Allow 4 hours

**ALONG THE PITT RIVER:**
Round trip 8.8 km (5.5 mi)          Allow 3 hours

Dykes, streets and trails          Good all year

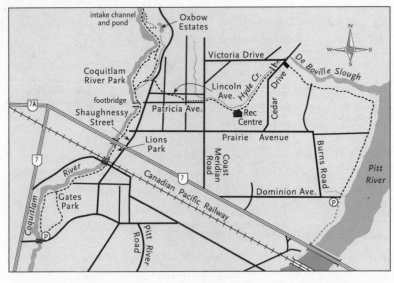

IN MARCH 1970, the idea was conceived of a walk round the municipality of Port Coquitlam, with trails running east and west to link the two south-flowing rivers, the Pitt and the Coquitlam, that enclose it. Sadly, development has played havoc with the original design, reducing the part that is still pleasant for pedestrians to little more than a semicircle confined to the northern half, with transportation necessary to connect the two ends or with your walk limited to one or the other of its segments.

One possible starting point, if you wish to focus on the Coquitlam River, is reached by turning east on Pitt River Road from Highway 7 (Lougheed Highway), crossing the river on the "Red Bridge" and going left into a parking area just beyond the bridge. From here, you have two options: the wide, paved multi-use path starts by going east from the bridge then curving back towards the river at Gates Park, over which you have a fine view of Golden

Restored stream in Coquitlam River Park.

Ears. You find the more interesting walking trail by going in the opposite direction, dropping towards the passage under the road, opposite which the trail starts into the trees using old dykes to stay above the marshlands bordering the river. Quite soon the two routes come together at Gates Park and you have on your right some new condominium developments as you near and pass under the railway with the popular Lions Park just beyond.

Continue to walk upstream using a pedestrian underpass at the highway, cottonwood trees on your right screening much of the urban growth as well as perfuming the air in spring. A short distance beyond the footbridge at the end of Patricia Avenue, you come to Coquitlam River Park, in which the federal Department of Fisheries and Oceans along with local groups has reclaimed historic stream channels, ponds and wetlands. The area is a maze of old roads and trails, but confined between the river and the Oxbow Sidechannel, it is easily negotiable. Leaving the PoCo Trail and travelling through mixed forest, you pass a former equestrian centre, a small pond beside a trailer parking lot and a dead-end trail into an oxbow lake in the midst of a private development before reaching the northern end of the project at the intake channel flowing into a dyked pond.

Alternatively, you might have stayed with the PoCo Trail, now also designated part of the Trans Canada Trail (TCT), crossing Shaughnessy Street onto a track into the trees and walking clear across the municipality from west to east, following park and woodland trails to Lincoln and Patricia Avenues, then along Hyde Creek through its nature reserve and past a recreation centre and a hatchery to Cedar Drive and the head of De Boville Slough.

The slough itself—a wetland habitat for a variety of birds, fish and animals—is a respectable 1.5 km (0.9 mi) in length, and it could be the destination of a walk along the Pitt River, its start at the turnaround at the end of Dominion Avenue which you reach by going north of Highway 7 (Lougheed Highway) on Ottawa Street and east on Dominion. This stretch of dyke gives unimpeded views of farmland and mountains to the east and north, and its marshlands provide a contrast to the treed banks of its neighbour stream. On its own, this route makes a return trip of 7.2 km (4.5 mi) along the river dyke between Pitt River Bridge and the mouth of the slough, an area that is popular with bird and nature watchers.

# WOODLAND WALKS (LOWER BURKE RIDGE)

**WOODLAND WALK:**

| | |
|---|---|
| **Round trip** 8 km (5 mi) | **Allow** 3 hours |
| **Elevation gain** 180 m (590 ft) | **High point** 500 m (1640 ft) |
| **Trails and roads** | **Best May to November** |

**COQUITLAM LAKE VIEWPOINT:**

| | |
|---|---|
| **Round trip** 9.5 km (5.9 mi) | **Allow** 5 hours |
| **Elevation gain** 610 m (2000 ft) | **High point** 930 m (3050 ft) |

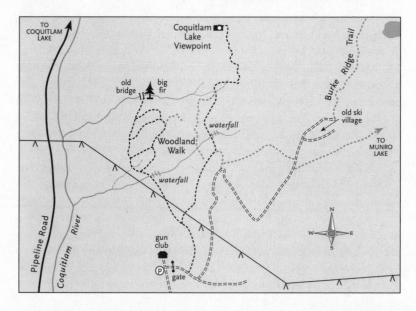

HERE IS A perfect walk for a hot summer's day, with shade to protect you and filtered sunshine to relieve any gloom cast by the massive stumps. The Woodland Walk is the gentlest route of several created by the Burke Mountain Naturalists from the maze of abandoned logging and skid roads on the ridge to introduce walkers to its treasures, biological and historical.

To start, go north off Highway 7 (Lougheed Highway) on Coast Meridian Road and continue for 5 km (3.1 mi) to Harper Road; turn right and drive another 2 km (1.2 mi) to a parking spot near the entrance to the gun club. Walk up the road on the right for about 10 minutes beyond the gate, then go left for a short distance to another fork. The left branch is unmarked;

Shady Woodland Walk.

the right bears a wooden sign inscribed "Coquitlam Lake View and Burke Ridge."

Go left, following the blue markers, staying on the old logging road through second-growth forest and ignoring small bike trails that cross your route. Soon you come into the open at a power-line cut, which you cross, entering the woods on a path that leads to a stream with a missing bridge. Stop here for a few minutes to enjoy the waterfall. To cross the stream, walk up the bank to the makeshift log bridge or farther uphill to step across on stones. Once across, you embark on a circuit on which going right at successive forks gives you the longest loop. The trail rises quite high among huge stumps and lengthy deadfalls before descending to another old road. Going right brings you to a halt at a ravine, where, near a great Douglas-fir on the verge, a mossy, ruined bridge crosses above a spectacular waterfall.

With no means to go ahead, you must turn back. This time, stay with the road when you pass the turnoff to several loop trails until, after bypassing a collapsed bridge, you find yourself at the beginning of your circuit, not far from the power line, where a right turn sets you off on the home stretch.

Another possibility in this area, if you want a more challenging route, is the Coquitlam Lake View Trail, which goes right at the second fork. Travelling in concert with the Burke Ridge route, it heads uphill, eventually reaching an opening at the power line. Ignore the small trail to your left, which leads downhill along the power line, and follow the trail under the power line and into the woods on the far side. The trail, an old logging road becoming washed out and overgrown, continues gently uphill to another fork with wooden signs, where you go left through a stretch of tall second-growth timber before arriving at an attractive little waterfall. Some 90 minutes from the start, this makes a satisfying destination for a short walk.

The hike all the way to the Coquitlam Lake Viewpoint is a more ambitious outing. To continue, ford the stream below the waterfall, go right at a fork, then right again shortly thereafter, ascending steeply on an old eroded road. Eventually, the grade eases and mosses and other plants carpet the trail as you approach your destination on a wooded knob. From it, you may enjoy excellent views of the lake with its surrounding ridges, though blighted by the sight of a gravel operation in the valley downstream.

# MINNEKHADA REGIONAL PARK

**Round trip** 6.5 km (4 mi)

**Elevation gain** 150 m (490 ft)

**Trails**

**Allow** 2.5 hours

**High point** 165 m (540 ft)

**Good most of the year**

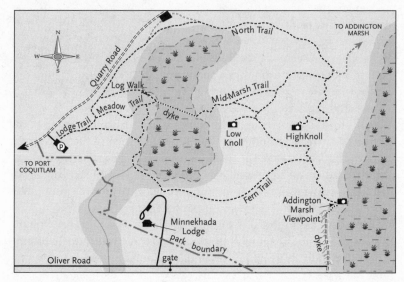

THIS FORMER ESTATE northwest of Port Coquitlam is now a regional park with a lodge that is sometimes open to the public and a trail system that supplies the walker with as much variety as anyone may desire, including a miniature mountain, steep enough to test many, and a viewing pavilion giving a wide outlook over the Pitt River Valley.

To reach the parking area, travel north for 2.5 km (1.5 mi) from Highway 7 (Lougheed Highway) on Coast Meridian Road in Port Coquitlam, go half right on Apel Drive and Victoria Drive, taking the left fork of Victoria, which later becomes Quarry Road. From the fork, continue for 3.5 km (2.2 mi) to parking on the right at the park entrance. The trail system starts here, with the choice of routes to either right or left.

Going right, you come to a marsh that you keep on your left, but after a picnic area and the approach road to the lodge on your right, the forest reasserts itself as you proceed on Fern Trail. Then comes the parting of the ways at a three-way crossing, the right-hand fork taking you to a striking viewpoint across Addington Marsh to the UBC Malcolm Knapp Research Forest with the great peaks of Golden Ears beyond. After gazing your fill, retrace

View over the marsh from Low Knoll.

your steps to the three-way crossing to rejoin the circle trail. Next, after a detour to the Low Knoll viewpoint over the central marsh, you reach a major junction: left here leads you across the marsh on a dyke before returning you via Log Walk or Meadow Trail to your starting point; right commits you to the long perimeter trail.

Going right, you soon come to yet another fork, the right-hand branch of which sends you panting to the top of the sharp rise to High Knoll lookout, from which once more the valley lies before you. On your return to the T-junction, go first right, then left, gaining height and losing it again as you turn west on North Trail. At the next fork, right heads away uphill towards Quarry Road, while you go left and down to marsh level, enjoying the profusion of marsh plants along the way until you merge into Quarry Trail, which parallels the road south. Of all the trails, the one alongside Quarry Road is probably the least attractive, so you may well decide to depart from it on Log Walk, which brings you to the dyke separating Upper from Lower Marsh. From there, you may make your way south on the view trail above Lower Marsh to go right on Lodge Trail for the final stretch back.

Note that the house, Minnekhada Lodge, previously owned by two lieutenant-governors of British Columbia, is now open to the public on the first Sunday afternoon of the month and most other Sundays from February to December. It may also be booked for private functions. (For details, call 604-432-6352.)

# WHYTECLIFF

**Round trip** 5 km (3.1 mi) or less      **Allow** 2 hours

**Trails and roads**      **Good all year**

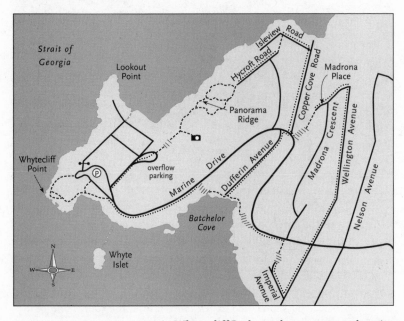

**FROM THE VIEWPOINT** in Whytecliff Park, on the most westerly point of West Vancouver, you may be content with a view across Howe Sound to Bowen Island or, if the tide is favourable, a walk over the causeway to Whyte Islet. But your activity need not be confined to the park's southerly area; a high ridge, aptly named Panorama Ridge, may be a satisfying outing in itself or the start to more ambitious walks.

Travelling west along Highway 1/99 (Upper Levels Highway), take the Marine Drive exit at the Eagleridge interchange, veer left to cross the overpass, then stay with Marine Drive as it winds its picturesque way round Batchelor Cove and ends in Whytecliff Park.

On foot, head towards the overflow parking lot on the fringe of the forest. There, find the start of the steepish trail to Panorama Ridge, with first, on your right, a diversion to a viewpoint over Batchelor Cove. Back on the route, you may enjoy the mixture of trees, arbutus being prominent, before emerging on top for views of Howe Sound and its surrounding mountains. Choosing left forks as you progress brings you to the northern margin of the

Whyte Islet.

park. If you wish only a short outing, turn back right, then left, rejoining your outward route for a return to the busier regions of the park, this time, perhaps, dropping down to the shore at Whyte Bay, then working up the steps and round the point to savour every aspect of Whytecliff.

For longer circuits, when you reach the park's northern extremity, descend Hycroft Road, going left at its bend on a track connecting with Isleview Road, down which you continue to its junction with Copper Cove Road, sharing as you go the fine views of the local homeowners. Next, travel right on Copper Cove to its meeting with Marine Drive, and here again you have a choice. A jog right, then a left turn down Dufferin Avenue brings you to Batchelor Cove, a secluded little beach enclosed by rocky cliffs, a pleasant spot for a swim or a picnic. But if you prefer to explore even farther, back at Marine Drive, go briefly right to find and ascend an inconspicuous track up to Madrona Place, thence to Madrona Crescent on which you go left to Wellington Avenue.

Now, it's plain sailing as you stride down Wellington with the occasional backwards glance over your left shoulder at Mount Harvey and Brunswick Mountain. Next, you cross Rosebery Avenue and Marine Drive in quick succession, then, just when you think you are approaching a dead end, you go right on Imperial Avenue, another cul-de-sac! But don't despair. The stone stairs between house numbers 6265 and 6268 are public and will take you back to Marine Drive. Nor are you yet condemned to walk that busy road, for a few metres to your left you may escape down another set of steps— down, down to Batchelor Cove.

But by whichever route you arrive here, there's no escaping a final walk along Marine Drive if you want to complete the circuit, so climb the steps at the west end onto the road, here bereft of sidewalk, turn left and cautiously make your way back to Whytecliff Park.

# SEAVIEW / LARSEN BAY

**Round trip** 6 km (3.7 mi)
**Trails and roads**

**Allow** 2.5 hours
**Good all year**

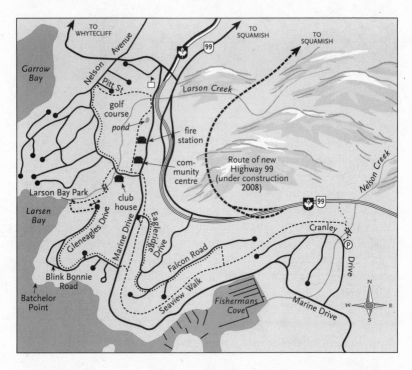

THE SEAVIEW WALK follows an abandoned railway right-of-way, and in order to remedy its lack of destination, your itinerary also includes a few residential streets and a trip down to secluded little Larsen Bay.

The eastern end of this excursion is in Eagle Harbour, approached by travelling west along Highway 1/99 (Upper Levels Highway) to the Marine Drive exit at the Eagleridge interchange. Turn east onto Marine Drive, then make a left turn in the 5700 block onto Cranley Drive, for which a bus stop is also convenient. Cranley takes you uphill to a crossing of Nelson Creek, and it is here, east of the stream, that a path takes off on the road's north side, crossing the waterway on a footbridge and continuing upwards to a flat stretch below the viaduct that carries the highway. A glance to the right shows the rerouted railway disappearing into the tunnel that replaced the right-of-way following a 1972 derailment caused by the sharp change of

Seaview Walk on a winter's day.

direction from southwest to north. Here, too, the Trans Canada Trail (TCT) departs uphill to the right on its long journey across the continent.

Although your main preoccupation on the Seaview Walk is surely with the marine views, you may be fascinated as well by the modern-day cliff dwellings and the plants, notably the arbutus and the mosses, which cling to the rocks on your right. Soon, however, shortly after the 1.5 km marker, you may leave the level walk and turn up a short track that takes you onto Falcon Road, where you turn left, heading more or less parallel to the trail below and ignoring cul-de-sacs on the left until you reach Eagleridge Drive. Here, having savoured the fine views en route, you go left and downhill to rejoin the Seaview trail just short of Marine Drive.

Now you turn right on the Seaview to the crosswalk, where you cross and drop to the path going right alongside the golf course, past the Gleneagles Community Centre, a skateboard park and a fire station, until you come to a sign that informs you that you are at km 1 of the Trans Canada Trail (TCT). Stay with the TCT beyond an ornamental pond and a bridge, then turn into the playground of Gleneagles Elementary School, still following the golf course boundary. At the far side, a rough track first leads you through a fringe of trees, then behind Pitt Street to Nelson Avenue, on which you go left, then left again on St. Georges Avenue. Continue on this road until you come to a golfers' crossing. Here you take the path that descends to the right of the fairway and onto a track dropping into a delightful little glen by the creek. Ignoring all the trails on your left, keep descending until you emerge at Larsen Bay. Here you may want to linger, perhaps to swim.

From this peaceful spot, you may return to St. Georges, which curves into Orchill Road and meets Marine Drive opposite the western end of Seaview Walk. From here you enjoy the length of the walk with sea and mountain vistas as you return to your transportation. Another possibility presents itself, however. From the shore, head right on the service track rising to Gleneagles Drive, and go right following it as it works through this pleasant residential area to meet Marine Drive just beside a bus stop. Across the way you will discern a steep track, which you climb to intersect and go right on the Seaview Walk to complete your outing.

# TRANS CANADA TRAIL / NELSON CREEK LOOP

**Round trip** 9 km (5.6 mi)

**Allow** 3.5 hours

**Elevation gain** 418 m (1370 ft)

**High point** 460 m (1510 ft)

**Trails and roads**

**Good most of the year**

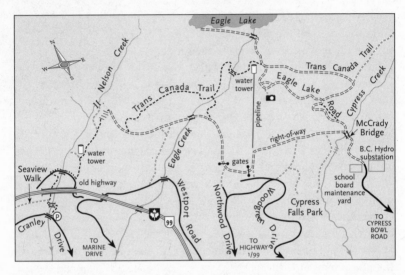

IF YOU HAVE traversed the Seaview Walk east from Horseshoe Bay (Walk 40), you have already sampled the most westerly mainland section of the Trans Canada Trail. Now comes the next, more demanding part, which starts you off on the trail's upsy-downsy march across the face of the North Shore mountains.

Start as you did for the Seaview Walk (Walk 40) by driving north off Marine Drive on Cranley Drive to the trailhead at Nelson Creek. On foot, you cross the creek and rise to the Seaview Walk, where you turn right and immediately mount to a vantage point above the entrance to the tunnel that replaced the original right-of-way. Then you continue to ascend, passing under the present Highway 1/99 (Upper Levels Highway) to reach the roadbed of its predecessor. Here, you may enjoy a brief respite as you cross the 1956-vintage bridge with a view down Nelson Creek under the viaduct.

Beyond the bridge, the route goes left and climbs towards another water tower, to the right of which you embark on a delightful trail through ancient forest above the canyon of Nelson Creek, climbing steadily through

Forest edge above Nelson Canyon.

the fine old trees to arrive at the end of an abandoned road. This you follow for a few minutes before the trail heads off left, zigzagging a little at first to gain altitude and oftentimes making use of old forest roads, for you are now among quite large second-growth trees. Descending into a damp bottom, you approach, then swing left away from a small creek (Eagle Creek), arriving at a fork where turning right offers you a shorter circuit. Electing to go left, you stay with the Trans Canada Trail as it rises, finally crossing the creek on a sturdy bridge and emerging shortly thereafter on the grassy right-of-way of a water pipe, just below a tower.

From here, you go right twice, following the old Eagle Lake Road to meet the new, on which you go right again to a three-way split. Here, the new road heads east taking the Trans Canada Trail with it, while you keep right to find a track to a bluff top with a splendid view. After this break, continue downhill to a wide turnaround where the former route of the Trans Canada Trail goes left, ascending steeply for another 500 m (1640 ft) on the route of the original access into Cypress Bowl. Your goal is lower, however, and you turn downhill again—on the road, if you wish, though you may cut the first corner using a faint trail that drops off on the east side, following a washed-out forest road. Whichever route you choose, you will eventually arrive at a junction close to the McCrady Bridge over Cypress Creek. Now, you go right on the wide right-of-way to another T-junction. Turn left here and down before going right above a residential area, your path adorned with a disclaimer of liability by British Properties, its owner.

Next, after passing a second gate with another warning, you note a track angling in from your right—the route you would have taken had you bailed out earlier—and then you continue westwards across Eagle Creek and gently upwards to rejoin the Trans Canada Trail and retrace your steps to Cranley Drive.

# LIGHTHOUSE PARK

**SHORT CIRCUIT: Round trip** 5 km (3.1 mi)   **Allow** 2 hours
**LONG CIRCUIT: Round trip** 9 km (5.6 mi)   **Allow** 3.5 hours
**Trails**   **Good all year**

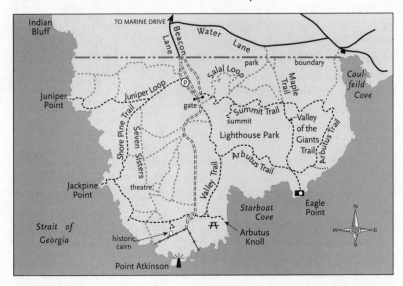

EVEN URBAN TROGLODYTES who emerge only infrequently from the built-up sections of Vancouver must be aware of Point Atkinson, the landmark on the north shore of Burrard Inlet, if for no other reason than that its lighthouse sends friendly beams of light over the waters during the hours of darkness. But Point Atkinson is well worth a visit for its own sake, located as it is at the southern tip of Lighthouse Park, which features old-growth coastal forest, rocky headlands and narrow bays. It is the haunt of varied wildlife, from the humble organisms of the intertidal zone to majestic birds.

To reach the park, drive or take the bus west along Marine Drive from the north end of the Lions Gate Bridge for a distance of just over 9.6 km (6 mi). A little past a firehall, after a small rise in the road, Beacon Lane lies on the left. Turn and follow it to the designated parking area, at the end of which a gate bars further progress, though a service road does continue beyond it. Below the gate, a main trail goes off through tall conifers towards the southwest, leading to the lighthouse.

For a trouble-free walk that leaves the lighthouse until later, you may walk back through the parking lot to a second gate about halfway down on

Point Atkinson lighthouse from the historic cairn.

your left. Simply follow this main trail as it circles the park counterclockwise, adding little excursions seawards as fancy takes you. You may, for instance, follow Juniper Loop as it goes off right beside an interesting cedar and works its way out to Juniper Point and a fine view; then, at the next divergence, you may go right and descend gradually to an attractive cove with dykes of igneous rock penetrating the granite and contrasting with it. A little farther south, another short diversion right leads to Jackpine Point, giving views across to Bowen Island and exhibiting all the beauty of a combined marine and forest landscape. Here, too, note the grooves in the rock, mute evidence of past glaciation.

As you turn southeastwards towards the point, you get your first sight of the lighthouse, and soon you find yourself on the rock just behind it, where a plaque gives its history, dating back over a century, though the present tower was erected only in 1912. Once you start back, your direct route is to the right (east) and virtually parallel with the service road.

Side trips are possible, the first being the short detour right to Arbutus Knoll, a rounded bluff overlooking Starboat Cove. Once you have rejoined the trail, the trip back to the gate at the south end of the parking area does not take long; that is, if you have not followed another track heading up from Valley Trail and linking up with the trail system on the park's east side.

If you do follow this track, the Arbutus Trail, cross the bridge on your right and begin to rise quite steeply over a little ridge, then descending again just as steeply on the other side to two intersections in quick succession. At the first a trail with the descriptive name Valley of the Giants goes left, while at the next a short diversion takes you right to Eagle Point, which is rich with lilies in the spring and well worth a visit regardless of the main trails you intend to follow. Both are rewarding routes which meet again farther along with Arbutus Trail. You continue on this trail past meetings with Maple, Summit and Deer Fern Trails to join Salal Loop, which will take you back to the final turn down to the parking lot no matter which direction you choose.

# SAHALEE / CAULFEILD LOOP

**Round trip** 5 km (3.1 mi)

**Elevation gain** 177 m (580 ft)

**Trails and roads**

**Allow** 2.5 hours

**High point** 220 m (720 ft)

**Good all year**

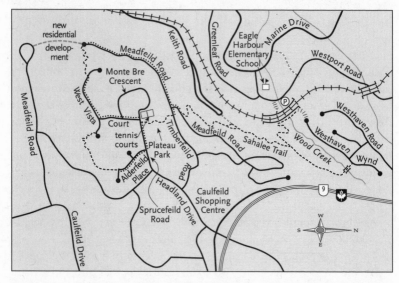

THE SAHALEE TRAIL must be one of the best little trails in West Vancouver, its trouble being just that—it is little, too short to make a full day's outing. Still, if what you want is a quick up-and-back, this is perfect, and rising as it does from just above Marine Drive to Upper Caulfeild, it provides sufficient challenge to compensate for its brevity.

Driving or taking the bus west along Marine Drive from the north end of the Lions Gate Bridge, you may reach the trailhead in Eagle Harbour by turning right just before Eagle Harbour Elementary School onto Westport Road. Continue past Greenleaf Road to the next bend, on which there is limited parking space by a small stream. It is here that you start up a steep flight of stairs on the right (south) side of the creek, then you pass under a railway bridge and come to a T-junction. If you go left across a footbridge and up many steps, you will very soon find yourself at the dead end of Westhaven Wynd (and indeed if you should do this it's no great matter, for you may continue uphill on the Wynd to house number 5367, where you will find another flight of steps leading to a track heading back across the creek and onto the Sahalee Trail).

Natural statue at the top of the trail.

The main route, however, goes right and ascends steadily on a rocky, zig-zagging trail in lush forest. At a sharp elbow bend to the right with a hand rail on the lower side, you may remark a fairly obscure route going straight ahead. This is the trail mentioned above. Keep right, therefore, staying with the rocky track until you come to a high bridge over a bushy ravine, after which the trail is smooth and gently descending. About halfway down the slope a rough shortcut goes left and avoids the re-ascent necessary if you stay with the easy route. Eventually, just before you arrive at Meadfeild Road, a level stretch provides you with views to the west, to Bowen Island and the Rainy River Peaks and, nearer at hand, to the Eagle Ridge area. For a short walk of about an hour, this would be a good place to turn.

However, by making use of some connecting roadways you may pro-long your outing and enjoy even better views. To do this, go right (south) on Meadfeild for about 500 m and watch for a "Trail" sign on the left. Here you head up the rocks on a steep track assisted frequently by equally steep stairways, with numerous viewpoints to west and south en route. Finally you arrive on a wide, grassy verge bordering a neighbourhood road, with a natural statue to admire as you draw breath.

Now turn right and follow what you discover is West Vista Court, which meets Sprucefeild Road opposite some tennis courts to the right of which is your next bit of trail. This descends to Timberfeild Road near its junction with Meadfeild and round the corner from the Sahalee, on which you begin your return either directly or by the detour via Westhaven Wynd.

Yet another possibility presents itself, however. If you relish a little adven-ture on a rocky, upsy-downsy route running along the edge of an escarp-ment, take the marked trail disappearing down to the right soon after you turn down West Vista Court from the high point. On this you work round the slope, enjoying some fine arbutus trees and smaller rock plants before emerging on Alderfeild Place, where going left twice brings you back to Sprucefeild, then to the tennis courts and the trail down.

# CAULFEILD TRAIL / KLOOTCHMAN PARK

**Round trip** 7.2 km (4.5 mi)     **Allow** 3 hours

**Trails and roads**     **Good all year**

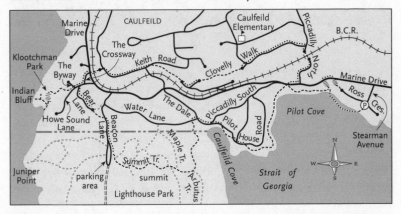

HERE ARE TWO parks, the first an ocean-side trail winding through mature trees, the second a forested gem approached by a narrow trail and a stairway which drop steeply to the rocks by the ocean. Each is a delight on its own but to visit both in a single outing, try this loop with Klootchman as your destination for a lunch stop.

Drive or take the bus along Marine Drive from the north end of the Lions Gate Bridge to just west of the Cypress Park Market area, turn south on Stearman Avenue, then go right briefly on Ross Crescent to parking on the left. From here, if the tide is right, you may walk along the beach and clamber up the rocks to the trail. Otherwise, continue west along Ross to its end, and climb the steps to Marine Drive, along which you walk a few paces to descend again just before house number 4518.

Now your route undulates along the foreshore, out over rocky promontories and back into the mature trees between water and road, with after some 15 minutes another entry point from Marine Drive and shortly thereafter a track down to a sandy beach. Finally the trail emerges in a clearing, the site of a pioneer homestead and pilot house, with, on the right, an anchor embedded in a large rock with a plaque commemorating Francis William Caulfeild. Here, after just over 1 km (0.6 mi), ends the Caulfeild Trail. Continue west on Pilot House Road and Piccadilly South, observing on the left the dock overlooking Caulfeild Cove, and over to the right the

View up Howe Sound from Klootchman Park.

popular Anglican church, St. Francis in the Woods, before you come to the junction with Water Lane and The Dale.

Now you must decide. You may stay with Water Lane to its far end; but for variety and interest, take the sporting little track going off into The Dale Park and rising steeply into Lighthouse Park. Thus you proceed, surrounded by mature Douglas-firs and hemlock to a three-way junction. Go right and, losing some of the height you have just gained, descend to another cross-roads, where you stay straight ahead on Arbutus Trail, then almost immediately fork left on Summit Trail, which as the name suggests leads you to the highest point in the park. After a short detour left to the bare, rounded hillock, continue to meet Salal Trail on which go left, then right, down to the parking lot.

Leave the park on Beacon Lane from which, on your left, you find a short track connecting with Bear Lane, your route through an attractive residential area. At the next junction, go left on Howe Sound Lane, pass The Byway and immediately on the right is the entrance to Klootchman Park. From here, a narrow path and a set of steps descend the cliff leading to the ocean side with its rocky coves and outcrops, where you may explore, picnic or just relax and ponder what woman, as the word "klootchman" means in Chinook, gave the park its name.

After this break, you must retrace your steps to Howe Sound Lane where you go left as far as The Crossway, which takes you to a crossing of the railway and on up to Keith Road. Here you turn east beyond a T-junction to a fork, where you go right into a cul de sac at the end of which the Clovelly Walk begins. Now you stay with Clovelly as it alternates between trail and paved lane, passing en route a bijou park with sea views on the right and a new residential development on the left. Then, after another stretch of wildness, you descend to meet and go right on Piccadilly North, recrossing the railway and dropping to Marine Drive on which you turn right briefly to reach an entry to the Caulfeild Trail. A left turn starts you on the last lap of your outing.

# WHYTE LAKE LOOP

**Round trip** 7 km (4.3 mi)         **Allow** 3.5 hours

**Elevation gain** 280 m (920 ft)      **High point** 310 m (1015 ft)

**Trails**                             **Good most of the year**

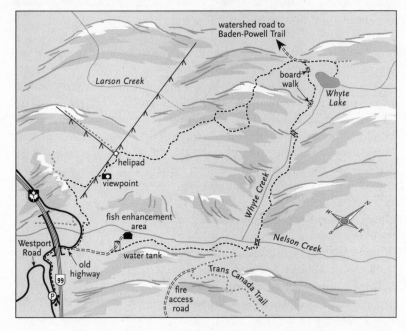

WHEN ROAD CONSTRUCTION in 2007 obliterated the western terminus of the Baden-Powell Centennial Trail, a substitute was soon found. A new route was devised using part of the Trans Canada Trail (TCT) and a recently restored trail up Whyte Creek. As well, the one-time route up the bluffs at Eagleridge—popular in spring for a fine display of wildflowers—was partly compensated by a new start farther east. Together, these innovations make possible a very attractive loop.

To start, leave Highway 1/99 (Upper Levels Highway) for Caulfeild (Exit 4); drive west on Westport Road and, for the next 2 km (1.2 mi), experience the original Upper Levels Highway as it was in the middle of the last century. Immediately after passing under the highway's present incarnation, go right on the TCT bicycle route to park by the roadside. On foot, continue along the old road past a yellow gate and under the highway yet again to reach the road bridge built high above Nelson Creek in 1956. (Note that if you travel

Boardwalk near Whyte Lake.

by bus, the approach would be by Marine Drive and Cranley Drive to the trailhead at Nelson Creek as described in Walk 41, then along the Trans Canada Trail as far as the 1956 bridge.) Here, beginning with the more demanding part of the circuit first, you will find the trail disappearing into the bush at the west end of the bridge on the north side of the old road.

Now you begin to climb, zigzagging upwards and trending generally westwards to pass under a power line before coming to a fork at which you turn back sharp right over rocks, many bare of soil, but with enough sustenance here and there to encourage a few flowers in spring—white camas and tiny yellow mimulus to surprise and delight. Then you emerge on the power line again with a view over the highway to Caulfeild Plateau, before plunging back into the forest for a short distance to reach a meeting place of power lines with a helipad—a good place to draw breath.

Next comes a very pleasant stretch, meandering and undulating through the woods on a trail, so far not heavily used. At a T-junction some 15 minutes later, left is the shorter route, though you may opt for either since they meet again farther on and finally descend to meet the old watershed road to Whyte Lake. Going left here takes you down to connect with the Baden-Powell Trail, but staying right brings you in a few steps to another fork, with a fine new boardwalk going off at right angles on what was an old logging road. That will be your return route; but for now, continue straight ahead and watch for a track going right and down to Whyte Lake.

After your sojourn at the lake, return to the boardwalk—which takes you south of the lake to cross its outlet, Whyte Creek—then make your way down the left bank through a stretch of magnificent old-growth forest. Finally, still among the forest giants, you come to Nelson Creek and a bridge completed in 2008 that is much less interesting than the previous crossing on a wide log that spanned the creek comfortably a little upstream. Once across the creek, you stay with it for a short distance, enjoying excellent views down into its canyon. Then you head uphill to join the Trans Canada Trail and go down it, leaving the forest near a water tank and descending on a service road to the old highway and its 1956 bridge. Now you retrace your steps under the highway and so back to your transportation.

# CYPRESS FALLS PARK

**Round trip** 3 km (1.9 mi) or more

**Trails and roads**

**Allow** 1 hour

**Good all year**

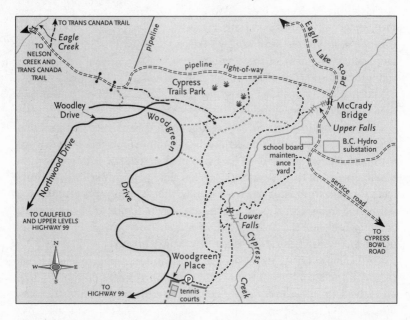

GIVEN THAT THE semi-wilderness Cypress Falls Park, with its groves of fine Douglas-fir, is little more than a stone's throw above Highway 1/99 (Upper Levels Highway), it is not as well known as it might be. For access to it, take the Caulfeild–Woodgreen Drive turnoff (Exit 4) from the highway, turn right, then right again at Woodgreen Place to park in the open area on the left beyond the tennis courts. Cross the clearing towards the forest, then turn left and uphill, but for the best view of the lower falls, abandon this trail almost immediately and drop to an old pipeline route on a bench just below on the right.

On this, you soon reach a fine viewpoint overlooking the tumbling waters in their little canyon. Then you must scramble up to your left to regain the main trail, which descends to a lookout above the waterfall. Next, a footbridge takes you across the creek to its east side and you start rising, eventually emerging on a service road with various power lines leading to a power station. Turn left and uphill towards that installation and a School Board facilities workshop opposite it. Ignoring a B.C. Hydro service road on your

Sword fern.

right, in a few more minutes recross the creek on the stout McCrady Bridge. Then, go left on the pipeline right-of-way where Eagle Lake Road goes right, rising quite steeply. A little more than 100 m along, a trail to the left takes you to a view of the upper falls, particularly impressive during spring runoff. From here, many routes descend through the park, providing opportunities for viewing its grand old trees. Staying left at forks, however, brings you down close to the creek, with glimpses of its rapids an added bonus. At a fork within sight of your first bridge, you may go right, rising slightly to pass a final few large Douglas-firs and a grove of young hemlocks before descending to rejoin the main trail within steps of the clearing from which you set out.

This, however, by no means exhausts the area's possibilities. Given that the park route abuts on the previously described Trans Canada Trail/Nelson Creek Loop (Walk 41), you may wish to incorporate part of that walk into your outing. For instance, you may set out afresh on the main trail then go left and up, making your way north along the western side of the park with occasional glimpses of dwellings as Woodgreen Drive makes one of its easterly swings. Keep left at the first major intersection then right at a second and continue along the front of a rocky face, descending slightly and rising again, finally veering west to emerge on the old road from Cypress Trails Park. Now go right past a British Properties gate with its disclaimer of liability, and a few paces beyond take a faint track heading into the bush on the left and across a small stream. Next, make your way between houses on your left and wetlands on your right until you join an access road near a second gate. Then after passing yet another gate, watch for a track angling up to the right at a widening of the road. This leads to the Trans Canada Trail.

Now, you may choose whether to go left towards Nelson Creek, returning on the British Properties road, or to go right, rising to the high point at the water tower and descending by Eagle Lake Road. Either way, you arrive back at the right-of-way with the previously described alternatives through the park at your disposal. And either way, you will have more than doubled the basic park outing, so allow lots of time.

# HOLLYBURN MOUNTAIN

**Round trip** 8 km (5 mi)

**Elevation gain** 425 m (1395 ft)

**Trail**

**Allow** 3 hours

**Highpoint** 1325 m (4345 ft)

**Best July to November**

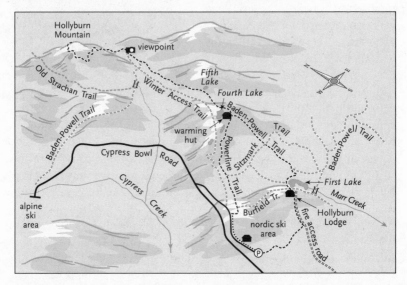

THE CREATION OF Cypress Provincial Park in 1975 and the accompanying vehicle access makes the ascent of Hollyburn today an easy outing for most people. But this was not always so. Early in the last century, Hollyburn was already a mecca for outdoor enthusiasts from Vancouver who ascended the mountain from the ferry at sea level to First Lake and beyond. Later, after construction of the Lions Gate Bridge and the development of British Properties, the routes became shorter as roads pushed higher up the slopes. Today, the ascent is less than a third of that facing the early mountaineers.

A good place to start today's short version and to savour a little of the past is at the cross-country ski parking area. Travelling west along Highway 1/99 (Upper Levels Highway), take the exit for Cypress Bowl Road (Exit 8), which you follow for 13 km (8 mi) as it winds around the mountain. Turn right off this road and drive beyond the ski buildings as far as you can. Note that parking fees are in effect throughout the summer months. At the far end of the lot, a trail heads off into the trees and rises to meet the old fire access road to Hollyburn Lodge. On this old road, you go left and continue uphill past a few cabins visible here and there in the trees. Soon you reach the old

The Lions seen from the top of Hollyburn Mountain.

lodge, now designated a heritage building, and First Lake, beside which is a picnic table adorned with plaques commemorating Hollyburn's pioneers. Circle the lake on its north side and join the Baden-Powell Trail, which supersedes a very worn original path which you may have noted to the west on the route of the present wintertime Telemark Trail.

Going left and uphill on the Baden-Powell brings you to a power line and a warming hut near Fourth Lake, then continues past Fifth Lake, winding back and forth across the ski clearing and into the trees. Then you come to a fork where you depart from the Baden-Powell and go right, rising to a mound where once stood the Nickey Creek Water Board cabin, only a few nails remaining as a reminder of its presence. With a view south to the lowlands of the Fraser delta, this spot makes a satisfactory destination for a round trip of some 4 km (2.5 mi) with an altitude gain of about 170 m (560 ft).

If you go on, the trail first drops very slightly to the right then swings back across the bush-covered slope and into the trees on the west side, becoming steeper as you zigzag upwards. Dodging little bits of trail erosion to arrive at a beautiful little meadow and a small pond, you enjoy a respite before a final scramble to the peak with its panoramic views and the pair of resident ravens that have dispossessed the one-time pan-handling whisky jacks.

To return, retrace your steps down the ridge, rejoining the Baden-Powell and continuing as far as the power line, where you have a choice: instead of returning by the Hollyburn Lodge, you may descend on the trail down the power line with views of the Strait of Georgia and as far as the Olympic Peninsula and Vancouver Island mountains—a fine end to your trip.

Although this walk is only possible during the months when the mountain is free of snow, a hikers' access route has been established for the ski season when the rest of the area is reserved for fee-paying skiers and snowshoers. This free route, which is marked with wands, starts near the information kiosk before the ticket office and rises steeply along the margin of the forest to the left of the power line, descends briefly, then just short of Third Lake, veers off left into the trees. After ascending independently for a short distance it approaches and works along the west side of first the Triangle Lakes then the Romstad ski trails and finally up the wide open swath to the peak.

# LOWER HOLLYBURN

**Round trip** 12 km (7.5 mi) or less

**Elevation gain** 500 m (1640 ft)

**Trails and roads**

**Allow** 4.5 hours

**High point** 930 m (3050 ft)

**Best May to November**

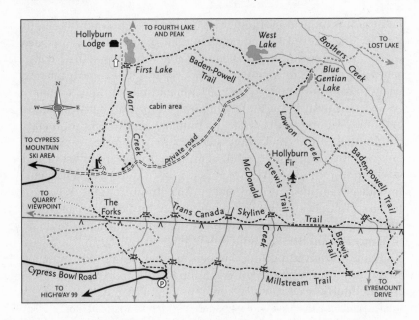

WITH SNOW LYING late on Hollyburn's higher reaches, it is fortunate that a well-established trail system on its south-facing lower slopes permits an earlier start to the hiking season. The bad news is that the trails are wet early in the year, the good that the tree shade makes this a wise choice for hot days in summer.

For a start, leave Highway 1/99 (Upper Levels Highway) at Cypress Bowl Road (Exit 8) and drive to Highview Lookout at the second hairpin bend. Note that parking fees are in effect here throughout the summer months. Cut across the corner to pick up your trail on the north side of the highway and almost immediately note the trail coming downhill from the left; it will be your return route. Next, your track, the Millstream Trail, rises then drops sharply to cross a stream and rise again, repeating the process for a second creek before it settles to a gradual descent on its way eastwards. Then, some 30 minutes along, a narrow track signed "Brewis Trail" leads up to the Skyline Trail if you want a shortcut. The main route continues east to

Hollyburn Lodge.

a T-junction not far from the junction of Eyremount Drive and Millstream Road.

Go left on the trail, rising steadily on the eroded surface and, ignoring a right fork to the Shields Incline Railway (Walk 51), eventually reaching the fork where your route parts from the Brothers Creek Trail. Keep left, making a second left just beyond a power line. From here, you are on the Skyline Trail, now also designated the Trans Canada Trail, sometimes in the open close to the power line, sometimes in the forest as you cross one creek after another, with, before long, signs for the Brewis Trail again, the uphill leg this time leading to the former Westlake Lodge road via the Hollyburn Douglas-fir.

At last comes a four-way fork adorned with a pile of stones that used to support the historic Old Forks sign as well as some newer ones. Here you turn left and follow the steepish trail downhill, emerging just above the original lookout for a round trip of 6.8 km (4.2 mi), having risen in all the best part of a thousand feet.

For a longer walk, stay right at the fork above the power line and follow the Baden-Powell Trail uphill, ignoring the Crossover Trail, which you intersect en route to the next decisive fork. Going straight ahead and still on the Boy Scout trail, you would pass the site of the one-time Westlake Lodge, then continue on the Grand National ski trail. But right is more attractive, leading you quite soon to Blue Gentian Lake, where the damp environment encourages a healthy growth of that plant plus other moisture-lovers. From here, turn left and uphill to West Lake, beyond which you may travel via the Jack Spratt ski trail until it too joins the Grand National, on which you reach the literal high point of your walk: the outlet from First Lake and the old Hollyburn Lodge. Just across the creek and close to the ranger station, turn left on the one-time main trail, descending through the cabin area and staying right at the first two forks, then going left at the third.

At the next, however, take the steep, dark and narrow track going down right to Westlake Road just west of and below a TV relay tower. Now jog right some thirty paces, then continue downhill on the foot trail, cross a very old road and finally turn left on an eroded stretch of logging road to the Forks. From here, your downhill route duplicates that of the shorter circuit.

# MCDONALD CREEK / LAWSON CREEK LOOP

**Round trip** 5.5 km (3.4 mi)

**Elevation gain** 265 m (870 ft)

**Road and trails**

**Allow** 2.5 hours

**High point** 440 m (1445 ft)

**Good most of the year**

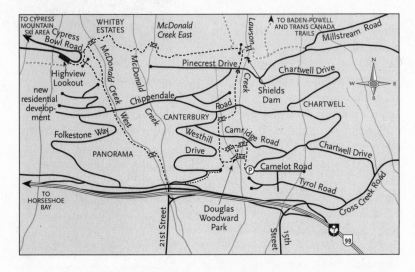

HERE IS A hike that may be done in either direction starting from Woodward Park, a patch of original forest gifted to the municipality by Mr. and Mrs. P.A. Woodward in memory of their son Douglas. Indeed the park alone with its grand trees, tumbling streams and several trails makes a fine destination for those lucky enough to live within walking distance. Otherwise, travelling west on Highway 1/99 (Upper Levels Highway), take the exit at 15th Street/Cross Creek Road (Exit 11) and go right on Cross Creek Road. At the next intersection, turn left onto Tyrol Road, right on 15th Street and left on Camelot Road, which leads you to the small parking lot for the park.

Now on foot, follow the trail along the west side of Lawson Creek to a footbridge, beyond which you turn left briefly before working west to a junction. Go left and downhill out of the park onto Westhill Place, which joins Westhill Drive. Still descending slightly, suffer this stretch of road until you reach the traffic light at the top of 21st Street. Cross the road and continue a few steps west to find a trail going uphill on your right. At first your path rises to the west of one branch of McDonald Creek in the

Along Lawson Creek in Woodward Park.

remnants of an old park, but soon more recent developments begin to impinge on your senses, though they are generally held at bay by a fringe of forest. Then you swing to the west and cross yet another branch of the creek before turning right and uphill once more. Thus you proceed, the pleasant sound of the creek on your right, while you reach and cross two roads leading to new developments. Finally you leave houses behind and ascend on a rough track to meet the Millstream Trail near the point where it meets the Cypress Bowl Road near Highview Lookout. En route to this point you have been enjoying fine views at each successive road crossing; but for the finest view of all, make your way behind the retaining wall to the lookout with its signs and information.

After this diversion, return to Millstream and proceed to negotiate the ups and downs over the eroding banks of two branches of McDonald Creek until you reach easy walking on what was originally a logging road, named Donald's Road after an early resident. Another pioneer is commemorated by the Brewis Trail, which you see going uphill just before you reach a British Properties gate. Here you leave Millstream Trail and descend past the historic Shields Dam on Lawson Creek to reach Pinecrest Drive, under which you pass alongside the creek in a huge culvert. Stay with the creek as you continue downhill until you reach and cross Chippendale Road below which the trail veers west and crosses another fork of Lawson Creek. Stay on this side of the creek all the way to Woodward Park, which you enter along a narrow path below Camridge Road.

Now you may choose one of four routes back to your transportation. Straight ahead goes down to join your outward trail, so go left along the top of the park to just beyond the footbridge over the west fork. From here, right goes back across the middle of the park. Staying left you continue along the edge of the forest until you reach the main stream, where going right takes you down the west bank to your original crossing. Alternatively, taking the bridge ahead brings you back on the east side of both creek and park to complete the circuit.

# BROTHERS CREEK TRAILS

**Round trip** 11 km (6.8 mi) or less

**Elevation gain** 435 m (1425 ft)

**Trails**

**Allow** 4 hours

**High point** 800 m (2625 ft)

**Best May to November**

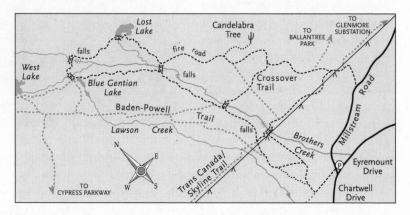

ONE NICE POINT about the trip described here is that the route's elongated shape allows you to sample slices of suitable length if you do not wish to indulge in the whole delicacy. It provides rich variety, too: maturing second-growth forest with, here and there, survivors of the original giant trees, a creek with three sets of falls and canyons, and two forest lakes as well, if you make the longest trip.

To reach its starting point, from Highway 1/99 (Upper Levels Highway) at Taylor Way (Exit 13), continue north into the British Properties, turn left at the T-junction and pick up Highland Drive at the first four-way stop. Stay on Highland until, finally, you turn left on Eyremount Drive and continue to its junction with Millstream Road. Park here close to a gated forest road with West Vancouver Parks trail signs and map. Take this trail, and in about 5 minutes turn right and uphill for another 5 minutes to a fork where you have a choice: to go right on Shields Incline Railway trail that meets the Skyline Trail close by Brothers Creek and then take a jog left; or left on the traditional route, going right at the next fork signposted for Brothers Creek and Lost Lake and, a few minutes thereafter, crossing a power line right-of-way and the variously named Skyline Trail, Baden-Powell Trail or Trans Canada Trail.

Now you plunge into forest, the creek well below you on your right, and thus you remain until, after track and waterway have both levelled slightly,

Lost Lake.

you come to the second point of decision: a footbridge takes you right, over the creek on the Crossover Trail, to a meeting with the return route, giving a round trip of 6 km (3.7 mi) for which you should allow about 2 hours.

If you stay left and continue up the main trail, you have first of all a level stretch where the creek is just another pleasant forest stream, but then you rise again and soon view your first set of falls, above which you face another choice: to cross the creek or not. Here again, you may return by staying right after you have crossed to the east bank, then descending on a fire road to link up with the lower circuit trail for a round trip of 8.7 km (5.4 mi) and a time of nearly 3 hours.

For the longest walk, stay west of the creek. Another 20 minutes or so of walking brings you to pretty little Blue Gentian Lake, where there are, in season, an abundance of water-lily flowers as well as the gentians for which the lake is named. From the lake, stay right, drop a little to cross a small creek, then cross Brothers Creek, just beyond which are interesting views into the gorge of the upper falls. After a half-hour walk on a sometimes rough, eroding track, traverse the outlet of the lake you are seeking, another possible stopping point.

For your return trip, use the trail downhill on the east side of Brothers Creek to join and descend the fire road. On this stretch, the road coincides briefly with an old cable-railway bed (Walk 51) before parting again at the next bend. Lower still, the Crossover Trail enters from the right and departs a few bends later for Ballantree by the site of a one-time sawmill. Keep right and continue down to the power line, turn right on Skyline Trail, rise some 100 m (330 ft), then drop sharply to Brothers Creek's lower falls. Here, you recross the creek, rise equally fast out of its ravine and return to your starting point by whichever route you choose, your walk on Brothers (once Sisters) Creek over.

If, when you reach the power line on the fire road, you want no more climbing, you could go straight ahead, crossing Skyline (Baden-Powell) Trail out to Millstream Road and thence back to your car.

# HOLLYBURN HERITAGE TRAILS

**Round trip** 6.7 km (4.2 mi)

**Elevation gain** 314 m (1030 ft)

**Trails**

**Allow** 3.5 hours

**High point** 665 m (2180 ft)

**Best May to November**

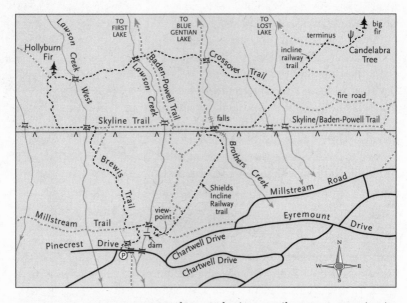

HOLLYBURN HAS NOT one but two heritage trails commemorating its logging history, with self-guiding brochures available from West Vancouver Parks and Community Services (for copies, call 604-925-7200). The walk suggested here combines the two to produce one satisfying ramble that avoids as far as possible those sections of routes described elsewhere (Walks 48 and 50).

To start, leave Highway 1/99 (Upper Levels Highway) at 15th Street/ Cross Creek Road (Exit 11) and go right on Cross Creek Road, then left onto Chartwell Drive. Stay on Chartwell, winding uphill until, just after the fifth elbow bend, you go left (west) on Pinecrest Drive. A small cairn and the distinctive blue-and-green heritage trail sign mark the beginning on the west side of the bridge spanning Lawson Creek.

Almost immediately, you reach a viewpoint for the Shields Log Dam and pass on up the pleasant woodland trail to meet Millstream Trail, an old logging road. Turn right and across Lawson Creek to a T-junction, where you go left. Stay on this, an old truck road, for about 5 minutes to the next

View downstream under Pinecrest Drive.

fork, leaving it for what was the route of an inclined cable railway, the Shields Incline Railway, running straight ahead until it reaches the banks of Brothers Creek, the remains of an old bridge still visible across the stream. Following the deepening canyon, you next come to the Skyline (Baden-Powell) Trail and turn right, dropping steeply to cross Brothers Creek and rising again to continue past a small lookout with views over the city to a fork at the foot of another section of cable railway, again straight and smooth except at creeks where old trestles have collapsed and disappeared. Next, you cross a transverse trail (Crossover Trail) and shortly thereafter join a fire road occupying the place of the railway for a short distance to the next bend, where you go straight ahead on the railbed to its upper terminal, only a few scattered artifacts to mark the one-time loading site. After visualizing the scene in the 1920s, return downhill almost to the fire road and descend by a rough trail on the left (east) for about 5 minutes to a large Douglas-fir, now dead and called the "Candelabra" tree for its distinctive forklike shape. Continuing downhill, the track passes several other huge snags before ending at an old-growth Douglas-fir, a living giant among the dead.

Next, retrace your steps to the fire road, and thereafter to the former railbed as far as the Crossover Trail, where you turn right, heading gently uphill towards Brothers Creek and its trail beyond the bridge. A few metres right on this brings you to the continuation of the Crossover Trail, now making for the Baden-Powell Trail and Lawson Creek and across both on the way to the high point of your outing—the Hollyburn Douglas-fir, a giant quietly growing here for nearly eleven hundred years.

Close by, Brewis Trail runs roughly north-south, north eventually arriving at the old Westlake Road via the McDonald Canyon, but today turn left and south, descending quite steeply to the Skyline Trail. Go left on it for a short distance before resuming your downhill plunge on Brewis, which returns you in short order to the Millstream Trail. Going left again soon brings you back to your outward route from Pinecrest Drive.

> ## 52  West Vancouver

# BALLANTREE

**Round trip** 3 km (1.9 mi)

**Elevation gain** 145 m (475 ft)

**Roads and trails**

**Allow** 1.5 hours

**High point** 465 m (1525 ft)

**Best April to November**

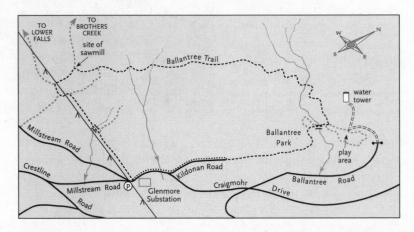

LOOKING FOR A short walk within easy reach of the British Properties? Try this circular outing on the lower slopes of Hollyburn Mountain for
a forest trail ending in Ballantree Park with a return through the woodland
above the homes of the area and views across to Crown Mountain, to Grouse
Mountain, and over the city and inner harbour.

As with Brothers Creek (Walk 50), your approach through the British
Properties is via Highland Drive and Eyremount Drive. This time, however, turn right off Eyremount onto Crestline Road. Follow Crestline to its
junction with Millstream Road, where you go left to the next junction. Park
there a little before the Glenmore power station, then ascend the power line
westwards, noting that it carries the Baden-Powell Trail sign and the markers for the Trans Canada Trail. Ignore a faint trail on the right alongside
a creek that you reach after about 10 minutes and keep left again shortly
thereafter, but do go right on the fire access road.

At the next fork, you pass several pieces of B.C. logging history—a stone
foundation, all that is left of a long-gone sawmill, and the remains of a donkey engine hidden in the bush opposite. Turn right at this point on Ballantree Trail, which takes you north and east through the forest towards the
watershed boundary. Finally, you come down off the trail, very eroded in

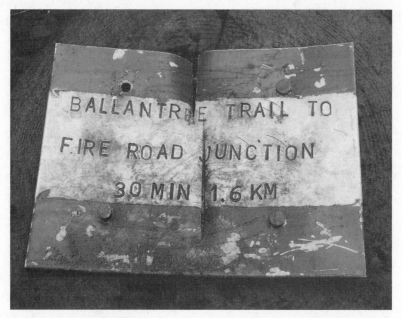

Sign made by early trailbuilder Paul Binkert.

the last section, into an open space, part of Ballantree Park. With the trail sign behind you, turn right again over a bridge and cross a clearing prior to picking up a trail that runs southwards above the houses on the west side of Ballantree Road itself.

The route you are following brings you out at the end of Kildonan Road, and a short walk along it and Craigmohr returns you to your parking spot. Incidentally, given that most of the street names have a Scottish flavour, it looks as though "Ballantree" may be a slightly distorted version of "Ballantrae," the setting of Robert Louis Stevenson's historical romance.

Another and more practical point: since this walk abuts on the Brothers Creek one (Walk 50), you may combine parts of that outing with the trail just described. For example, stay with the Baden-Powell (Skyline) Trail beyond the fire-road crossing, go up to the Brothers Creek Trail just west of the lower falls and go right on it. Recross the creek at the first junction and follow the Crossover Trail downhill through the forest to the fire road. Descend on that road for about 5 minutes until you reach the Ballantree Trail going off left. Since this extension would more than double the length of the walk, adding roughly 5 km (3.1 mi), and would also double the elevation gain, you should allow an extra 1.5 hours.

# CAPILANO CANYON

**TO DAM FROM PARK ROAD:**
**Round trip** 4.5 km (2.8 mi)          **Allow** 2 hours

**TO DAM FROM KEITH ROAD:**
**Round trip** 8 km (5 mi)          Allow 3 hours

**TO DAM FROM AMBLESIDE PARK:**
Round trip 12 km (7.5 mi)          **Allow** 4 hours

**Trails**          **Good all year**

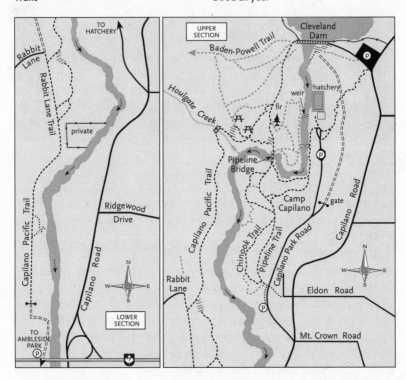

THIS SCENIC VALLEY lying between North and West Vancouver offers a number of outings, from circuits in Capilano River Regional Park to an upriver approach, following in part a one-time logging-railway right-of-way that links Keith Road in West Vancouver with the Cleveland Dam.

For walks within the park, drive or take the bus north on Capilano Road in North Vancouver. Fork left onto Capilano Park Road from a little north of the traffic light at Edgemont Boulevard and park near a salmon hatchery on the valley floor below the dam. For another approach, with views across the

Pipeline Bridge.

reservoir northwest to The Lions, turn left at the top of Capilano Road where it curves into Nancy Greene Way.

From the former, you may complete a circuit below the dam taking Coho Loop, a short level loop using the park's two foot-bridges. Of course, once on the river's west bank, you may take one or other of the trails leading to the dam top. A detour to the Second Canyon Viewpoint provides a fine spot for appreciating the canyon's grandeur, and an extension, Giant Fir Trail, gives you a sight of that monster conifer as well. Thereafter, having crossed the spillway, you may return by one of the routes on the east bank.

For a walk from the south, you may use the Capilano Pacific Trail, start-ing from Keith Road, itself reached by going east from Taylor Way in West Vancouver. From here, after parking a little beyond the underpass of High-way 1/99 (Upper Levels Highway), you head upstream on the old railway grade, then leave it for forest, meeting Rabbit Lane Trail farther on. High above the river, the park trail hugs the side hill, majestic trees all around until Houlgate Creek causes a detour, after which you must make a choice: stay high for the dam or drop into the valley. For the dam, the second trail to the left, still Capilano Pacific, provides a relatively level route, with the trails from the valley joining from the right as you rise to the dam.

A more ambitious walk, adding a good 4 km (2.5 mi) to the round trip, follows the Capilano Pacific Trail all the way from Ambleside Park, which you reach by turning south from Marine Drive on 13th Street. From your start eastwards along the seawall, you swing north, following the river's west bank until, after crossing Brothers Creek at its mouth near Capilano Care Centre, you approach the Woodcroft residential complex. Now, you go left and uphill to meet and go right on Keith Road, continuing as above.

To explore the downstream trails on the east side, start on Capilano Park Road at a small parking area about 200 m beyond the turnoff from Capi-lano Road and walk north on the sidewalk to where the trails, Chinook and Pipeline, go off left. Both take you to Pipeline Bridge, with Chinook winding up and down closer to the river. North of the Pipeline Bridge, you may join Capilano Pacific Trail on its way upstream to the dam crossing, with a return via the hatchery and Camp Capilano on the river's east side. Then, back on Pipeline Trail, your outing ends with a gentle little rise back to the road.

# BOWSER TRAIL

**Round trip** 7.5 km (4.7 mi) or more

**Trails and streets**

**Allow** 3 hours

**Good all year**

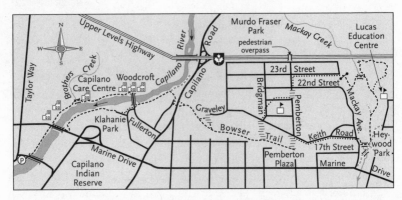

IN ITS OFFICIAL entirety, this trail running along the foot of the slope north of Marine Drive and linking Capilano Road with Pemberton Avenue has one drawback: it is too short, less than 30 minutes being required for the complete walk. Fortunately, it does lend itself to expansion at either end.

You may, for instance, start from the parking lot by the Capilano River at the end of Taylor Way in Park Royal south of Marine Drive. From here take the trail heading upstream and passing under two roads, the second of which is Marine Drive. Here you double back and up onto the sidewalk, crossing the river to its east bank where you drop down to the trail that makes its way among the boulders of various periods of the river's shifting history. Finally, at the far end of the playing fields, leave the riverbank, traverse a parking lot and step over the retaining wall onto Glenaire Drive on which you go left to its intersection with Fullerton Drive. Now go left again to the near side of the bridge leading across the Capilano River to the Woodcroft residential complex. Without crossing the bridge, drop to the riverbank and follow the track that runs along it, some townhouses on your right and the Highway 1/99 (Upper Levels Highway) bridge ahead of you, with the ridge running north from Grouse Mountain as a background.

Just beyond the last house, a track takes you right among some young conifers to Sundown Place and hence to Capilano Road. This you must negotiate with care, given the speedy traffic, to reach the start of the trail proper. Along it, you walk in a screen of tall trees, noting on your way the high flight of steps from Pemberton Heights by which you may return.

View upstream to Crown Mountain beyond the Upper Levels bridge.

Finally, behind a shopping centre at Pemberton Avenue, the official trail ends; however, you may continue by ascending the many flights of wooden steps upwards to the attractive little Ashdown Park, with its view of Vancouver's inner harbour.

Now you go right on Keith Road, starting to lose the height you just gained, as you pass 19th Street and reach Mackay, with a track into Heywood Park just opposite. Once in the park, you descend to cross Mackay Creek and its grassy valley before you turn north to experience its ravine. Ignore the first steps heading upwards to the right, taking instead the second set to emerge on the plateau by Lucas Education Centre.

Your business is not with education, though, and you continue north along some playing fields, with the choice of recrossing Mackay Creek directly or of looking for a track starting just behind the right-hand goalpost of the soccer field. This detour gives another experience of mini-wilderness, the illusion spoiled only by the sounds of traffic on the Upper Levels Highway. Descend gently to the creek on this forest trail and rejoin the direct route at a bridge. Here, you are faced with the inevitable climb out of the ravine, after which, by turning right at the edge of the trees, you emerge on 23rd Street at a little sports field. Now on quiet treed residential streets, work your way west on 23rd, then south on Pemberton, its pedestrian steps taking you a little uphill before again you turn west then south, cross Keith Road and descend by the 200-odd steps from the end of Bridgman Avenue to the Bowser Trail again.

Retrace your steps as far as Fullerton but this time cross the river, turn back left on the Woodcroft side and follow the west bank downstream, past the Capilano Care Centre and the mouth of Brothers Creek, under Marine Drive and thus back to your transport.

# BADEN-POWELL TRAIL (GROUSE MOUNTAIN)

**CURRENT ROUTE: Round trip** 5 km (3.1 mi)  **Allow** 2 hours

**Elevation gain** 215 m (705 ft)  **High point** 533 m (1750 ft)

**ORIGINAL ROUTE: Round trip** 6 km (3.7 mi)  **Allow** 3 hours

**Elevation gain** 380 m (1245 ft)  **High point** 686 m (2250 ft)

**Trails and roads**  **Best April to November**

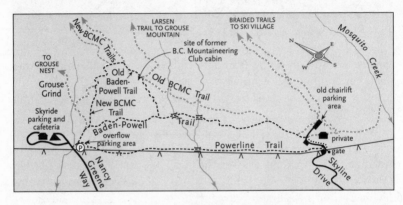

THE BASIC WALK on this circuit linking the Grouse Mountain Skyride with Skyline Drive uses the current Baden-Powell Trail one way with a return trip on B.C. Hydro's power line right-of-way for a round trip of 5 km (3.1 mi) and an altitude gain of 215 m (705 ft). If, however, you do not mind having to gain some extra height on a rough trail with a bit of a drop-off here and there, you may add to your options by hiking part of Baden-Powell's original route.

Whatever your choice, a start from the west end is preferable, despite its greater altitude gain, for on the return along the power line you face views southwest to the Strait of Georgia and northwest to The Lions. To begin, therefore, drive or take the bus to the Skyride area at the top of Nancy Greene Way. Just above the overflow parking lot, you will find the trailhead blazoned with statistical data for the much-touted Grouse Grind with the blue fleur-de-lis on orange background, the distinctive Boy Scout sign, taking second place.

Rising quite steeply at first, in a few minutes you reach a fork. The Grouse Grind heads up even more steeply to the left, while the Baden-Powell Trail works its way along the front of the slope in deep forest. Finally levelling, you come to a junction with signs, the steep trail on your left to the

The Lions seen from Powerline Trail.

old British Columbia Mountaineering Club (BCMC) cabin site being assigned a deceptive 300 m only. Continuing, you undulate along until you arrive on the verge of a washed-out ravine, its bridge swept away in a savage flood. At low water, however, the creek, Mackay Creek, is negotiable with care, as are several more spots where slippage has occurred. Carry on, gradually descending to the next significant fork, where the Baden-Powell Trail heads left towards Mosquito Creek. But you go down right, emerging in a few minutes on a bend at the top of Skyline Drive and going right again to the second bend down the road, where a gated track starts along the power line right-of-way. With nothing now to worry about but the views, you are soon back at the Skyride and the end of your circuit.

And what of the older route of the Baden-Powell? For this, start as before. The actual route of the old trail has been usurped by the much-touted Grouse Grind but, for a less crowded and more peaceful experience, go a few paces beyond the Grind turnoff then turn left on a trail marked with red BCMC markers. This route zigzags upwards until, again within sight of the Grind below on the left, it is joined unobtrusively by the original Baden-Powell coming up the side of the ravine. Still climbing, you turn away eastwards to a junction where you go right on an older edition of this BCMC Trail, following it a little higher before departing from it and dropping gently to an open bluff with views over Burrard Inlet and the cities along its shores.

Close by is the site of the former BCMC cabin and the meeting of several trails: left and uphill, the Larsen Trail to Grouse Mountain; straight ahead, the joint BCMC and former Baden-Powell Trail, not recommended now because of a massive landslide at Mackay Creek and a few trouble spots farther on. To complete your circuit, therefore, you should keep right and descend the steep 300-m trail to join the current Baden-Powell, going east with it as before described or, if you wish a shorter outing, turning back west for a direct return to the Skyride.

# MOSQUITO CREEK

**Round trip** 6.8 km (4.2 mi)

**Elevation gain** 206 m (675 ft)

**Trails and streets**

**Allow** 2.5 hours

**High point** 220 m (720 ft)

**Good all year**

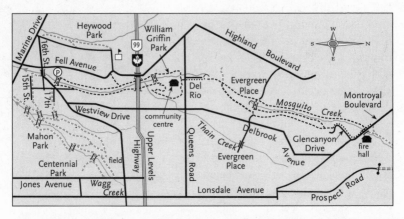

LIKE ITS NEIGHBOUR to the west, Mackay Creek, some of the Mosquito Creek valley has been preserved as parkland, the most scenic sections stretching upstream from Mosquito Creek Park on its west side at the intersection of Fell Avenue and Larson Road, just north of Marine Drive.

To reach the parking area, drive east on Marine Drive from the north end of the Lions Gate Bridge, turn left (north) onto Fell Avenue and look for the parking area on the right after 16th Street.

At first the route coincides with the Trans Canada Trail (TCT), but you may leave that in a few moments to go left on an interesting diversion through a riparian restoration area, with numerous native plants as well as the rejuvenated waters of a little stream to catch your attention. All too soon, however, this pleasant track makes its way back to the main multipurpose trail near a viewpoint by the creek. Next you travel beneath the Upper Levels Highway, after which you find yourself in William Griffin Park, with its recreation centre on Queens Road.

For a short outing, you may walk uphill east of the centre towards some trees before turning south on a little upland ridge separating Mosquito Creek from its tributary, Thain Creek, and dropping down again to the path alongside the playing field. Continuing round the margin of the field, you reach a bridge that provides a return to the main trail and eventually your

Mosquito Creek.

starting point. However, in summer you may vary that final return by veering left round the lacrosse box and upstream along the bank of Thain Creek to a ford with a rickety bridge, leading to a trail that runs down the east bank of Mosquito Creek. The first part can be extremely muddy and unpleasant, so it is only viable after a prolonged period of dry weather. South of the highway, bridge conditions gradually improve and eventually you reach a well-made path with access from Bewicke Avenue, continuing south to the park. On whichever side of the stream you elect to return, you will have completed a walk of about 3.2 km (2 mi).

If you wish to continue, however, you must cross Queens Road for the dead-ended Del Rio Drive, where the trail resumes, the creek invisible in a culvert extending uphill as far as Evergreen Place. Beyond here the stream, now carefully tailored, is in a surprisingly wide valley, the route beside it taking you as far as Montroyal Boulevard, a little beyond which it deteriorates into a very rough and difficult track connecting with the Baden-Powell Trail higher up. Leaving that option for another day, you may, however, vary your downstream return by climbing the steps to Montroyal, crossing to the east side, then going right on Glencanyon Drive until that street turns away left at a sign saying "Mosquito Creek Walking Trail." Descend on this trail until you arrive at the track from Evergreen Place, where, instead of crossing the footbridge to join your outward route, you may choose to go straight ahead on a rough track that works its way gradually back to the main trail. Thereafter, retrace your steps to William Griffin Park and your return as for the shorter option.

Note that only experienced and confident walkers should attempt the track leading from Montroyal to the Baden-Powell Trail. It is not long, being only about 800 m, and adds minimally to the altitude gain, but it needs extreme care, as you must scramble up and over rocks, haul yourself up by tree roots or rope and cross potentially slippery logs, always with a rushing torrent not far away on your right.

# MAHON PARK

**Round trip** 6 km (3.7 mi)

**Trails and roads**

**Allow** 1.5 hours

**Good all year**

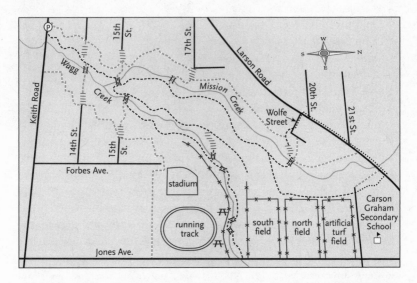

AT THE TRAILHEADS on both Keith Road and Jones Avenue, you are provided with much useful information of historic as well as contemporary interest. Here you have the genesis of the North Vancouver Park system, the brainchild of one of North Vancouver's pioneers, Edward Mahon, who sold some of his land in 1910 to North Vancouver to create a park. When it opened four years later, the park's emphasis was on mass entertainment, a far cry from today's attention to eradicating exotic species and restoring native plants in the valleys, leaving the plateau area to sports fields and playgrounds.

However, the park is small, so to get the most out of this "jewel of the city," here are two loops that allow you to experience most of what the park has to offer. To do this, the best place to start is at the trailhead on the north side of Keith Road just east of the traffic lights at Bewicke Avenue. To get there, drive east on Marine Drive from the north end of the Lions Gate Bridge. Turn left onto Keith Road and look for the parking area on the left. From the entrance, you plunge immediately into trees on a well-made path following Wagg Creek upstream in its little ravine and ignoring steps leading

Wagg Creek.

up to subsidiary trailheads on neighbouring streets. Cross at the second
bridge near the confluence of Wagg
and its tributary, Mission Creek, and
keep right, then left, ascending to
the crest of the ridge between the
creeks and, after passing a flight of
steps going down to join the valley
trail, you emerge on the edge of a
grassy plain, a playing field to your
right. Make your way half left, then
swing round to work between playing fields eastwards to Jones Avenue,
where you go right to reach another
entrance to Mahon Park. Now you
go downstream on a truly delightful
section of Wagg Creek, staying left when you come to a bridge connecting
with the stairs you noted earlier from above. At the next bridge you must
cross and climb the steps to retrace your outward route until you round the
corner and approach the bridge over Mission Creek, where you embark on
the second loop exploring the western side of the park.

Turn right, therefore, and rise steadily on the east bank of Mission Creek
until you come to a fork where you keep right to arrive at the playing fields
again. This time take the path heading north to the Carson Graham Secondary School and, staying west of the buildings, follow a track through a gap
in the fence to come out on busy Larson Road, down which you march for
a few minutes to enter a cul-de-sac, Wolfe Street. A few paces along, a path
goes right and down into the valley of Mission Creek which you cross, then
you ascend to meet your outward route. Back at this fork, you now have the
choice of three routes back to Keith Road and your transportation with the
possibility, if you return by Wagg Creek from the Jones Avenue entrance, of
checking out those steps leading up onto the ridge between Wagg and its
tributary.

# LYNN HEADWATERS LOOP

**LYNN LOOP TRAIL:**
Round trip 5.1 km (3.2 mi)                    **Allow** 1.5 hours

**TO DEBRIS CHUTE:**
Round trip 9.5 km (5.9 mi)                    **Allow** 3 hours

Elevation gain 168 m (550 ft)                 High point 380 m (1245 ft)

Trails and roads                              Good most of the year

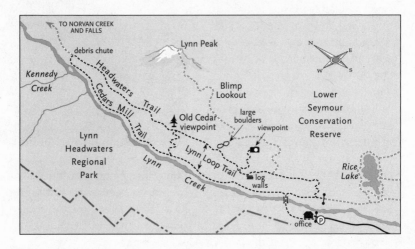

ALTHOUGH THIS REGIONAL park is intended to provide a wilderness experience, some of its trails are short enough to make satisfying walks, notably certain combinations of Lynn Loop, Cedars Mill and the lower section of Headwaters itself. Nor is it difficult of access: just leave Highway 1/99 (Upper Levels Highway) at Lynn Valley Road (Exit 19) and travel north, passing the approach to Lynn Canyon Park on your right and continuing along the one-time Intake Road by going straight ahead where Dempsey Road goes off left. The final part of your approach to the park is somewhat winding and narrow, so you should exercise caution as you approach the main parking lot close to the bridge over the creek and the start of your walk.

Having crossed the creek, you must choose whether to turn left and follow it upstream or, for a more demanding walk, to go right and uphill, turning left just before the gate to the Lower Seymour Conservation Reserve (LSCR) at the south end of the Lynn Loop Trail and following it back along a raised bench, the moss-covered trees giving an indication of the high rainfall in the area. Along the route, you will see areas of blowdowns, the result

Bridge and cascades near start of walk.

of the December 2006 storm. Some way along, a hiking trail to Lynn Peak goes off to the right, then a little later a short, steep track rises some 70 m (230 ft) to a viewpoint overlooking the Seymour Valley and Burrard Inlet. Still later, another path to the right takes you on a side trip to a pair of huge boulders, erratics left by a retreating glacier. Next comes another point of decision: to continue north on what will be Headwaters Trail or to complete Lynn Loop by dropping to the creek via a steep connector, a left turn at its foot giving you a round trip of 5.1 km (3.2 mi).

If you decide to go forward, you reach first of all, beside an ancient cedar, a viewpoint over the valley to the wooded slopes of Mount Fromme (named for the founder of the company that logged the area). Then, you gradually start descending, the trail crossing one or two debris torrents, perhaps dangerous when in spate during spring runoff. At the third such feature, a major one, you drop to the open ground by the creek, where the lower trail joins the upper that you had been on. From here, Headwaters Trail continues north, but the round trip to Norvan Falls, the next objective, involves an extra 5.5 km (3.4 mi), so this may be a satisfactory destination, with its superb view across the valley towards Kennedy Creek and the wild country north of Grouse Mountain.

A return downstream from here on the creekside trail has you passing the site of the long-vanished Cedars Mill, the only signs of its existence a few pieces of rusty machinery. Somewhat farther downstream, you reach the T-junction at the lower end of the Lynn Loop connector, and from here back to the dam your walk is enlivened by the sight of wire coils, remnants of wire stave pipes that carried water to North Vancouver.

# RICE LAKE

**FROM LSCR: Round trip** 3 km (1.9 mi)     **Allow** 1.5 hours

**FROM LYNN HEADWATERS:**
**Round trip** 8 km (5 mi)     **Allow** 2.5 hours

**Trails and roads**     **Good most of the year**

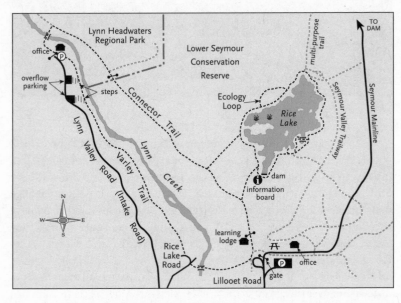

THIS FEATURE OF the Metro Vancouver Regional Parks Department's Lower Seymour Conservation Reserve (LSCR) is a major recreation area within the outdoor educational complex, and as such is worth a visit in its own right. It is readily accessible from the entrance at the north end of Lillooet Road; in fact, many walkers may argue that the approach is too easy to ensure a reasonable walk even when that distance is added to the lake circuit, which is wheelchair accessible to boot. Fortunately, that objection may be met in some part by starting not from the forest gate but from the neighbouring Lynn Headwaters Regional Park (Walk 58) instead.

For the direct approach to Rice Lake, leave Highway 1/99 (Upper Levels Highway) at the Capilano College exit (Exit 22) and drive north on Lillooet Road, travelling through a cemetery with a concealed pipe on its east side. The public part of the road veers right to a parking lot just short of the gate that bars access to the upper valley. From the parking lot, you cross

Mount Seymour reflected in Rice Lake.

the picnic area heading towards a yellow-painted gate beyond the Learning Lodge at the north end, with the lake trail next on the right.

Starting from Lynn Headwaters Regional Park, cross the bridge and turn right as though you were making for the south end of the Lynn Loop Trail (Walk 58), but where it branches off to the left, pass through the boundary gate between the two parks, after which you have a possible access going left to the lake. You may, however, wait for the next approach, which brings you to the shoreline farther south, as does the trail from Lillooet Road, having passed a flume and shinglebolt demonstration en route.

Making your circuit clockwise, your next point of interest is the Forest Ecology Loop Trail, which makes a short detour on your left. Then, working your way round to the east, you see a broad multi-purpose trail heading north and come to a path going left to connect with it. Staying with the lake, you next come to a fork where you may go right along the shore or straight ahead to arrive at the Douglas Mowat Memorial Special Fisheries Wharf. Shortly thereafter comes the dam at the south end of the lake and reunion with your outward route. Now, you may start your return to Lynn Headwaters, first making your way out to the connector, then going right on it.

However, you may add distance and variety by electing to return by the Varley Trail, dedicated in 1998 to the memory of Frederick H. Varley, a founding member of the Group of Seven. To do this, start by going left on the Lynn Headwaters connector and back to the LSCR entrance. Now go west on the track that descends to cross Lynn Creek on a footbridge high above its turbulent waters. Turn right immediately on crossing and follow the road briefly to where the signed trail begins and heads northwards along the low-lying lands west of the creek, rising finally to the main parking lot and the end of your outing.

# TWO-CANYON LOOP

**Round trip** 8 km (5 mi)
**Trails and roads**

**Allow** 3 hours
**Good most of the year**

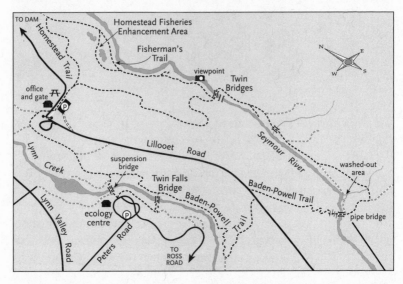

THE PROXIMITY OF the Lynn Creek and Seymour River canyons near North Vancouver makes a scenic circuit possible with the use of connecting trails in Lynn Canyon Park and the Lower Seymour Conservation Reserve (LSCR), plus a stretch of the Baden-Powell Trail for good measure.

For this loop, the best departure point is Lynn Canyon Park. To get to it from the west, leave Highway 1/99 (Upper Levels Highway) at Lynn Valley Road (Exit 19), go northeast and cross Mountain Highway, then turn right at the park sign on Peters Road and drive to the parking lot near the Ecology Centre. Arriving from the east, depart Highway 1/99 at Mountain Highway (Exit 21), drive north on Mountain Highway and go half right on Lynn Valley Road. Turn left on Peters Road and park in one of the many lots near the ecology centre.

First, you cross Lynn Creek on its suspension bridge, walk forward away from the canyon, then turn left on a trail that takes you to the entrance of the LSCR at the north end of Lillooet Road. From there, cross the main access road and work along the edge of the parking lot to join a trail bound for Twin Bridges.

Looking up Seymour River from the viewpoint.

Soon, Homestead Trail goes off left, and on this you may descend to the river before turning right to go downstream, passing the mossy gate of a long-abandoned settlement on your left and the Homestead Fisheries Enhancement Area on your right. At the surviving Twin Bridge, if you opt for a shorter walk, you may turn uphill on the road back to the gate and thence to Lynn Canyon Park for an outing of some 6.5 km (4 mi). (An even shorter outing of 4.8 km (3 mi) would start at the LSCR entrance itself.) If, however, you are not seduced by the appeal of an early return, cross the river and head downstream on the remnants of a road cut into the canyon walls with viewpoints here and there to the river far below. And, on the last stretch, where a small tributary has washed away most of the original trail, angle off left through the forest to intersect the Baden-Powell Trail.

On this, you turn right, heading downhill for the river, crossing on a pipe bridge at a point where the narrowness of the canyon causes the water to come through with explosive force. But now comes retribution, for you must mount a steep flight of steps then zigzag upwards, gaining some 110 m (360 ft) in the process, until you emerge on a power line right-of-way, Mount Seymour standing up proudly on your right. Continue west, cross Lillooet Road and stay with the Baden-Powell Trail as it takes you through open forest, until, just above Lynn Creek, you turn right for the descent into the depths of a small side valley, then use the boardwalk to return to the creek by a gravel beach.

From here, you must regain your lost height. This you can do on either side of the creek, staying on its east side to the suspension bridge or crossing Twin Falls Bridge for your return on the west side at the end of an energetic but rewarding outing.

# FISHERMAN'S TRAIL

**Round trip** 11.5 km (7.1 mi)          **Allow** 4 hours

**Trails and road**          **Good most of the year**

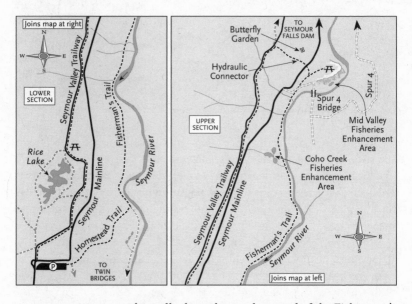

IF YOU ENJOYED the walk along the southern end of the Fisherman's Trail in the preceding walk (Walk 60), you will surely want to try this northern section up the Seymour River valley with its unusual views of Mounts Seymour and Elsay. Dog Mountain, too, rising abruptly from across the valley, looks very different from our usual conception of it as a non-mountain. That this is an area enjoying a heavy rainfall may be surmised by the healthy growth of moss, old man's beard and other moisture-loving plants, such as the skunk cabbage that is a sight to behold in spring. As well, the walker's enjoyment of this attractive valley has been enhanced by the upgrading of the one-time muddy trail, with sturdy bridges over the many tributary streams and boardwalks to protect the area from the trampling of many feet.

To begin, leave Highway 1/99 (Upper Levels Highway) at the Capilano College exit (Exit 22) and drive north on Lillooet Road through a cemetery. The public part of the road veers right to a parking lot just short of a turning circle and a gate barring access to the upper valley. On foot, you start eastwards along the Twin Bridges Trail, going left in a few minutes on the Homestead Trail, which descends to meet the Fisherman's Trail. Here you

Mount Seymour from Mid Valley Viewpoint.

turn left (north) on the well-made path, soon to find it passing through maturing second-growth conifers, interspersed with large, moss-covered stumps from the original forest. Then you break out into the open on the riverbank with the great bulk of Dog Mountain over on your right and Mounts Seymour and Elsay farther north along the ridge. Now the trail follows the windings of the river, but never bereft of trees, the many deciduous among them to colour the fall. And as you proceed you may note at the crossing of one of the many streams that this is the outlet from the Coho Creek Fisheries Enhancement Area. Eventually, after crossing the oddly named Hydraulic Creek and the forest road to Spur 4 Bridge, you go straight ahead and up to the end of your trail on a miniature plateau, a suitable site for the Mid Valley Viewpoint and a picnic area located to take advantage of the fine views of mountain and valley. Down below, visible in the backwaters of a great bend of the river, lies yet another fisheries enhancement project.

With the time to depart comes the need to decide on your return route. The more scenic alternative is to return as you came by the winding, undulating trail beside the river, with the mildly daunting little ascent on Homestead Trail near the end. You may, however, make a circuit by following the Hydraulic Connector west to join and go left (south) on the Seymour Valley Trailway, a paved, multi-purpose route that runs almost straight as a die back to the park entrance. Whichever is your choice, however, before you take your leave of the area, walk along the Connector Trail a short distance to see how fares the Butterfly Garden, a volunteer effort to create an environment that is attractive to these colourful insects.

# MAPLEWOOD FLATS
# WILDLIFE SANCTUARY

**Round trip** 3.3 km (2 mi)  |  **Allow** 1 hour or more

**Paths**  |  **Good all year**

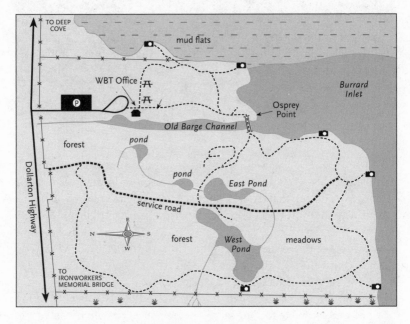

HERE IS A walk for the bird watcher—indeed for the lover of any aspect of the natural world—and perhaps also for the history buff. From the early 1900s Burrard Inlet has been the scene of a rapidly growing ocean-going trade, and its shores have experienced a variety of industrial activities associated with the port as well as with the logging taking place on the landward side. Long-time residents of North Vancouver have seen industries come and go in this area but more recently have witnessed its transformation from a post-industrial wasteland to the present healthy wildlife sanctuary thanks to the success of a local community group in preserving the site and then to the members of the Wild Bird Trust who have developed a network of trails and viewing spots—but for human visitors only, so NO DOGS.

To see how Maplewood is restoring itself, drive or take the bus for 2 km (1.2 mi) east of the Ironworkers Memorial Bridge on the Dollarton Highway and turn right to the Pacific Environmental Science Centre. (If you are

Looking east over Burrard Inlet towards Burnaby Mountain.

either very early or very late and the gate is closed, you may find parking by the roadside opposite the Crab Shack.) Start at the Wild Bird Trust office, where you find information and a self-guiding map, then proceed south towards Burrard Inlet and cross the Old Barge Channel on a fine bridge to your right. Now go left and keep working south then west along the shore with little jaunts to viewpoints over the inlet. Next you circle a small inland marsh and swing northwards along the western boundary, a meadow to your right and the structures of a busy terminal across the marsh to the left. Soon you come to a viewing area overlooking a pond fringed with reeds and other moisture-loving plants and with several waterfowl in residence.

Beyond the pond you enter an area of forest, cottonwoods and other deciduous trees, mostly with flowering shrubs interspersed among ferns and other lowly plants. Follow the trail as it turns eastwards, paralleling the road until you reach a tiny bit of paved road, an old access, now a service road on which you turn south alongside the remnants of past building. Stay with this route until you can depart to the left on a trail passing between two ponds and continuing to yet another left fork leading to a miniature summit with views of the conservation area and across the inlet. Then, you descend to rejoin the trail back to the Old Barge Channel and its bridge, beyond which you may wish to pause in spring at Osprey Point, in the hope of spotting nesting ospreys on the offshore dolphins (mooring buoys).

The eastern part of the sanctuary is quite small, with paths leading to lookouts, where you may observe the life of the intertidal marshes and the vast mud flats stretching out across the bay. Finally your path leads you back past the buildings of the Environmental Science Centre to a picnic area near the sanctuary office and the end of an enjoyable and instructive outing.

To enhance your enjoyment of the area, the Wild Bird Trust sponsors free guided walks on the second Saturday of every month, featuring topics appropriate to the season in the sanctuary. (For more information, call 604-924-2581 or visit the Web site: www.wildbirdtrust.org.)

# NORTHLANDS BRIDLE PATH

**Round trip** 11 km (6.8 mi)

**Elevation gain** 245 m (800 ft)

**Trails**

**Allow** 4.5 hours

**High point** 268 m (880 ft)

**Good most of the year**

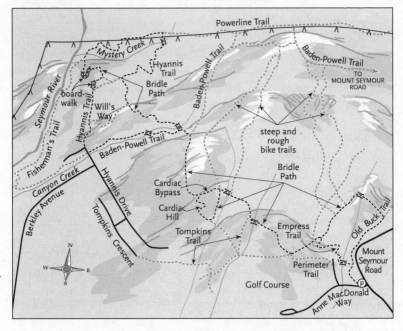

THE BRIDLE PATH is one of the oldest trails in the Northlands area, created on the remnants of earlier logging tracks, in the days when horse riding was more popular than walking, and bicycles were machines for children and eccentrics.

To reach the start, turn off Highway 1/99 (Upper Levels Highway) at Mount Seymour Parkway (Exit 22), drive east on the parkway, then go left on Mount Seymour Road and left again onto Anne MacDonald Way, where there is a small parking area on the right for the Old Buck trailhead. This area is in the provincial park, so there is a parking fee during the summer months unless you can find parking on the public road—or travel by bus to the Parkgate Village Shopping Centre.

On foot, you start on the Old Buck Trail, itself a restored logging road, then go left on the Empress Trail, the most recently constructed path on today's loop. After crossing Taylor Creek, it winds steeply uphill to meet the

Bridle Path on which you go left to the next point of decision: a 3-way junction where Perimeter and Old Golf Course trails lie below on the left. But you go right and uphill, following the orange fluorescent markers as the trail undulates towards a second creek crossing. You then pass the Tompkins Trail on the left, later a bike trail uphill on the right and immediately after that another bridge, beyond which you reach a T-junction. If you jog right then go left, you will have a shortcut that saves a few uphill metres; but the Bridle Path itself goes left and downhill to meet the Blair Range Trail. There it turns back sharp right on Cardiac Hill, heading back to meet the shortcut—Cardiac Bypass—and go on to the Baden-Powell Trail, which pre-empts the route of Bridle Path for the next 70 m.

From this junction, go left, descending slightly from what is the high point of this walk, to where Bridle Path goes right to cross Canyon Creek. Follow the twisting route through mixed forest, pass Will's Way and arrive at Hyannis Trail. Here, turn right, staying with the trail as it fords a small tributary, then swings round to cross Mystery Creek on a bridge and proceeds uphill to emerge on Powerline Trail. Now you go west until just before the next pylon, where you go left and down the side of the shady Mystery Creek ravine to Fisherman's Trail, on the verge of the Seymour River canyon.

Now you are at your low point, but not for long. A few minutes beyond the bridge over Mystery Creek, go left and ascend on Bridle Path, traversing a long, curving boardwalk that takes you back towards the south rim of Mystery Creek ravine. Then you turn away, and the trail levels in a fine stretch of old forest. Going right at the next T-junction, then left over another boardwalk brings you back onto Hyannis Trail and soon thereafter to the Hyannis Point trailhead, from which a short walk along the road takes you to the Baden-Powell trailhead on the left. Here you set out eastwards on the aging trail, closely watching for Baden-Powell Trail signs to keep you on track at forks until you regain the point where Bridle Path departs to the right.

Now you may retrace your steps; or, for variety, you may opt for the Cardiac Bypass en route, and as well, when you reach the Empress Trail junction, you may choose the slightly longer route, staying with Bridle Path to Old Buck, where a right turn takes you back to your transportation.

# HISTORIC MUSHROOM LOOP

**Round trip** 6.4 km (4 mi)

**Elevation gain** 275 m (900 ft)

**Trails**

**Allow** 2 hours

**High point** 580 m (1900 ft)

**Best May to early November**

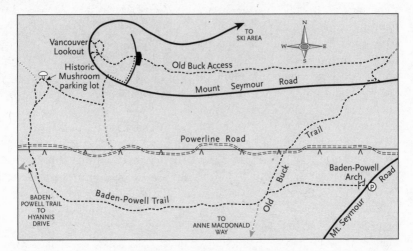

HERE IS AN accommodating walk in Mount Seymour Provincial Park that allows you to enjoy the lower reaches of the park when higher trails are snowbound earlier and later in the season. In addition to the Historic Mushroom parking lot, you may experience some of the park's logging history and yet another stretch of the Baden-Powell Trail at the outset. Turn off Highway 1/99 (Upper Levels Highway) at Mount Seymour Parkway (Exit 22) and drive east on Mount Seymour Parkway, then go left and uphill on Mount Seymour Road to reach your start at the little parking lot opposite the Boy Scout trailhead about 2.5 km (1.6 mi) from the park entrance. Note that parking fees are in effect here.

Once over the road, you rise gently in forest westwards to an intersection with the Old Buck Trail that is your return route, then after about 30 minutes, you forsake the Baden-Powell Trail to go right across a power line right-of-way. Shortly thereafter comes your trip into the past as you inspect the Historic Mushroom, that stump rich in memories for earlier generations of mountain lovers, who, condemned to hike from this point if they wished to go higher, used it to leave messages for others.

Though you may turn back from here, the remaining distance to the so-called Vancouver Lookout is not great. Continuing, you soon reach the

Sign describing the Historic Mushroom.

park highway, to find that the view is being obscured by the growing forest. To get the best glimpses, you should cross the road to the little picnic site above the corner, where the route back starts on a connector with the Old Buck Trail via a picnic area with a history of its own. It is situated on the one-time road to the upper parking lot that was superseded by today's highway.

You are now on one of the most pleasant parts of your route, descending gently round the spine of the mountain to the junction with your return trail. A right turn here on the Old Buck, once a logging road, takes you down to the highway, where you must walk a short distance uphill for the trail's continuation. As on your outward trip, you must cross the open power line, the right-of-way giving you a view eastwards over Indian Arm to Buntzen Ridge, with Eagle Ridge behind. Re-entering the forest, you continue to descend. Watch for the sharp turn left onto your original trail, which will bring you back to your starting point, a change of direction signalled by the distinctive Baden-Powell Trail signs.

For a walk taking another hour or so, you may start lower on the mountain, going left off Mount Seymour Road onto Anne MacDonald Way, then right into a small parking lot at the Old Buck trailhead. From here, the rehabilitated Old Buck Trail rises 215 m (705 ft) in 2.3 km (1.4 mi) to meet the Baden-Powell Trail.

# THREE CHOP / OLD BUCK LOOP

**SHORT LOOP: Round trip** 9.5 km (5.9 mi)  **Allow** 4 hours

**LONG LOOP: Round trip** 13 km (8 mi)  **Allow** 5 hours

**Elevation gain** 558 m (1830 ft)  **High point** 783 m (2570 ft)

**Trails**  **Best June to November**

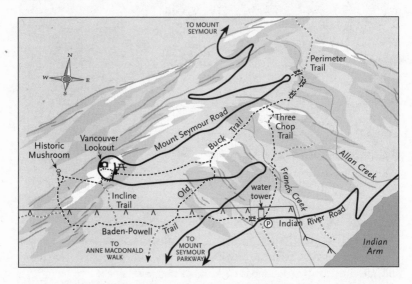

IF YOU ARE looking for a shorter and less crowded hike on the North Shore than the Grouse Grind, this may be the walk for you. Located on the lower slopes of Mount Seymour, this walk avoids the higher trails where snow lies late as well as those high-use areas of the provincial park.

To reach the start, turn off Highway 1/99 (Upper Levels Highway) at Mount Seymour Parkway (Exit 22) and drive east on the parkway; then just beyond the Parkgate Village Shopping Centre, go left towards the provincial park, then sharp right on Indian River Road. After 700 m, go left on Indian River Crescent and stay on it as it merges with Indian River Road again, until, just after the 2 km marker you see facing you a B.C. Hydro access road, with a Baden-Powell Trail sign on your left and a water tower between. Park on the right where there is a small parking space, then walk up the rough Hydro road to the power line right-of-way.

The trail is directly in front of you as you walk underneath the wires towards the forested slope ahead. From here you ascend steadily in fairly old second-growth trees, until you come to Francis Creek which is fordable,

Bridge over Allan Creek.

with care, most of the year. After the creek crossing, the grade steepens and the trail is eroded, but eventually relief comes just as the forest becomes mainly deciduous with berry bushes and ferns crowding in on the trail. Now, too, you may be able to spot some of the three-chop marks used to blaze the original route. Then you work to the left to join the Old Buck Trail and go right on the rehabilitated logging road, continuing on its gentler grade towards the Perimeter Trail, with fine views of many little waterfalls en route. At the junction you turn right over a final bridge with a view both up- and downstream of the falling waters of Allan Creek. Then you arrive at Deep Cove Lookout on the Mount Seymour Road—

at first a seemingly anti-climactic destination. Walk round the perimeter, however, and there lies before you the wide sweep of the Fraser Valley and delta, from Mount Baker to the southern Gulf Islands across the Strait of Georgia. Only Deep Cove is missing—the trees having grown since it was first named.

Returning from the lookout, take the Old Buck Trail, staying with it as it swings gradually west across the face of the mountain, bridging numerous streams, until, a short distance above the park highway, you come to a fork to the right. It does not matter which route you choose; both lead to the Baden-Powell, on which you eventually return to your starting point. If you stay with the Old Buck, you drop to the highway, cross it, walk 50 m uphill to pick up the route again, keep on to the power line and cross that as well. Then continue down to the Baden-Powell and turn left when you reach it. Soon you descend to and cross the park road, keeping on down on an easy grade through the attractive forest beyond it back to your starting point.

On the other, longer, route to the right, you rise gently to the Vancouver Lookout picnic area and parking lot. From here, go down to the main park road, cross and walk uphill a few paces, then descend the steep and eroded Incline Trail, which drops precipitously to the Mushroom Trail on which you go right to the site of that historic parking lot (Walk 64). From here, one of two converging tracks takes you down to the power line and across it to join the Baden-Powell Trail. Now you turn eastwards on the Boy Scout trail to rejoin the shorter route and enjoy a wonderfully relaxed ending to your day.

# GOLDIE LAKE

**COMBINED LOOPS:**

**Round trip** 6 km (3.7 mi)　　　　　　　**Allow** 2.5 hours

**Elevation gain** 150 m (490 ft)　　　　　**High point** 1000 m (3280 ft)

**Trails and roads**　　　　　　　　　　　**Best June to October**

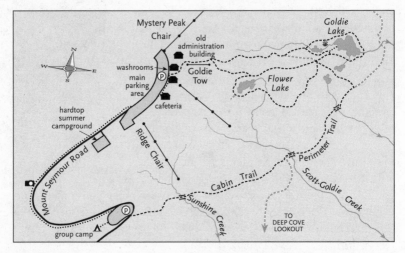

"WHAT DO YOU know of Seymour, who only Seymour knows?" Such a question may well be asked of the many visitors to Mount Seymour Provincial Park who drive to the top parking area, inspect the downhill ski facilities around it, then depart wondering what all the fuss is about. As an interesting way of finding out more, this hike over park trails may provide an answer, taking you as it does through cool forest to a small picturesque lake situated a little below the level of the parking area and to the east of it.

For the start of your journey of exploration, leave Highway 1/99 (Upper Levels Highway) at Mount Seymour Parkway (Excit 22) and drive east on the parkway until, just beyond the Parkgate Village Shopping Centre, you go left on Mount Seymour Road. Drive 11 km (6.8 mi) up this road to the parking lot on the west side of the hairpin bend, the prominent "Cabin Trail" sign just before the bend being another point of identification. Note that parking fees are in effect here. Cross to the highway's east side at the corner and pick up the trail as it angles off downhill to bypass the lower end of a ski run. After this, the forest reasserts itself and the only signs of human activity among the trees are some elderly log cabins, survivors of the days before this area acquired park status. When you come to a trail junction,

Looking southwest over Goldie Lake.

go left on Perimeter Trail, designed, as its name suggests, for straying ski-ers. To give B.C. Parks credit, it has carried out some improvements with-out making them too obvious, providing footing in soft spots and bridging creeks where necessary. The first crossing, reached just after the junction, is over Scott-Goldie Creek, where you may admire a miniature canyon before you continue northwards.

After some 50 minutes, you leave Perimeter, going left to Goldie Lake and arriving at a trail junction by two small ponds just south of your objec-tive. For the nature trail round Goldie, you may go in either direction (each is attractive). You finish your circuit at this same junction with two choices: staying right for a direct walk to the upper parking lot via Goldie Tow, or going left and taking in the pretty little Flower Lake as well before heading for the parking area with its cafeteria and comfort stations.

From here, you may retrace your steps, but for a succession of views stretching from the southern islands in the Strait of Georgia to the peaks and ridges of Mount Seymour's companions on the North Shore, you may cross to the west side of the parking lot and walk back to your vehicle on the park highway's broad shoulder, this return being much shorter also—less than 1 km (0.6 mi).

Should the outing just described seem a little strenuous, you may try a shorter circuit of the lakes themselves from the top parking lot, starting on the sawdust track parallel with the rope tow. To include Flower Lake in your walk, go right at the first and second junctions, the circuit being a modest 3.5 km (2.2 mi) with no great change of elevation involved.

# DOG MOUNTAIN

**DIRECT: Round trip** 6 km (3.7 mi)  **Allow** 2.5 hours

**VIA DINKEY PEAK: Round trip** 8 km (5 mi)  **Allow** 3 hours

Trails  **Best July to October**

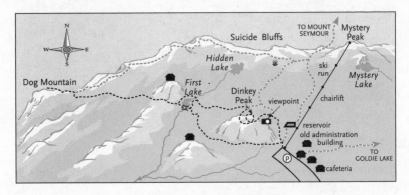

THIS WALK, WITH virtually no climbing involved despite its title, takes you from the top parking area in Mount Seymour Provincial Park to a point overlooking the Seymour River, one that gives breathtaking views of Vancouver and its sister municipalities to the south and west, of Mount Garibaldi and Mamquam Mountain to the north, while Mount Baker provides a majestic backdrop to the eastern Fraser Valley. The trail itself is pleasant also, lying in open forest for much of its length and interrupted only by First Lake, set in its subalpine meadow.

To start, approach as per Goldie Lake (Walk 66), driving to the end of the road and parking near the chairlift terminal at the north end of the main parking area. Remember to purchase your parking permit before setting out. Just left of the chairlift, the main Alpine Trail heads off northwards to Mount Seymour. Follow this briefly, then turn left en route to your own mountain, and very soon the works of humans are left behind. After some 20 minutes, you reach the little lake, its name sadly uninspired in terms of its surroundings—a picturesque wooded basin with, surprisingly, quite a large cabin perched on a bluff above.

Cross at the lake outlet, noting as you do the trails that join from the right, as they can provide a variation of your return route. Again, you enter forest and in it you remain until, practically at your destination, you emerge on a rocky outcrop with an almost sheer drop to the valley below. Here is

Westward view from Dog Mountain.

the panoramic view of the features already mentioned as well as the great mass of Cathedral Mountain to the northwest and—to move from the great to the small—the remains of a cabin just in front of you, a relic of the time when the Vancouver Water District kept a lookout here.

When you start your return journey on the main trail, you may, if you are experienced and properly equipped and the season is summer, follow the taped route that stays left, going straight ahead where the path turns right. This, however, winds up and down—sometimes quite steeply—over several minor summits; it is, besides, on occasion somewhat close to Suicide Bluffs for comfort, so if you decide against it but wish a slightly longer walk on your return, there is another possible variant from First Lake, with a miniature mountain, Dinkey Peak, for good measure.

At the lake, therefore, turn left and north, then east following the trail uphill. Gradually, you rise towards the main Mount Seymour Trail, coming to a T-junction as the trail levels. Go right here and soon you are enjoying a series of views, culminating in a vantage point directly above the parking lot. Thereafter, continue to the junction with the main trail, on which a right turn brings you back to your original starting point.

# MYSTERY LAKE AND PEAK

**TO LAKE: Round trip** 3 km (1.9 mi)  **Allow** 1.5 hours

**TO PEAK: Round trip** 4.5 km (2.8 mi)  **Allow** 2.5 hours

**Elevation gain** 215 m (705 ft)  **High point** 1220 m (4000 ft)

**Trails**  **Best July to October**

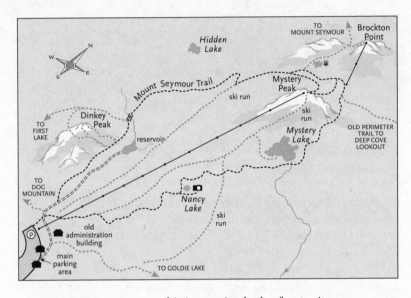

WHAT MYSTERY GAVE this interesting body of water its name we are not now likely to uncover. At all events, the lake does provide a pleasant stopover point on what may be a circular hike or a straight there-and-back outing starting from the upper parking lot in Mount Seymour Provincial Park. Approach as for Dog Mountain (Walk 67). Remember that parking fees are in effect within the park.

From the lower terminal of the Mystery Peak chairlift, take the marked trail right across the little basin beneath the right-of-way, beyond which you start rising among trees, soon losing sight of pylons and, indeed, of all human activity. After 20 minutes or so of walking, you pass tiny Nancy Lake, with a rocky outcrop above it to the south. A brief detour to this viewpoint rewards you with views of Vancouver and the Fraser lowlands. On resuming, take the trail round the west side of the lake, following it north, crossing a ski run and heading along a nice ledge with small cliffs on your left and

Near the outlet on the lake's east side.

forest elsewhere. As you advance, the trees gradually thin, and the surroundings become subalpine as you near your objective in its rocky basin.

Here is a spot for rest and contemplation, even if the intrusion of the chairlift does spoil the setting to the west. Otherwise, all is natural, and it is pleasant to sit on clean rock and let the peace wash over you. Now, however, comes the moment of decision: to return by the trail you have just traversed, a total distance of 3 km (1.9 mi) for the trip; or, if you are energetic and adventurous, to continue round the back of Mystery Peak to reach the main Mount Seymour Trail.

To do this, follow the track north on the lake's east side, rising slightly, dropping, then rising again to the foot of the Brockton Point chairlift. From here, a sign points to Mount Seymour, and you may follow its route round to the junction with the main trail. If, however, you want to enjoy the all-round views from Mystery Peak, you should leave this on a ski run rising steeply on your left and circling round to the summit. After you have savoured the panorama, your descent takes you north on the Manning ski run before you swing west and join the main Mount Seymour Trail, on which you go left.

Nor need you tramp down the ski run, barren as it is of shade and vegetation. If you look carefully to its right as it starts to descend, you will see below you the original well-used Mount Seymour Trail, which takes you down a little valley. On your way down the hiking route and not far from the parking lot, you will pass the two ends of the Dinkey Peak Loop Trail (Walk 67), an interesting little outing in its own right or a means to prolong your exploration of the hidden corners of this popular park.

# BADEN-POWELL TRAIL (DEEP COVE)

**Round trip** 5.3 km (3.3 mi)

**High point** 200 m (655 ft)

**Trails and roads**

**Allow** 2.5 hours

**Good all year**

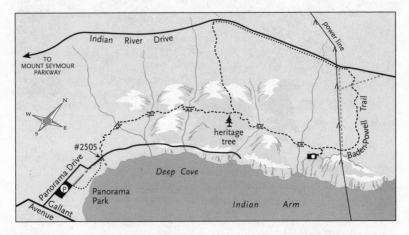

ONE POSSIBLE DESTINATION for this walk, a high bluff overlooking Deep Cove, is actually visible from your starting point in Panorama Park, but to make the most of the Baden-Powell Trail's most easterly section, you should continue farther, turning part of your walk into a loop. The park itself, a popular recreation area fronting Indian Arm in Deep Cove, is actually a little south of your trail's beginning, but parking on Panorama Drive's 2500 block is so limited and the view from the park so interesting that leaving from it is recommended. You can also arrive by bus.

In any event, you arrive by Deep Cove Road, with a right on Gallant Avenue followed by a left on Panorama Drive. Then, on foot, you may descend to the waterfront and rise again to Panorama on the north side of some private dwellings to where the trail goes off uphill left, with a few houses at the start soon giving way to forest. After swinging right, continue to follow the Baden-Powell fleurs-de-lis that mark the route as you descend into and climb out of little ravines, until, after about 1.6 km (1 mi), you note a heritage Douglas-fir to the right and nearby a track going off uphill left—a possible return route.

After another kilometre, you reach a viewpoint on the right, the great bluff visible from Deep Cove. This is an ideal spot to rest and contemplate

View of Indian Arm from bluff viewpoint.

the scene before you: across the waters of Indian Arm to Belcarra on the left, Burnaby Mountain ahead and Deep Cove below you on the right. A short distance farther on comes a power line, its final pylon to the west of Indian Arm standing on a rocky eminence just to the right of the trail.

Here is another turning point if you do not wish to follow the Boy Scout route into the forest beyond the right-of-way as it turns uphill, parallel with the power line, to meet Indian River Drive. On this you make your way west for 500 m until, at the road's high point, beside a small water tower, the Baden-Powell Trail goes off right, making for Mount Seymour Road, while you go a few metres farther, then turn downhill on the opposite side from a fire hydrant.

This track, marked with red and yellow tapes, was the one that you passed on your outward journey, and it drops straight down through a windfall area to join the main trail. There, you turn right, once more on the Baden-Powell Trail, for your return to Deep Cove and its eastern terminus.

# INDIAN ARM PARKS

**SHORT CIRCUIT: Round trip** 4.5 km (2.8 mi)  **Allow** 1.5 hours
**LONG CIRCUIT: Round trip** 9 km (5.6 mi)  **Allow** 3 hours
**Streets and trails**  **Good all year**

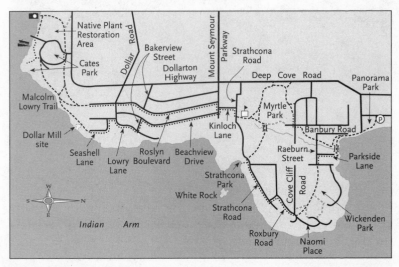

ALONG WITH CATES Park at its south end, lower Indian Arm boasts no fewer than five public recreation areas, the round of which, either in whole or in part, gives you an interesting variety of scenery. Cates Park on its own is reached from Dollarton Highway, but for its incorporation in the total outing, it may also be approached from the northern loop, where four smaller recreation areas vie for your attention.

From the north, the starting point is Panorama Park, accessible by bus or car from Deep Cove Road by going right on Gallant Avenue then left on Panorama Drive to the park. From here, you turn south, heading past a yacht club, following the shoreline on either of two routes through Deep Cove Park to a small creek. Cross this and turn south again on Parkside Lane to Raeburn Street, where you go left to cross Lockehaven Road and enter Wickenden, your third park. In it you continue east amid tall trees, staying first right over a bridge, then left up some steps, and right again to emerge a little above Roxbury Road. This you follow a short distance before jogging left onto Strathcona Road, which takes you to the tiny but very attractive Strathcona Park in its little bay.

From it, a track takes you westwards across Noble Bridge to Myrtle Park.

Indian Arm.

Staying left allows you to make a clockwise circuit to emerge on Cove Cliff Road near Banbury Road, on which you go north briefly before turning right on a path behind Cove Cliff Elementary School. Ignoring a bridge on your right, traverse a children's playground on the way to a small parking lot and thus to Raeburn Street again. Cross this and walk north on a track flanked by a creek on your right. Once more in Deep Cove Park, a left turn takes you back to your transportation.

To include Cates Park in this outing, go left after Noble Bridge, then left again through a narrow screen of trees to cut through the grounds of Seycove Secondary School and down Norah's Lane to Strathcona Road. Here, walk right to Kinloch Lane, thence to Mount Seymour Parkway. Jog left to Beachview Drive and continue south before going left on Bakerview and right on Lowry Lane to a viewpoint on a corner. Now, you must return to Beachview for one block, then drop down again to Seashell Lane and your entry to Cates Park, site of the First World War Dollar Logging Mill and once the home of the novelist Malcolm Lowry.

To sample this park's trails, you might try a "figure of eight" course. Start along the path above the shoreline then, just after a bridge, swing right, ascend a series of steps to join Upper Trail and continue left then right on the track leading towards the parking lot by the main entrance. Across the paved area, Upper Trail resumes and circles past a native plant restoration area to a viewpoint just above water's edge.

Your return route takes you along the waterside past a boat-launching ramp, the main recreation area, with a rock and a plaque with the words "International Maritime Bicentennial, 1792–1992" commemorating the First Nations' welcome to the first white explorers, and a Native war canoe. Then you come to the Malcolm Lowry Trail, on which you stay until, immediately beyond the bridge, you arrive at another fork. To vary your return, take the left inland route to rejoin Upper Trail near the margin of the park, then walk back on Roslyn Boulevard, enjoying vistas of mountain and sea. After Mount Seymour Parkway comes Kinloch Lane again, and thereafter your return to Myrtle Park and continuation to your left of the shorter circle route back to Deep Cove.

# LULU ISLAND DYKES

**MIDDLE ARM AND TERRA NOVA LOOP:**
**Round trip** 9 km (5.6 mi)                    **Allow** 3 hours

**WEST DYKE ONLY:**
**Round trip** 12 km (7.5 mi)                  **Allow** 3.5 hours

**MIDDLE ARM AND WEST DYKE:**
**One-way trip** 10 km (6.2 mi)              **Allow** 3.5 hours

Dykes                                              Good all year

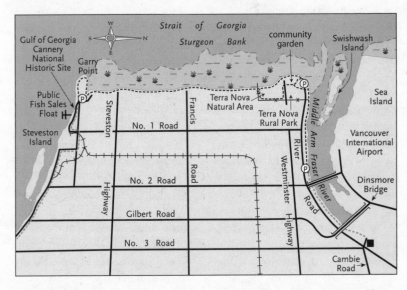

THIS EXCURSION REPRESENTS at least two walks, with a self-contained downriver portion along the Fraser's Middle Arm and an equally self-contained walk along the West Dyke Trail overlooking Sturgeon Bank, though they may be combined in a single lengthy outing or, better still, a one-way walk with a bus ride back.

To reach the start of each walk from the north, leave Highway 99 at the Bridgeport Road turnoff (Exit 39A), which takes you onto Sea Island Way. Turn south on No. 3 Road, right on Cambie Road and then left on River Road. Parking is limited until west of No. 2 Road Bridge, so start at the skateboard park by Lynas Lane if you intend to walk downstream; otherwise, continue to the parking lot near the river's mouth at Terra Nova Rural Park, the location of a long-gone cannery. From the south, however, stay on Highway 99 to Steveston Highway (Exit 32) and drive west on Steveston Highway, almost

Scotch Pond, with the North Shore
mountains in the distance.

to its end, before going left on 7th Avenue
to Chatham Street, where a right turn leads
to parking in Garry Point Park.

From Lynas Lane on Middle Arm Dyke,
soon you come to a viewing pier, then a
marsh enhancement project, followed by
a natural stretch of shore pine, briars and
broom. Waterfowl are present in numbers.
On your elevated walkway, you travel past
Swishwash Island to the mouth of the river, with its little park and the
connection with the rest of the walk. If recent developments at Terra Nova
tempt you, across the road from the nearest parking lot take the path that
departs south from here into the Terra Nova Rural Park and winds its way
round and over a slough before heading off eastwards into the community
garden where various gardening techniques are demonstrated. The south
end of the gardens abuts on Westminster Highway and a path parallel to
the road heads east for a block before turning south again into the Terra
Nova Natural Area, a wide ditch separating the trail from the old field habitat now being colonized by shrubs and deciduous trees. Then, when a golf
course becomes visible through the screen of trees, the route turns westwards and arrives on the West Dyke trail about 1 km (0.6 mi) south of the
Terra Nova trailhead, to which your return along Middle Arm makes a satisfactory outing.

However, if you have an appetite for more, turn south on West Dyke, at
this point separated by low trees from the rich tidal marshes of Sturgeon
Bank, with its abundance of birds. Towards the south end of your walk, a line
of radar-reflecting towers warns passing ships of the proximity of the mud
flats. On the landward side, townhouse developments threaten to engulf the
old farmhouse home of the Steves family, at the end of Steveston Highway.

Next, you reach a lagoon, beyond which is Garry Point Park, recently created from a long strip of sand at the mouth of the river. Now, much altered
by humans, it boasts a Japanese garden honouring the citizens of the old
Steveston, for whom also a Fisherman's Memorial is located at the man-
made point to the south, overlooking the entrance to Steveston Harbour.

With its sea and mountain views, this spot makes a fine destination for
your walk, though to return by bus, continue eastwards into Steveston Village as far as No. 1 Road, along which buses run north to and along Westminster Highway and pass Lynas Lane only a block from your car.

# RICHMOND SOUTH DYKE TRAIL

**Round trip** 12 km (7.5 mi)

**Dykes, trails and roads**

**Allow** 3 hours

**Good all year**

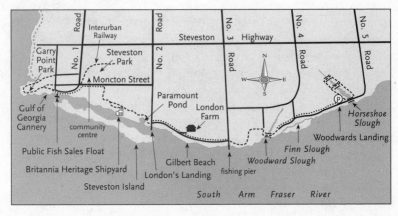

ON THIS OUTING along the South Arm of the Fraser River, walkers must share the trail with cyclists and, on the road sections, with motorists as well, but that should be no deterrent to the cooperatively minded. It is an ideal cool-weather walk when shade is of no consequence, for there is none; it is also a walk that may be started at either end, and even partway along, for there are numerous access points.

To reach the upstream end, drive south through Richmond on Highway 99, turn off west on Steveston Highway (Exit 32), then almost immediately go left on No. 5 Road, driving south to its end, where it veers right into River Road. Continue past the Dominion Bridge building to just beyond the bridge over a slough to find parking by the Woodwards Landing picnic area.

Horseshoe Slough, as it is called, boasts a little 15-minute trail up one side and down the other, the commercial buildings nearby obscured by a line of trees, whose reflections in the water enhance its attractiveness, as do the pedestrian bridges from which you may take in the scene, before you finally cross on the third one to return to the river. The next section, though nominally part of the South Dyke Trail, is on paved road, so unless you are a purist and would disdain to compromise, you may drive the next 1.7 km (1 mi) to No. 4 Road and begin your walk proper at Finn Slough, a narrow backwater with a fascinating array of old buildings on stilts, some rescued from decay and still lived in, some with evocative names such as Dinner Plate Island School.

Old pilings in the Fraser River.

Continuing westwards you arrive at Woodward Slough, slanting down to the Fraser beside a discharge building, and begin a detour around a packaging plant that has usurped the waterside. Cross Garden City Road at the farthest point before returning to the riverbank a short distance from No. 3 Road, with its pier and picnic area. The next stretch is well endowed with picnic tables, attesting to its popularity in summer for its fishing, beach-combing and nature observation as well as for its historic interest at London Farm, a late-nineteenth-century farmhouse, the restored building gracious in its spacious garden. The first land dyked and cultivated on Lulu Island was in this area.

Opposite, on the riverside, you may also dally at Gilbert Beach or continue to London's Landing, which, established in 1885 as a government wharf, is part of the fabric of local fishing and canning history. Since its purchase by Richmond in 1994, the pier has been upgraded and its immediate surroundings developed as a little park, commemorating the area's past. Here, at the foot of No. 2 Road, with Mount Baker dominating the upstream landscape, is an attractive destination for your walk down the river.

If, however, you have arranged transport farther west in Steveston or at Garry Point Park, you may make this a one-way trip and continue westwards past Paramount Pond, with its many and varied craft, and past the Pacific Coast Cannery, en route to the Britannia Heritage Shipyard, thence to Steveston Park and the village community centre. From here, you may head directly to Garry Point or detour to take in the sights and sounds of the waterfront, a popular area on a fine summer's weekend. (See also Walk 71.)

# RICHMOND NATURE PARK

**Round trip** 3.2 km (2 mi)

**Trails**

**Allow** 1.5 hours

**Good all year**

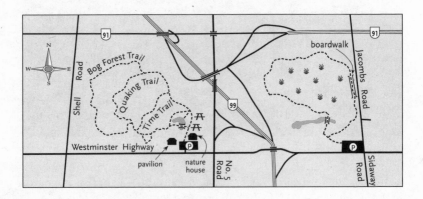

MOTORISTS SPEEDING SOUTH from Vancouver on Highway 99 are very likely unaware of the outdoor pleasure available to them only a few yards from the highway in Richmond. Here, fronting Westminster Highway, is Richmond Nature Park, the creation of a devoted group of conservationists.

To find this hidden treasure, leave Highway 99 on the Shell Road turn-off (Exit 38), veer right and drive south to the traffic light at Westminster Highway, where you go left to the park entrance, also on the left. Across the parking lot lies the park office, in which various useful guides are available, as are bags of seeds for the inhabitants of the waterfowl pond nearby. There is a picnic area for humans, too, if you wish to make a leisurely round and need sustenance afterwards.

Although the park's total area is small, it is so skillfully laid out that covering its three interwoven circuits in their entirety provides a satisfying walk. For a start, stay left to cross the end of the bird pond, take in the scene from the viewing platform, then set off on Time Trail, the short, 30-minute self-guiding nature loop, armed with its accompanying pamphlet. This course in nature study complete, you may set out, with your newly assimilated knowledge, on Quaking Trail, keeping the other circuit, Bog Forest Trail, for the third and last. By now, you should have acquired some familiarity with, at least, the commonest features of the area, from its shore pines to the shrub Labrador tea, a plant particularly colourful in spring.

On Bog Forest Trail.

And these shrubs that overtop you on many of the trails? These are interlopers—descendants of domestic blueberries blown in from neighbouring fields many years ago.

But this is not all, should you be in the mood for exploring, for you may still walk the circuit of the Richmond Nature Study Centre, situated on the east side of Highway 99. To reach this relatively undeveloped tract by car, turn left from the nature park onto Westminster Highway. Go left again on Jacombs Road, its east side adorned by an auto sales mall but its west side mercifully untouched. Immediately after turning, go left again into the small parking lot for the study centre, a more natural area than its neighbour across the way.

Twenty years ago and more, with few improvements to modify the environment, you were able to glean from the marshlike surroundings here some idea of the nature of the peat bog that covered much of Richmond in the past. Today that's not so easy, for the proliferation of construction of all kinds on the fringes of the sanctuary has accelerated the drying up of the ponds which have become so overgrown as to be well-nigh invisible. However, the Nature Park Society has embarked (in 2008) on a program to restore some of the old trails and to build new bridges and boardwalks, so that once again the casual visitor may appreciate this relatively untouched piece of Richmond.

# DEAS ISLAND

**Round trip** 4.4 km (2.7 mi)

**Trails**

**Allow** 1.5 hours

**Good all year**

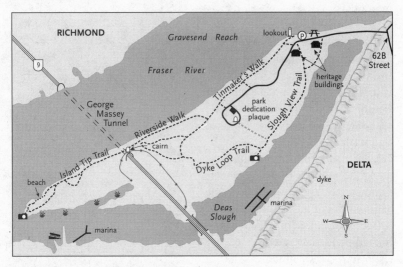

THOUGH THIS IS an island in name only, a causeway now connecting the regional park with the mainland south of the Fraser, it still has sufficient water around it to maintain the illusion of its former status. Another interesting feature is that on your walk westwards you cross the southern entrance to the George Massey Tunnel, giving you a view from above of Highway 99, the route on which you travel south from Vancouver to undertake this outing. This walk is especially rewarding in winter when the trees are bare and river views are at their best.

Turn off Tsawwassen Highway (Highway 17)/River Road (Exit 28), follow the River Road (62B Street) sign back left across the overpass and continue east for 2.5 km (1.5 mi). Turn left off this road a little before a sand-and-gravel operation and enter the park, leaving your vehicle at the first designated parking area on the left. Here, you are close to the heritage Inverholme Schoolhouse, and beyond it, also on the left, are two more heritage buildings, the imposing Burrvilla and its plain neighbour, the Delta Agricultural Hall. To your right, at the Tinmaker's Walk trailhead, are a commemorative tablet and a lookout tower, the tower providing fine views of the river's main channel below Gravesend Reach.

Burrvilla, a heritage house built in 1906.

As you proceed, you pass another parking area on your left, and here you may see the plaque—mounted on an old piston-drive air compressor—that commemorates the park's opening. Continuing, you arrive at a fork, the left arm of which, Dyke Loop Trail, takes you back by Deas Slough to your point of departure. By staying right on Riverside Walk, however, you veer closer to the river, being joined quite soon and in quick succession by Island Tip Trail and Sand Dune Trail, which is a combined horse and hiking trail. Thereafter, horses and hikers travel in tandem as the trail crosses the tunnel access, passing the cairn that commemorates its opening in 1959 by Queen Elizabeth. Your trail west stays close to the river now as you make for the island's tip, passing an attractive little beach en route.

From there, you look south across the mouth of Deas Slough, with its marina lying just to the east of Ladner Marsh. Southwest lies Kirkland Island, a navigation beacon marking its shoal waters. North, of course, is the river, and Lulu Island beyond, the shoreline marked by commercial and industrial operations—freight terminals and the like—though the B.C. Ferries refitting dock does add a touch of maritime romance to the scene.

On your return across the tunnel, you want to go right on Sand Dune Trail and again on Dyke Loop Trail to complete your circular tour of the park. At first, you have an interesting sample of dune ecology; next, you have views south across the waterway that is Deas Slough. At the second viewpoint, stay right on Slough View Trail as another trail forks left to the central picnic area at Fisher's Field and plod along the sandy route with the recreational activity on the slough to entertain you. Then, just behind Burrvilla, keep right again and cross the bridge on Tidal Pond Trail, the pond replete with vegetation and a blaze of colour in summer. All too soon, you emerge at the picnic area near which you started, your expedition over.

# BOUNDARY BAY REGIONAL PARK

**NORTH SECTION:** Round trip 8 km (5 mi)   **Allow** 3 hours
**SOUTH SECTION:** Round trip 4 km (2.5 mi)   **Allow** 1.5 hours
**Dykes and trails**   **Good all year**

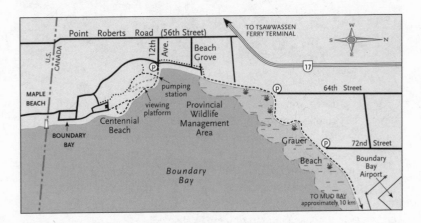

SINCE THE TOTAL distance from Mud Bay in the east to Beach Grove at the bay's western end is 16 km (9.9 mi), only the superfit, cyclists and two-car groups are likely to attempt this route in its entirety. Fortunately, there are numerous intermediate access points, so you may choose the distance you wish to cover in this interesting regional park, with its marine and mountain views and variety of birds.

The whole area is particularly rich in birdlife and is of international importance to migrating and wintering birds. Waterfowl and shorebirds are common, but you may come across a snowy owl if you are lucky, and hawks and eagles may also be seen on the stretch between the dyke and the sands of the bay. There, too, you may spot small mammals such as the coyote.

From Highway 99 a short distance south of the George Massey Tunnel, go right on Highway 17 (Tsawwassen Highway) at Exit 28 and follow it for 2.3 km (1.4 mi) to its intersection with Highway 10 (Ladner Trunk Road). Turn left here and, as you drive eastwards, the various beach access roads are on your right. The first, 64th Street, provides a short walk to the southwest before the dyke ends at Beach Grove Spit. The next, 72nd Street, gives you a nice round trip west and southwest covering nearly 8 km (5 mi), just the thing to bring colour to your cheeks on a cool winter day.

Pond at Centennial Beach.

Eastwards from 72nd lie Boundary Bay Airport and Delta Air Park and, possible noise apart, the uniformity of the landscape towards Mud Bay makes access from 88th, 96th, 104th and 112th Streets less than inviting unless you are a keep-fit buff with distance covered your main object.

At the west end, between 12th Avenue and Delta Centennial Beach, you may use the shore dyke for one leg of your trip and another, a little farther inland, as a start for your return route. For this section, turn left off Highway 17 on 56th Street (Point Roberts Road), go left again on 12th Avenue and drive east to the small parking area at road end. Once through the gate, follow the dyke east then south, noting on your right a track coming in from across the drainage ditch at the pumping station.

As you continue and your dyke becomes indistinguishable from the beach, a trail veers inland heading towards the facilities at Centennial Beach, a loop on the left providing instruction on dune ecology. Then, to vary your return and enjoy an undeveloped part of marshland, make your way towards the Park Entrance Road where you take a rough track just outside the boundary and work north, a ditch to your left and a narrow strip of bush separating you from the parking lot on your right. Soon you join the Savannah Trail that leads you back eastwards to the main Raptor Trail. Thereafter, you should keep left until, close to the main dyke, you veer right to meet it by the pumping station you noted near the beginning of your walk.

Yet another possibility exists, should you wish to connect the two ends in one long walk: when the dyke ends at Beach Grove on your trip from 72nd or 64th Street, continue beyond the gate along the lane leading to Beach Grove Road and walk the kilometre or so south to 12th Avenue, where the dyke resumes.

# ELGIN HERITAGE PARK

**Round trip** 8 km (5 mi)

**Trails and boardwalks**

**Allow** 2.5 hours or more

**Good all year**

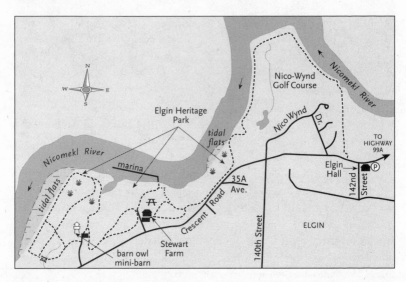

HERE IS A walk along the winding Nicomekl River in an area of both eco-logical and historical significance. To get there, drive south on Highway 99 to Highway 99A (King George Highway) at Exit 10, follow the signs for Cres-cent Road, then watch for the old Elgin Hall on the left. Park here and before you depart take time to study the information board with its introduction to the human history of the Elgin district.

Now cross Crescent Road to its north side, where you will find a trail passing between residential areas and heading towards the Nico-Wynd golf course, a pleasantly landscaped area which you pass on three sides, viewing it from the river dyke, where, though above and separate from it, you are not immune to straying golf balls. Beyond the golf course, your trail turns inland to skirt a marshy bit of tidal wetland, then comes to a fork. The left and longer branch takes you west parallel to the roadway; the right, more direct, soon arrives on the riverside lawns lying between the marina—with its main interest in non-motorized craft like canoes and kayaks—and the buildings of the historic farm and its fine Victorian mansion. The farm and mansion date from the late 19th century when the Stewart family first set-tled and developed a lucrative hay farm.

Springtime wildflowers attract attention.

Leaving the buildings for closer examination later, continue past the parking lot westwards through a forested area with many large trees, keeping an eye open for signs of culturally modified trees and burial mounds of the Aboriginal communities that pre-dated the Stewart farm. Beyond a second parking lot your route follows dykes and boardwalks round marshes and across tidal sloughs, habitat for a variety of birds, from the patient great blue heron and majestic bald eagle down to the tiny wren. Across one wet meadow you spot an intriguing building on stilts, a "barn owl mini-barn."

Finally, when further progress to the west is halted by the fences guarding the tailored lawns of some private houses, you make your way back to the heart of the Heritage Park at the Stewart Farm, there to indulge your curiosity about what life and farming was like in this part of British Columbia in the early years of last century. Then you must retrace your steps to Elgin Hall through forest and by swamp, through natural environments and man-made landscapes to end a varied and interesting outing.

# REDWOOD PARK

**Round trip** up to 5 km (3.1 mi)          **Allow** 1.5 hours

**Forest trails and lawns**               **Good all year**

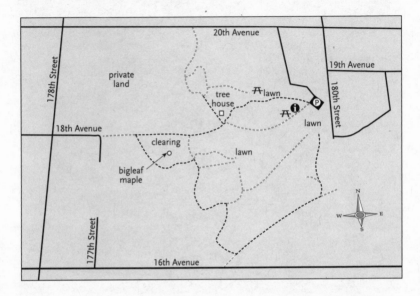

DON'T BE PUT off by the small area of this park, which is only 26 ha (64 acres). Because of the park's unique and attractive collection of trees bordering on shady lawns, you may easily follow its varied trails for a good hour or more.

Redwood Park more than lives up to its name. Its original owners—eccentric twin brothers Peter and David Brown—made a hobby of collecting the seeds of various trees and planting them in this property. Among these are redwoods from California, and though most of the trees are exotics such as the deciduous dawn redwoods from China near the parking lot, there are also more everyday species like our own native conifers and maples. It must be admitted, though, that part of the charm of the place is the memory of the pioneer Surrey family that lived here, finally ending up in a large tree house, unfortunately removed for safety reasons and replaced by a contemporary model.

The park is somewhat isolated considering that it is only 48 km (30 mi) southeast of Vancouver. One approach from Highway 99 is to go south on

The tree house.

Highway 99A (King George Highway) at Exit 10, east on 16th Avenue (North Bluff Road), then north again on 176th Street (Highway 15 / Pacific Highway) for 800 m to 20th Avenue, where you turn right and continue until you see the parking lot signs near the park's east side. Alternatively, you may find it less complicated to drive Highway 1 to 176th Street (Exit 53) and go south on Highway 15 (Pacific Highway) to 20th Avenue.

From the parking lot, head a little northwest to pick up a main trail (by the washroom) that leads you into the forest. Here you have a sense of the different trees in the park, and identification of them keeps you guessing. By turning a little south you come out on one of the open grassy areas with trees on all sides except to the southwest, where you look out to the Canada–United States border and the San Juan Islands. Close to one of these clearings is the tree house, with a short account of its history on a wooden signpost beside it.

Though you may put in your time here simply wandering the park trails at random, the following circular outing covers most of its features, once you have viewed the tree dwelling. From it, follow the trail west, admiring the giant bigleaf maple as you swing back along the lower edge of the clearing and into the woods. At the junction, turn right and head downhill. Next, go right on a path that curves back left along the edge of some private property and through a swampy area to an old railway grade a little north of North Bluff Road.

Follow this grade to the left as it rises northeastwards, then, after some 10 minutes, go left over a bridge on a trail back up into the park to emerge on the lawn a little south of the picnic tables and the parking area.

# SOUTH SURREY URBAN FORESTS

**SUNNYSIDE ACRES:**
**Round trip** 4 km (2.5 mi)

**Allow** 1 hour

**CRESCENT PARK:**
**Round trip** 4 km (2.5 mi)

**Allow** 1 hour

**Trails**

**Good all year**

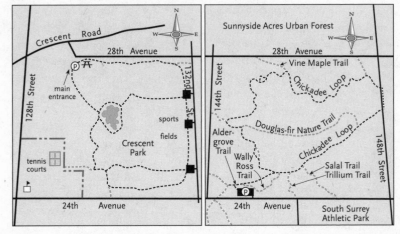

LOOKING FOR A shady walk on a hot summer's day? Why not try one or both of these delightful little oases located within a stone's throw of each other in South Surrey? To make a day's outing, you might start with Sunnyside Acres, a small area of second-growth forest rescued from development by the local heritage society, which provides guided tours and information about the plant and animal life of the forest; and afterwards move on to Crescent Park, which has picnic and sports facilities as well as trails.

Driving south from Vancouver, leave Highway 99 at Exit 10 for Highway 99A (King George Highway) and continue south to 24th Avenue where you go right (west) to a parking area on the north side of the road shortly after 148th Street just beyond the entry to the athletic park. You may also reach this spot from Highway 1 at 152nd Street (Exit 48) by going south on 152nd Street to 24th Avenue.

A large kiosk with trail maps and pictures of the plants and animals you may see stands at the trailhead. Especially useful is the *Interpretive Trail Map,* key to the numbered stops along the route. Having provided yourself with this information, plunge into the forest on Stellar's Jay trail, soon going right on Aldergrove, noting in passing the wheelchair-accessible

Mallards enjoying the duck pond.

Wally Ross Trail which meanders off on your right. Next you come to a
junction with Chickadee Loop, which circles the forest, so it is immaterial
in which direction you go. On this occasion, however, go right, passing the
other end of the Wally Ross Trail almost immediately. Thereafter, keep left
twice (right would take you back onto 24th Avenue), at first enjoying the
shade of Douglas-firs before, very soon you come to the Douglas-fir Nature
Trail, a little track, disappearing into the trees on your left. Then you enter
an area with a more open canopy and an abundance of bushes and shrubs.
Soon your path debouches on a busy street (148th), on which you go left,
fortunately for only a minute or two, before re-entering the forest. Still keeping left at main intersections and ignoring all unofficial tracks, make your
way past windfalls—some old, some recent—and great cedar stumps, relics
of the forest logged a century ago. Then the western end of the Douglas-
fir Nature Trail emerges from the forest on your left so you go right and
finally, when you come to a T-junction, right again, retracing your outward
route on Aldergrove Trail the short distance back to your car.

To follow with a visit to Crescent Park, turn right when you leave the
Sunnyside parking area and drive west to 132nd Street, then north to
28th Avenue, which leads you west to the park's main entrance. Here, you
are near a wide clearing and picnic area. For a short stroll to the heart of the
park, take the path to the right behind the washrooms, which leads to an
interesting little pond circled by several trails, from which you may view the
various water birds resident there.

Going left at the entrance, however, takes you onto a bridle trail to begin
a ramble round the perimeter of the park in fine second-growth forest, from
which you must emerge to pass several sports fields and their associated
parking lots along 132nd Street. At the third, you may opt to remain in the
open and follow the walkway westwards, from there going right at forks
and arriving at the central pond and its picturesque little bridge, on the
near side of which lies your return path; or you may prefer to remain with
the shady perimeter trail, on which you work round back to your start, your
exploration of two contrasting urban forests complete.

# GREEN TIMBERS URBAN FOREST

**WALK 1: Round trip** 6 km (3.7 mi)  **Allow** 2 hours

**WALK 2: Round trip** 5.5 km (3.4 mi)  **Allow** 2 hours

**Paths and trails**  **Good all year**

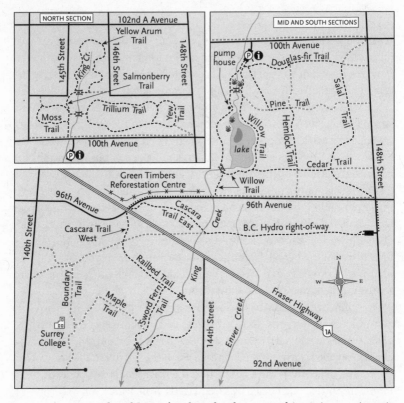

SET IN THE midst of Surrey's urban development, this oasis owes its existence to the efforts of the Green Timbers Heritage Society. Today this forest is a mix of natural regeneration and the remnants of B.C.'s first attempts at reforestation.

The main entry to the forest lies between 144th and 148th Streets on the south side of 100th Avenue, and you reach it by driving east from Highway 99A (King George Highway) or from Highway 1, by going off at 152nd Street (Exit 48), driving south on 152nd Street, then west on 100th. The forest is divided into three sections by 100th and 96th Avenues, each with a profusion of short trails with descriptive names. Here are two walks that together

Sun-dappled Salal Trail.

allow you to experience what this forest has to offer.

For the first, cross 100th Avenue to the trailhead, walk north on Salmonberry Trail, a one-time logging railway, then very soon go left on Moss Trail, which circles back to Salmonberry. Next you continue to Yellow Arum Trail, where you go left again, following it round the marsh in which King Creek is born, before returning to Salmonberry. This time go right and south to Trillium Trail which, with little Yew Trail, makes a wide loop through some fine Douglas-firs before coming back to the main Salmonberry on which you complete your circuit. Back at the parking lot, go left on Douglas-fir Trail, then south (right) on Salal to Cedar Trail. Turn right, then right again onto Hemlock, another nature trail heading north. At the crossing with Pine, you may go left to an unnamed trail, where you go half right and across a meadow towards the parking lot. But you haven't yet seen the little lake and its surrounding marshes, so go left and south again on Willow. Then you work west round the end of the lake and over its outlet to turn right and north on Birch Trail to complete this first walk.

For the second walk, head south on Willow Trail and left (east) on Cedar to a crossroads, where you go right on Salal and out onto 96th Avenue. Cross at the traffic light and walk south along the verge of 148th Street to a small parking space on a B.C. Hydro line. From here you proceed west along the open swath, until, after about 1 km (0.6 mi), you come to the Cascara Trail East on the right. Follow this trail as it curves to emerge on 96th Avenue at Fraser Highway, which you cross at the lights to find Cascara Trail West heading into the bush on your left. Soon you cross the power line onto Railbed Trail, which takes you through forest to a fork just before a bridge. If you go right on Sword Fern Trail, you first pass Maple Trail, then you cross King Creek and turn left (north) on King Creek Trail, which returns you to the bridge you noted previously. Now you retrace your steps to the Fraser Highway/96th Avenue junction, where you cross to the north side of 96th Avenue. A short walk beside this road soon brings you to Willow Trail, which you soon leave to cross the bridge over King Creek and then north on the shady Birch Trail, to end the walk.

# TYNEHEAD REGIONAL PARK

**Round trip** 4.8 km (3 mi)          **Allow** 2 hours

**Trails**                            **Good all year**

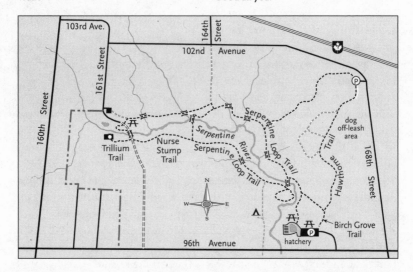

ITS STATISTICS SUGGEST that this walk may be a little lacking in distance. The relative shortness of the current trail system is, however, more than compensated for by the points of interest along the route, as you wend your way through lush meadows and mixed deciduous-coniferous forest among the headwater feeders of the Serpentine River, with, as culmination, the Tynehead Salmon Hatchery, open at certain times to the public. (Phone 604-589-9127 for details.)

To make the most of the little park's winding trail system, a start at the most northerly of its three parking areas is best. To reach it from Highway 1 going east, turn off at 104th Avenue (Exit 50), go left on 104th Avenue, right on 160th Street, then left again on 103rd Avenue, which curves south onto 161st. Go east again on 102nd Avenue, continuing until this road begins to turn south onto 168th Street and you see, on the right of the bend, the site of the one-time Tynehead House, now a shady parking lot equipped with information kiosk and brochures. Your trailhead is in the north side of the parking lot.

From here, your trail heads off roughly southwest shaded by interesting old trees, the bigleaf maples being particularly fine; and beyond the trees,

Bigleaf maple blossom.

glimpses of an old meadow gone wild. Then you reach the parting of the ways: left, the direct trail to the picnic area and salmon hatchery at its southeast end, the other reaching the same destination by a much longer route.

On this longer trail, the northern segment of the Serpentine Loop, you cross successive headwater tributaries of the river, normally dry in summer and seen at their best in early spring. After the third such crossing comes another fork with left leading to a bridge of the main waterway. Go right, however, then left, ignoring the trail out to 164th Street, and make your way along the southern margin of an attractive meadow, beyond which you soon come to a picnic area with tracks going off in various directions: right to a parking area on 161st Street and ahead round a butterfly garden and up the Trillium Trail to a viewing platform overlooking a small pond, a safe rearing area for coho and steelhead fry before they migrate to the ocean. Turning your back on the picnic area, you now start downstream on the aptly named Nurse Stump Trail, soon meeting the shorter Serpentine Loop, in trees mostly with one glimpse of a parklike area, home to the Raven's Nest group camp. Then you approach the river again and a fine arching bridge, on the near side of which you may investigate a short interpretive loop before crossing. Here, going right brings you into the open at another picnic area, another parking lot and the hatchery, while left continues the Loop and is a possible return route to the 168th Street parking lot.

However, for those who visit the hatchery and its picnic area, it is possible to avoid retracing any part of your outward route by returning on the Hawthorne Trail, which meanders back to the parking lot across the lush meadows of the dog off-leash area. To do this, look for the Birch Grove Trail at the far southeastern corner of the picnic area, then when it splits with left heading back to rejoin Hatchery Trail, go right and stay right thereafter on the last lap of your outing.

# DERBY REACH REGIONAL PARK

**Round trip** 8 km (5 mi)

**Trails**

**Allow** 2.5 hours

**Good all year**

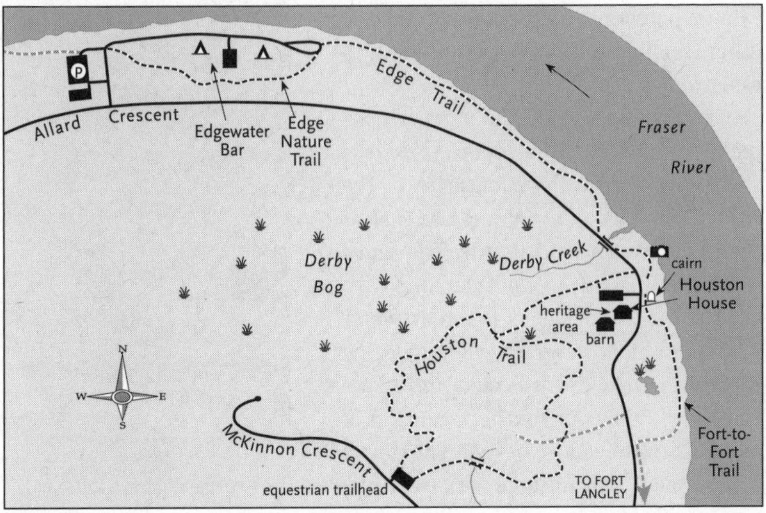

LONG A FAVOURITE destination for fishers and picnickers, Derby Reach
has become more attractive to those of us who like to stretch our legs now
that a trail along the river links the Edgewater fishing bar to the eastern section of this park at the cairn marking the location of the original Fort Langley. Built in 1827, in its heyday, the fort was a centre of pioneer agricultural
settlement and trade in the lower Fraser Valley. Today, from the heritage
area focussing on this early period, a short path connects with the Houston
Trail, a hiking and equestrian circuit meandering through forest.

To reach the park, leave Highway 1 on 200th Street (Exit 58), go north to
96th Avenue, then east to 208th Street, on which you go left (north), staying
with it as it curves east onto Allard Crescent. The entry to Edgewater Bar is
on your left. Park here.

Begin your walk by approaching the river, then going east to the right
of the campground on the Edge Trail and winding through woodland with
imposing cottonwood trees. Beyond the campground, the trail nears the
river again and continues upstream as part of the Fraser River Trail. Soon,
after a short diversion alongside the road and a crossing of Derby Creek,

Looking beyond the Fort-to-Fort Trail to Golden Ears.

you reach a viewpoint affording magnificent views across the Fraser River to the North Shore mountains and east to Mount Baker. A few metres on is the heritage area where you can pause to read the inscription on the commemorative cairn as well as the information boards.

The Houston Trail connector starts across the grass from the parking area opposite and meets the trail proper in some 10 minutes. If you go left, your trail borders some low-level meadow and swamp at first, passing through a mixed forest with some fine cedars and bigleaf maples, the leaves of the maples rustling underfoot in fall. Then, the path rises on the first of its many ups and downs, and you may glimpse the road below, with the river in the distance across a pond. Next comes a junction. Left will take you down to Allard Crescent where you must walk some 200 m east along the road to connect with the Fort-to-Fort Trail. So, you stay with the Houston Trail, which pursues its roller-coaster way, eventually arriving at another trailhead and the horse-unloading lot off McKinnon Crescent.

Across the parking area, some large maples welcome you to the final lap of the Houston Trail, which winds down towards the Derby Bog, skirting to the right of the swampy ground before coming to your original fork and the path back to the heritage area, from which your return lies downstream once more on Edge Trail.

Alternatively, instead of, or perhaps in addition to, your circuit of Houston Trail, you may wish to sample the Fort-to-Fort Trail, the beginning of which runs upstream within park boundaries for about 1 km (0.6 mi) from the heritage area. It is now possible to continue along this trail, following streets and trails beyond the park, another 4 km (2.5 mi) to the present-day Fort Langley, making possible a much longer walk—or with two cars—a one-way trip between these two historic points.

# CAMPBELL VALLEY

**Round trip** 12 km (7.5 mi) or less      **Allow** 4 hours

**Trails**      **Good most of the year**

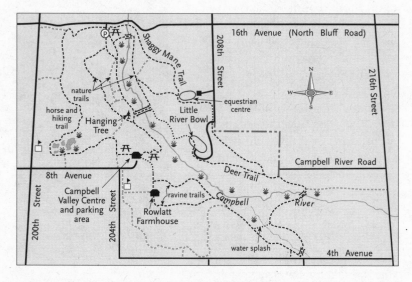

THE STREAM THAT flows through this regional park rises at the south end of Langley Township and pursues a gentle course westwards, running roughly parallel with the Canada–United States border except for one hair-pinlike swing to the north followed by a return to its original direction. Thereafter, it ends uneventfully in Semiahmoo Bay, just south of White Rock.

On its jig northwards, it is crossed by 16th Avenue (North Bluff Road), which you reach from Highway 1 by turning south on Highway 15 (Pacific Highway) at 176th Street (Exit 53) or 200th Street (Exit 58). A little east of 200th Street, the road drops into its valley, with the park's north entrance and parking area on the right. From here, you have several choices, ranging from a short walk on the valley floor to a half-day circuit of the whole park using Shaggy Mane Trail, open to both hikers and horseback riders.

For a short walk, simply head east past the picnic area, through tall trees to a raised boardwalk over the extensive wet meadows bordering the river. On the far side, your trail turns south, paralleling the verge of the marshland to another bridge, which returns you to a T-junction on the west side. Here,

Springtime in the marsh.

you turn north, heading back on the Little River Loop Trail and crossing a wide meadow, with the possibility of several detours through the woodlands on its east side for variety.

If you decide on the hiking and riding trail, you may head back north for a little before you turn east, crossing the stream just south of the road, then rising to level ground above. More attractive, however, is use of the pedestrian route across the boardwalk and south to a fork where a minor trail rises to the left out of the valley and joins Shaggy Mane Trail, passing south of an equestrian centre; or you may stay with the loop trail to the next junction, then go straight ahead across a meadow to enter the trees beyond. This route, aptly named Deer Trail, takes you southeast by the Little River Bowl, finally joining Shaggy Mane as it descends to the valley floor.

Next comes a turn to the right at a major fork and your crossing of the watercourse. A stretch of open country follows as you wind south, east, west and northwest, eventually leaving Shaggy Mane for the narrow Ravine Trail on your right. This takes you into a picturesque little valley where, just across a small creek, you come to a fork. Right takes you past a viewpoint over the marsh; left on the more recently constructed branch, which emerges in a meadow near the heritage Annand/Rowlatt Farmstead, with the one-time Lochiel Schoolhouse a little beyond. Leaving the farm, the trail heads north across the open field to a picnic area and the park's 8th Avenue Visitor Centre.

From here to your starting point, you may drop into the valley and take the west leg of the short Little River Loop Trail, its scenic meadow particularly attractive in its fall colours. Or you may stay above, on the rim of the valley, using Shaggy Mane Trail round the western perimeter before dropping to your starting point, thus completing your walk over the gently rolling countryside just north of Canada's border with the United States.

# ALDERGROVE LAKE REGIONAL PARK

**SHORT CIRCUIT: Round trip** 4 km (2.5 mi)   **Allow** 1 hour

**LONG CIRCUIT: Round trip** 7 km (4.3 mi)   **Allow** 2 hours

**Trails**   **Good all year**

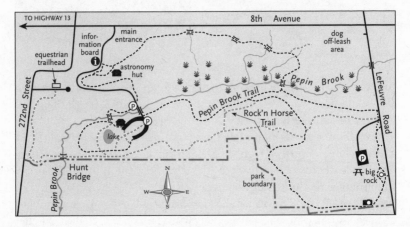

DO NOT BE misled by the presence of the word "lake" in the title. The body of water so designated is, in fact, no more than a large outdoor swimming pool. Still, Metro Vancouver Regional Parks Department is working to make the park fit its name by creating a more realistic lake with nature walks in its eastern purlieu where formerly was an unsightly quarry.

To reach this regional park from Highway 1, turn off at 264th Street (Exit 73) onto Highway 13 (Aldergrove–Bellingham Highway) and drive south to 8th Avenue, on which you go left. Then, just after 272nd Street, a right turn sees you descending into the valley, perhaps taking a few minutes to look at the information board about midway to your parking spot on the far side of the creek, where the trailhead for the Pepin Brook Trail is also found.

Shortly after getting underway on the pleasantly winding trail, you pass two trails to the right that connect with the bridle trail running higher up and farther to the south. Ignore these if you prefer the shorter walk and descend gently into the valley on the left to cross the long arching bridge over the brook and the adjacent marsh, an area oftentimes waterlogged thanks to the activity of beavers. As you start to rise again, you find that the route is more open now with one fairly narrow ridge, the legacy of

Pepin Brook and marsh.

glaciation. Finally approaching the park road at the information board, you turn south along the margin of a meadow, then east on the trail down the hill to another meadow, across the road from the picnic site. Now, you may simply follow the road back to your start or, to exploit the park to its fullest, circle behind the picnic shelter crossing the pedestrian bridge to the west and traversing the "lake" area before returning to your transportation.

For the longer circuit, leave the Pepin Brook Trail at the second fork, rising to join the Rock'n Horse Trail, a multipurpose route that heads south, leaving the comfort of the trees to emerge on the verge of the one-time gravel pit, now green with grass, bushes and a picnic area. But for now keep right, skirting the hollow and facing south, with berry fields on the other hand. Gradually, you work round to the east, into a treed valley and out again, eventually arriving at a viewpoint with trees behind and broad fields in front stretching south and east, with Mount Baker and the other great peaks of the Cascade Range as backdrop.

Resuming your walk, you turn north into the trees on a trail that undulates along, passing en route an enormous boulder, another instance of glacial deposition, and coming out onto a park road. Turn right towards LeFeuvre Road, where you turn left. Thirty metres along the road, you are able to escape back onto the pedestrian trail, travelling west above the marshy valley and descending finally to join the Pepin Brook Trail at its bridge. Now you may go left for a quick return or right as described previously for the short circuit.

# MATSQUI TRAIL

**One-way trip** 10.4 km (6.5 mi)

**Dykes and roads**

**Allow** 2.5 hours

**Good all year**

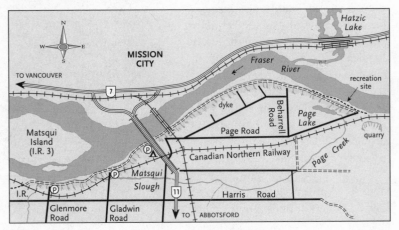

IF YOU WISH, you may stretch this walk into a return trip that will take you the better part of a day; there are, however, intermediate points with access to the river at which you may turn around once you feel you have had enough of this stretch of the Centennial Trail north of Abbotsford. If you can organize two cars, you may also turn this into a very pleasant one-way outing.

To reach the walk's western end in this regional park along the Fraser River, leave Highway 1 at the Mount Lehman Road interchange (Exit 83) and drive north to Harris Road. Turn right here and travel east 3 km (1.9 mi) to Glenmore Road, where you go left and cross the railway to the trailhead on the dyke. From here, you head upstream and, soon after passing that reminder of the less savoury aspects of human existence, the James Sewage Treatment Plant, you reach the Gladwin Road access point, another possible start, 1.6 km (1 mi) from the beginning. Then, 2.2 km (1.4 mi) more brings you to the Mission Bridge and the park facilities in its shadow, also reached directly from Highway 11 (Huntingdon–Mission Highway) via Harris Road and Riverside Street.

The next short stretch takes you beneath the highway bridge and over the CP Railway crossing, used at one time by the road as well to provide access to Mission from the south. On the dyke again, you come to Kelleher Road. Now the route begins bending from northeast to southeast, at the

Mission Bridge over the Fraser River.

same time drawing back from the main current sufficiently far to permit cottonwood trees to grow, with even one or two houses on the river side of the embankment close to Walters Road.

Another possible turnaround is at Beharrell Road, where dyke and river begin to come together again 4.5 km (2.8 mi) from the park's centre. A short walk to the top of the bank gives you a view of Westminster Abbey, the Benedictine foundation that dominates the countryside east of Mission.

If you intend to go all the way along the trail, you must still cover 2.5 km (1.6 mi) to reach Page Road, close to a quarry under the battlements of Sumas Mountain, having passed the small Page Lake on your right and an undeveloped recreation site between the dyke and the river on your left.

From here, you have nothing for it but to turn about for the journey downriver to whichever of the points you started from. The distance from Glenmore to Page Road suggests the advisability of a car shuttle to make the whole trail a one-way trip, not unlike a portage, reference to which may be a reminder that Matsqui itself means "portage," making the single-direction trip even more appropriate.

The recent addition of some 4 km (2.5 mi) westwards makes such a one-way trip still more attractive. Thanks to Metro Vancouver Regional Parks Department obtaining permission from the Matsqui First Nation to cross its reserve, you may now start at Douglas Taylor Park (formerly Olund Park), 2.7 km (1.7 mi) west of Glenmore on Harris Road, for a very different experience from the open dyke just described. This extension meanders up and down through woodland and pasture with the occasional glimpse of the Fraser River below before descending to river level just before the Glenmore trailhead. Alone or as part of a Matsqui Trail outing, this walk is likely to be a popular one, and its being part of the Fraser Valley Regional Trail as well as the Trans Canada Trail will almost certainly add to its attraction.

# SEVEN SISTERS TRAIL

**LOW LEVEL: Round trip** 4.8 km (3 mi)     **Allow** 1.5 hours

**HIGH LEVEL: Round trip** 10 km (6.2 mi)     **Allow** 4 hours

**Elevation gain** 290 m (950 ft)     **High point** 325 m (1065 ft)

**Trails**     **Best April to November**

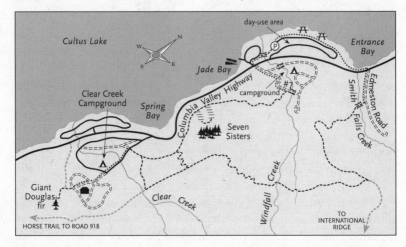

WHETHER YOU ARE staying in one of Cultus Lake's many campsites or
simply visiting the area for the day, you may find this walk's variations to
your liking. To reach the popular provincial park via Yarrow, leave Highway 1
at No. 3 Road (Exit 104); alternatively, go off at Vedder Road (Exit 119A)
for Sardis. Either way, you eventually find yourself driving the Columbia
Valley Highway past Cultus Lake village to the Entrance Bay day-use area,
where you may park, remembering to purchase your parking permit before
you set off.

Now on foot, turn west, passing through the screen of trees and over
Windfall Creek to the Jade Bay boat launch. Here, you go left, cross the highway and continue uphill to just around the corner past Campsite 7, where
your trail ascends out of the valley before levelling off in second-growth forest, the mixture suggesting the early days of logging, when the tree cover
was left to restore itself. Through this, the trail rises and falls gently until a
large Douglas-fir and a flight of steps announce your arrival at the grove of
the Seven Sisters, survivors of the original forest.

For a short stroll, you may return from this spot, but continuing to

Grove of the Seven Sisters.

Clear Creek campground gives you the chance to view a solitary giant at close quarters. On your way, you pass the ends of two trails on your left coming down from the bench above, and you may note these for future reference. Once in the campground, turn left and ascend the access road, crossing Clear Creek, staying left at a fork, and finally reaching a five-way junction with washrooms between the two middle roads.

Take the one just below the washrooms, and you soon reach the trail (between Campsites 49 and 50), which is joined by another from the right that comes up from the main road. The tree, when you reach it, is truly worth the effort, if only because of the details provided of its past, from its birth in the thirteenth century, long before this land was known to Europeans. After this, if you return by the same route, you will have had a walk of 4.8 km (3 mi).

If you are fit, experienced and have some time at your disposal, another possibility presents itself, though it does involve a rise of nearly 300 m (985 ft) and extends your round-trip distance considerably. This time, having made your way back through the campground onto the Seven Sisters Trail, turn uphill at the first fork on what was presumably a logging road, go left at the T-junction onto the high-level horse trail and, after about 15 minutes rising steadily, note yet another track joining from the left. This, of course, is the other trail you passed on your outward trip; it provides a possible return and a walk of 6 km (3.7 mi).

Should you continue to climb, your route eventually levels off as you reach the upper waters of Windfall Creek and realize the appropriateness of its name. After this, it is virtually downhill all the way until you reach what was obviously an old logging road now reverting nicely to nature. Here, you turn left and downhill until you come out upon Edmeston Road, a little above the highway at Lakeside Lodge. From here, a short turn back left brings you once more to the beach and, eventually, your car.

# TEAPOT HILL

**Round trip** 5 km (3.1 mi)

**Elevation gain** 250 m (820 ft)

**Trails and roads**

**Allow** 2 hours

**High point** 290 m (950 ft)

**Good most of the year**

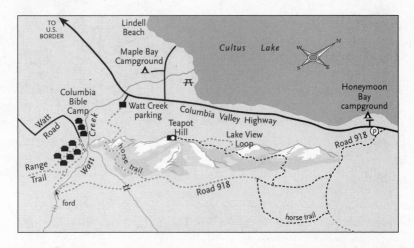

TO CLIMB THIS sporting little bump so quaintly named, you must park at the Teapot Hill trailhead parking lot in Cultus Lake Provincial Park, a short distance beyond the entrance to Clear Creek campground and just short of the entrance to the Honeymoon Bay group campgrounds. Parking fees are in effect here during the summer months, so purchase your permit before you begin your walk.

The trail rises quite steeply at first to join, within minutes, the service road. Several minutes later you pass the outhouse and a map of the trail system. The trail then settles down to a steady uphill grade. Next, you may note a trail joining from the left after some 800 m, with a sign to the horse trail. This could be your return route. Shortly after you arrive at your next intersection, where the trail to Teapot Hill goes right. Not long afterwards, a small sign board indicates some of the interesting flowers you should watch for on your walk.

The trail, rerouted in the past few years, no longer has a long flight of steps to daunt you, and you make your ascent along the side of a ridge instead of up its snout. Still, you eventually reach ridge level at a station with two points of interest. A sign tells the story of an instance of violence

View of the Fraser Valley from Teapot Hill.

in nature where a large Douglas-fir has been struck by a lightning bolt, the scar running all the way down its trunk. A few metres onward, you can enjoy a view over Cultus Lake and across it to the ridge of Vedder Mountain. Thereafter, the trail to the main summit proceeds uninterrupted.

At your destination, you find that B.C. Parks has decided that the drop-off is sufficiently steep to warrant the use of restraining wires, the side towards the lake being virtually sheer, and from here you have views that would do credit to a more lofty eminence. Immediately below you are the cabins and playing fields of the Columbia Bible Camp, whose campers created the southern, now abandoned, route to your miniature mountain; while farther off is the little residential settlement of Lindell Beach, with the Maple Bay picnic area and campground close to the south end of Cultus Lake. Farther south still lies the International Boundary while, as before, the ridges of Vedder Mountain block the view to the north. And the reason for the name of the hill? A brass teapot was found here when the trail was first built.

Your return is by the same route as far as the intersection with Road 918. Here, you may choose a somewhat longer and more energetic return than by the main trail. For this, jog right on Road 918 and then almost immediately go left on the horse trail. On this, you meander through the forest, surmounting its steep little undulations until after some 30 minutes you arrive at a fork. Leave the bridle trail here and go left, descending once more to Road 918, where a right turn brings you back to your parking spot just east of the Honeymoon Bay group campgrounds, a peculiar use, one would think, given the name of the location.

# CHATHAM REACH

**FROM ALOUETTE BRIDGE:**
**Round trip** 10 km (6.2 mi)   **Allow** 3 hours

**FROM END OF HARRIS ROAD:**
**Round trip** 4 km (2.5 mi)   **Allow** 1 hour

**Dykes**   **Good all year**

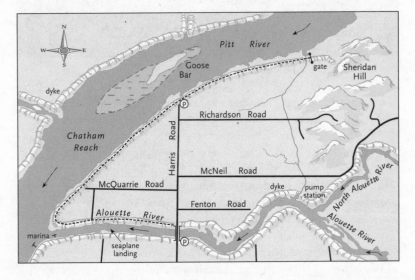

PITT RIVER WITH its succession of dykes offers many fine outings, and this one, with its superb upriver views, must rank high on any aesthetic scale. You have a choice of distance as well: a short trip of 4 km (2.5 mi) and another of more than double that length, the longer route providing you with a stretch of the Alouette River for good measure.

For the shorter excursion, turn north off Highway 7 (Lougheed Highway) on Dewdney Trunk Road just east of the Pitt River Bridge. Go left at the T-junction onto Harris Road and drive to the end of that thoroughfare at the river dyke, crossing the Alouette River en route. To embark on the longer walk, stop at the bridge over the Alouette; park in the lot just south of the bridge.

From the Alouette bridge, your walk begins with crossing to the north bank, prior to setting off westwards downstream. As you proceed, assorted small farms lie below you on your right; then, as you approach Pitt River, a variety of boathouses and pleasure craft sit on the water to your left. Having

View upstream to ridges enclosing Widgeon Slough.

arrived at the confluence of the tributary and the main stream, you begin your northward march along the Pitt, its tidal waters providing passage for tugs and small boats, its wide shoreline marshes home to a multitude of wildlife. Waterfowl of many kinds are present as well as herons and raptors; spring is a wonderful time, with nesting birds going about their business on every hand. At any time of the year, however, the prospect ahead would be hard to beat: the wide expanse of the Pitt River making its great bend that encloses Addington Marsh and, beyond that, the ridges and knolls surrounding Widgeon Slough with, as background to it all, the snow-capped mountains at the head of Pitt Lake. After a walk of some 35 minutes, you come to the starting point of the shorter walk and acquire a feeling of smugness in the thought of the extra exercise you are getting as well.

Proceeding, you observe that a narrow band of rough ground with trees and shrubs now separates the dyke from the various agricultural enterprises and homes on your right. Finally, you come to an information board announcing that this narrow strip of land has been left in its natural state for wildlife habitat—small recompense, it seems, for the many hectares lost to human endeavours. Then, just beyond, a gate bars further progress and you must turn around.

After your upstream views, you may find the return a little anticlimactic, the sight of new urban developments on the slopes west of the river no match for nature's work. Still, the countryside has its own quiet beauty, and city bustle seems far off as, after a visit to that part of the river that commemorates William Pitt, Earl of Chatham, you retrace your steps to whichever starting point you selected.

# ALOUETTE RIVER DYKES

**Round trip** 14.5 km (9 mi)

**Dykes**

**Allow** 4.5 hours

**Good all year**

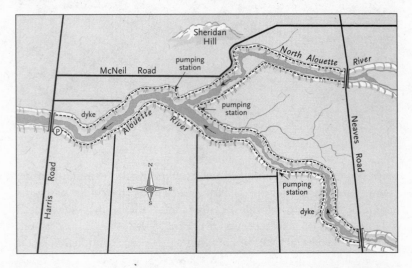

SITUATED IN THE heartland of Pitt Meadows, this walk has much to offer: low-level, easy walking and magnificent mountain scenery amid the peace and serenity of a countryside far removed from cities and highways. To reach the start, turn left off Highway 7 (Lougheed Highway) onto Dewdney Trunk Road just east of the Pitt River Bridge. Turn left again at the T-junction onto Harris Road and continue along it for 2.5 km (1.6 mi) to a bridge over the Alouette River. Park in the lot on the south bank.

Joined by the Trans Canada Trail, you head upstream on the busiest section of dyke, which carries recreationists of all sorts and conditions as well as the occasional farm machine, for the land south of here is highly developed agriculturally. After a short distance, you come to the confluence of the North Alouette and the main stream, both arms wide and slow-moving as they traverse the lowlands. Now your dyke turns southeast and even due south on occasion, following the windings of the river until finally, at a bridge, you meet the road you have been paralleling for the last short while.

Cross this bridge and, turning left onto the grassy dyke along the north side of the river, embark on the most peaceful, most delightful part of the

At the confluence.

trip, in the triangle enclosed between the two branches of the Alouette, some of the original marsh remaining though attempts at draining and cultivating are afoot. After about 30 minutes you are back at the meeting of the waters and turn northeast, with the peaks and ridges of Golden Ears in full view. On this stretch, the dyke runs straight, leaving a wide margin of marsh between you and the meanderings of the North Alouette. Quite soon, you change direction again and, closing the gap, head eastwards towards Neaves Road, once more with the river on one side and a drainage canal on the other. Now, you look clear to Mount Baker, agricultural development having levelled the cottonwood trees, sometime nesting place for the local herons. At the road, cross on its bridge and turn left, dodging around a small slough and some remaining cottonwoods before resuming your march along the grassy north bank, looking ahead now to Sheridan Hill, whose base you eventually reach before you swing away on the next stage of your walk.

Back on a gravelled dyke, make for the confluence of the two Alouettes, where you turn west towards the crossing of Harris Road and the end of your excursion, reflecting that the whole course has been Y shaped, with more or less equal distances between bridges; and that it has revealed to you two faces of Pitt Meadows: the original marsh with its abundance of wildlife, and the more recently reclaimed lands with their produce destined to meet human needs.

# GRANT NARROWS REGIONAL PARK

**SOUTHERN LOOP:** 4 km (2.5 mi)       **Allow** 1.5 hours

**KATZIE MARSH LOOP:** 6.5 km (4 mi)    **Allow** 2.5 hours

**LONG LOOP:** 12 km (7.5 mi)          **Allow** 4 hours

Dykes                                  Good all year

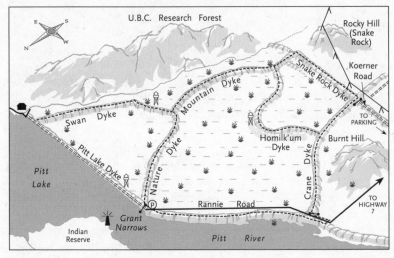

CHOOSE A CLEAR day for this walk to experience the full beauty of the majestic peaks enclosing the valley that houses Pitt Lake and the river draining from it. This is especially true in spring when the mountains are still snow-clad and when your way is sweetened by the scent of the balm from the surrounding cottonwoods. As well, much of the park is protected marshland, home to many species of birds and waterfowl, with winter visitors like the trumpeter swan adding interest in the cold season. And at all seasons there are opportunities from several interconnecting dyke trails to view a wide variety of wildlife and wetland plants.

To reach the start of your outing, go east on Dewdney Trunk Road and north on Harris Road as for the walk to Chatham Reach (Walk 87). Fork right off Harris on McNeil, which takes you east round the south end of Sheridan Hill. Thereafter you go left again on Rannie Road. For a southern access point, park north of the wide power line that crosses the whole valley and walk 1.7 km (1.1 mi) along Koerner Road to the beginning of the Snake Rock Dyke, setting your face in the direction of the bluffs that bound the marsh on its east side. Now you turn north for a short distance then go left

Boardwalk east from Snake Rock Dyke.

on Homilk'um Dyke which swings out into the heart of this southern part of the marsh, with an observation tower about halfway to provide an overlook of the area. Proceeding, you come to a T-junction where you go left again to return to the gate on Koerner Road and the slog back to your car.

To reach the northern access, continue on Rannie Road to its end at the lake where there is a boat launch and picnic area. From here the Pitt Lake Dyke stretches east but, less obvious, another, the tree-clad Nature Dyke, begins here also, diverging from the other and offering many opportunities to spot wildlife, or signs of their presence, as you make your way to the southeast on the rooty, sometimes muddy trail. After some 30 minutes you come to a viewing tower with lots of information about the birds and animals that are resident at different times of the year. Ignoring the trail that heads off to the south, work your way north past a screen of trees and on to the open Swan Dyke, with the fine mountain vista ahead and lush pond plants on either side. This route brings you back to the east end of the Pitt Lake Trail, along which you march to complete your circuit, observing the lake with its pleasure craft on one hand, and the marsh and its life on the other.

One long circuit starts on Pitt Lake Dyke, then turns south to meet Nature Dyke, on which you might also begin for a walk shorter by 1.9 km (1.2 mi). From this common point you continue south on Mountain Dyke to Homilk'um Dyke, which takes you westwards past an observation tower and brings you to a T-junction, where you go right once again. Now on the lush Crane Dyke, make your way to Rannie Road, on which you turn left for a short distance to a track leading onto the Pitt River Dyke on the far side of a ditch. Here you go right on the multi-purpose trail with views now across Pitt River to Widgeon Slough and its surrounding ridges as you make your way back to the lake outlet and your car.

Note that Crane and Homilk'um Dykes are closed during the nesting season from mid-March to mid-July, so choose your walks with this knowledge in mind.

# UBC MALCOLM KNAPP RESEARCH FOREST

**BLUE TRAIL TO KNOLL:**

**Round trip** 8 km (5 mi)

**Elevation gain** 298 m (980 ft)

**Roads and trails**

**Allow** 3.5 hours

**High point** 335 m (1100 ft)

**Good most of the year**

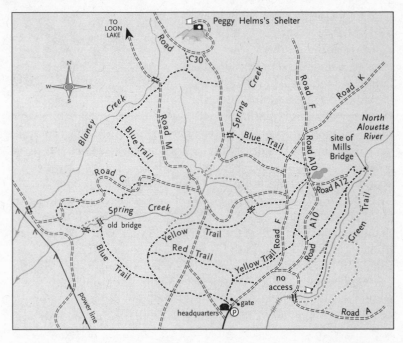

TO HONOUR ONE of its outstanding personalities, the University of British Columbia dedicated to Malcolm Knapp its research forest in Maple Ridge. And to introduce the layman to some aspects of forest management practices, the University Demonstration Forest occupying a small area at the south end has been created.

To reach the forest from Highway 7 (Lougheed Highway) in Maple Ridge, follow the signs for Golden Ears Provincial Park, staying with 232nd Street when the park road turns right after the bridge over the South Alouette River. Thereafter, a fork right on Silver Valley Road brings you to the parking area. To the left is the office, with maps and information about the forest.

Mills Bridge.

Thus armed, you may enjoy the demonstration forest on your own. (Please: no dogs or bikes.) The easy Red Trail takes up to an hour, Green a little longer; Yellow provides the most detailed information about various aspects of forestry and requires about 2 hours for its 3.2 km (2 mi). One possibility, once you have sampled the basic routes, is to follow Blue Trail, adding a side trip to a knoll with a view and ending with a detour down the North Alouette River.

Except for Green, all trails go left past the office, cross the arboretum and an old road, then enter the forest. Blue is the first to diverge, heading off left and losing altitude to cross Spring Creek and continues left to a forest road (G), which it crosses again and again as it winds through a managed plantation. After its seventh crossing comes a patch of scrub and then you approach Blaney Creek. Go right here, rising to cross yet another road (M), and continue your northward course to fork just as you start to turn east. Now, you deviate left and up a track to meet a road on which you go right, circling a small knoll whose summit and shelter cabin you finally attain from the north side. Here, you are rewarded with views northwards to Golden Ears and southwards to the whole sweep of the Fraser Valley.

You may return to the Blue Trail as you came or by the new logging road which intersects and replaces it for a short distance farther on. Then you re-enter the forest on the left, negotiate a rough piece of trail, cross two roads and finally link up with the Yellow Trail again beside a small pond. From here, go left on Road A12, then down to the river on a trail to the Mills Bridge, a graduation gift from forestry students, washed out some years ago. You have two options for your return: the Green Trail which you noted on your descent to the Alouette River; or, in dry weather, the little track running just above the bank downstream to a shelter just short of the road bridge, where you have views of some spectacular rapids.

The whole area between the bridge and the forest headquarters is closed, so you must plod up Road A to join the main Road F and go left not far from your starting point. Of course, you may cross the road to wander through the arboretum and its fine collection before taking leave of this teaching forest.

# MIKE LAKE

**Round trip** 5.6 km (3.5 mi)

**Elevation gain** 180 m (590 ft)

**Roads and trails**

**Allow** 2 hours

**High point** 430 m (1410 ft)

**Best March to November**

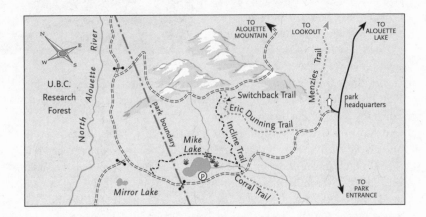

CONTRASTING WITH THE spectacular mountain scenery in much of the rest of Golden Ears Provincial Park are the surroundings of this unobtrusive body of water with its tall conifers, its only contact with the high country to the north being its parking lot where hikers and climbers begin their trips to Alouette Mountain or Blanshard Peak. Even if you have no such ambitions, you do have a choice of two trails, one a short round of the lake of 2 km (1.2 mi), the other a longer circuit mostly within the encircling forest.

To reach the start of these walks, follow the Golden Ears park signs north from Maple Ridge, and from the park entrance drive another 4.5 km (2.8 mi) along the main access road, then turn left at the park headquarters sign. Go left again after a short distance and travel on a dirt road for about 1.6 km (1 mi) to the parking area by the lake, some 200 m beyond the point where Incline Trail goes off to the right. Just west of the parking lot, a locked gate bars the road to vehicles, thereby ensuring peace for your walk along it.

The more gentle ascent in each case is clockwise, so, after having paid your parking fee and passed the locked gate, head west. Shortly before a notice that you are in the UBC research forest, Lakeside Trail goes off right. If you follow it, you soon realize why this was the preferred direction, as it dips to lake level in a series of switchbacks preparatory to crossing a marshy

Fishing in Mike Lake.

tract on a boardwalk. If you continue on the road, stay right at a fork and right again at the next junction, which has a locked gate to the left.

Next, turn right at a point where you glimpse Mount Blanshard, your only mountain view. Now you are heading back east, rising a little on the one-time railway grade, until you come to the park sign for Alouette Mountain and you recognize your return route, Incline Trail, dropping right downhill. This trail also owes its existence to logging days, when it was used as a route to skyline logs down to the lake from the railroad above.

On this stretch, you speedily lose the height gained so gently earlier, descending the steep Incline Trail and ignoring Eric Dunning Trail to your left. Finally, just before the bridge spanning the lake outlet, Lakeside Trail joins from your right, having stayed with low ground round the lake's north side. If you have followed the longer circuit to the junction yet still have lots of energy, you may cut back right on the lake trail instead of gently crossing the outlet and walking back along the road to your starting point. By so doing, however, you add 2 km (1.2 mi) to your trip and give yourself the short but sharp ascent from lake to road close to the end of your walk.

# ALOUETTE NATURE LOOP

**Round trip** 6 km (3.7 mi)

**Elevation gain** 170 m (560 ft)

**Trails**

**Allow** 2.5 hours

**High point** 320 m (1050 ft)

**Best March to November**

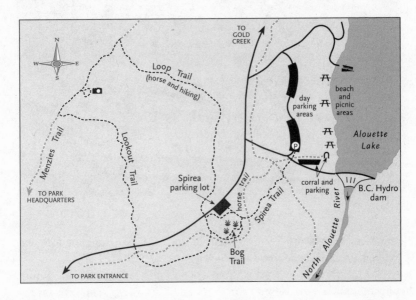

WHAT TITLE DO you give a walk that embraces sections of no fewer than five trails in Golden Ears Provincial Park: Spirea, Bog, Lookout, Menzies and Loop? Our suggestion, as above, takes account of the fact that part of the route is on the lower slopes of Alouette Mountain, that it provides a circuit and that much of it is a self-guiding nature trail, the placards increasing your knowledge of forest lore as you walk along. Add to those things interesting stretches of marsh complete with sphagnum moss and skunk cabbage, a seventy-year-old forest of hemlock that restored the tree cover after fire had devastated the valley, a lookout over Alouette Lake and even a picnic table by its shore at the end of your outing, if you so desire.

For the beginning of this intriguing mixture, follow the signs for Golden Ears park north from the east end of Haney. Continue for 7.2 km (4.5 mi) beyond the park entrance to a right turn into a day-use area, noting as you pass the Spirea Trail parking lot about 1 km (0.6 mi) before, a possible alternative starting point if you wish a shorter walk. In Lot 2, park as closely as possible to the south end and purchase your parking permit; your route,

Autumn display of mushrooms.

signed "Spirea Nature Trail," is on the opposite side of the access road and takes you into the woods. Almost immediately, you drop left to cross a small creek on a bridge. (If you go straight ahead on the bridle trail, you will have to ford the stream.) After crossing, you must traverse an access road to the Alouette Dam before re-entering the trees and beginning to rise in nice open forest, the bright green of the moss in the understorey attesting to generous precipitation in the valley.

After some 20 minutes, you come to a fork where the trail from the Spirea parking lot joins and now you are on Bog Trail, upgraded and renamed Spirea Universal Access Trail. Here, on boardwalks, you cross what would otherwise be very muddy ground. Shortly thereafter, as the path begins to curve right, go left at the sign "Lookout Trail," cross the horse trail for the umpteenth time, then the main access road and start rising again in forest. This trail is joined by Menzies Trail coming from your left. Soon after, a clearing to your right provides the view over the lake and towards Mount Crickmer, which you may enjoy from a seat on a little bluff.

Continuing, seek out a bridle trail coming uphill from the right for your descent; it will bring you back to the main road a short distance before the Spirea parking lot. Cross the road and go left on the horse trail, then left again on the pedestrian path. This takes you between road and bog along the final part of the nature walk until, within sight of the parking area, you swing away right onto its first part to rejoin your outward route east of the boardwalk. Now, you go left and retrace your steps downhill to your starting point.

Back at your car, you can drop down to the beach picnic area to refresh yourself; you may find all its tables occupied, though, on a fine summer weekend, for it is a popular area with Metro Vancouver residents.

# GOLD CREEK TRAILS

**GOLD CREEK LOOKOUT:**

| | |
|---|---|
| **Round trip** 8 km (5 mi) | **Allow** 3.5 hours |
| **Elevation gain** 150 m (490 ft) | **High point** 320 m (1050 ft) |
| **VIEWPOINT BEACH: Round trip** 8 km (5 mi) | **Allow** 3.5 hours |
| **Elevation gain** 180 m (590 ft) | **High point** 350 m (1150 ft) |
| **Trails** | **Good most of the year** |

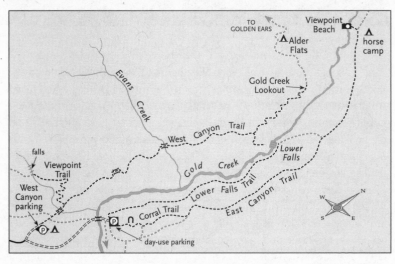

REMOVAL YEARS AGO of its popular Burma Bridge means that walks can be along only one side of Gold Creek at a time. Even so, there are many options if you are staying in Golden Ears Provincial Park and looking for a nice late-afternoon appetite-rouser; and many of the trails, alone or combined, are suitable for the day visitor eager for some exercise.

Having followed park signs north from Highway 7 (Lougheed Highway) in Maple Ridge, drive from the entrance along the main access road for 11.6 km (7.2 mi) to a fork. Go left then left again for the West Canyon parking lot, or left then right for the Gold Creek day-use area if you wish to sample the east-side trails. Parking fees are in effect throughout the park, so purchase your permit before you begin.

The West Canyon Trail follows an old railway grade with, for the observant, some interesting relics of the 1920s logging era along the way. On it, you proceed north for about 10 minutes until, after crossing a creek, you see

Alouette Lake is popular in the summer.

leading uphill to the left a path signed "Viewpoint Trail," a sporting little trail and pleasant, but alas, its views obscured by a growing forest.

Continuing, your route rises gently northwards bordered by mixed deciduous and coniferous trees until, having crossed two major creeks and the impressive erosion associated with them, you reach the railway's end at a fork. Going right, you descend by a rough track to Gold Creek and a viewing spot just below its Lower Falls; on the left branch, you head up steeply on the Golden Ears Trail to a lookout over the upper Gold Creek valley. Either viewpoint makes a satisfying destination for your excursion up the West Canyon.

The best views, however, are to be enjoyed from the east side, where you may follow the Lower Falls Trail running more or less parallel to the creek. Eventually, after nearly an hour, you arrive at the spray-enshrouded and mighty Lower Falls, awe-inspiring in their power.

But, although the Lower Falls Trail is undoubtedly the most popular of the east-side walks, it is short—only a 5.4-km (3.4-mi) round trip—so you may wish to try the multi-purpose East Canyon Trail to Viewpoint Beach. For the East Canyon Trail, start on Corral Trail, which not surprisingly goes off from the corral just north of the parking lots. Very soon this meets the main East Canyon Trail and you go left, rising gently and, in spring, fording innumerable streamlets until, after some 30 minutes, you pass a huge washout and come to an old gate, a reminder that your route was once a logging road. Next, the trail crests at a spot with a glimpse of Blanshard Peak through the trees before it descends to river level; then, at a fork just beyond a horse camp, left takes you to Viewpoint Beach, a truly spectacular destination. Here, you may pause to enjoy the magnificent view of the aptly named Edge Peak and the mountain that gave the park its name.

# KANAKA CREEK

**RIVERFRONT TRAIL:**
Round trip 3 km (1.9 mi)                    **Allow** 1 hour

**CANYON LOOP: Round trip** 3.5 km (2.2 mi)    **Allow** 1.5 hours

Trails                                       Good all year

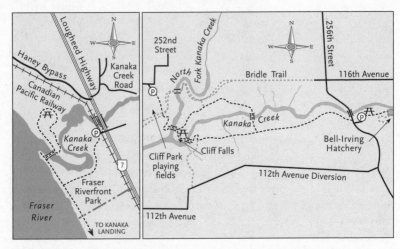

KANAKA CREEK REGIONAL Park, extending in a narrow band
upstream from the creek's mouth just east of Haney to north of the Dewdney Trunk Road on the lower slopes of Blue Mountain, is still in the making.
Although a trail system along the whole of the park is yet only a plan, the
more accessible sections, notably the Fraser Riverfront, Cliff Falls and Bell-
Irving Fish Hatchery, are already well provided with pathways that show off
its many faces, from canyons and cliffs to meadows and marsh.

For the Fraser Riverfront entrance on River Road, turn right off Highway 7
(Lougheed Highway) just east of its junction with the Haney Bypass. From
the parking lot, you set off through trees, very soon coming to a viewpoint
over the creek, here wide and slow as it winds towards its demise in the
Fraser River. Next, you reach a T-junction beside the Fraser itself, the left
branch taking you upstream and out of the park, following the riverbank to a
small-craft harbour at Kanaka Landing. Staying right within the park, however, brings you to a high-arching bridge where a plaque informs you that the
Kanaka (Hawaiians) were once employed by the Hudson's Bay Company at
Fort Langley across the Fraser, hence the creek's name. Now, you circle the
marshy peninsula created by the stream's final meander, passing meadows,

Cliff Falls.

lush berry bushes and impressive cottonwood trees en route back to the bridge.
From here, you return as you came, with,
perhaps, one last look down the Fraser
from the neighbouring viewpoint.

To reach the other regions of the park,
for the time being you need your car;
turn right onto Lougheed Highway and
drive to the Albion traffic light, where
you go left on 240th Street, driving
north to cross Kanaka Creek near the Fish Fence, another park feature. Stay
with 240th a little farther, then go right onto 112th Avenue, following signs
for the hatchery as you wind your way to 256th Street and the entrance to
the parking lot on its right side.

On foot, cross 256th Street, where at a yellow gate you embark on Canyon Trail, which gradually rises above creek level amid mostly deciduous
trees, with maples to make fall resplendent and cottonwoods to scent the
spring air. Quite soon, you come to a fork where, if you go right towards
the North Fork Loop, you drop to cross a footbridge over the canyon, then
rise again to another fork, where left takes you into a wide clearing and picnic area situated between the main stream and its north fork. Across the
bridge over the north fork to the west, you may visit viewpoints overlooking the rapids and falls tumbling over cliffs and waterworn rocks before you
return to the meadow and beyond it the crossing where the Canyon Trail
departs, affording a grandstand view of the main gorge. Then, ignoring all
deviations from the trail as you travel upstream, you are soon back at the
hatchery, your excursion over.

Note that should you wish to visit the Fish Fence en route to the hatchery,
you may go left (west) off 240th Street onto Kanaka Creek Road and look for
it on your left. But that is not all. Continue west to where 238th Street goes
right: facing you is a gated path skirting the riverside marsh and heading
westwards to meet the Trans Canada Trail. After absorbing the information
at the intersection, go right to the Rainbow Bridge, a fine destination for a
short side trip with superlative views of the creek and its bordering wetlands. To resume your journey to the hatchery, simply continue northwards
on 238th and go right on Kanaka Way, which becomes 112th Avenue after
crossing 140th Street.

# HAYWARD LAKE

**RAILWAY TRAIL:**
**Round trip** 12 km (7.5 mi)                    Allow 3.5 hours

**HAYWARD RESERVOIR CIRCUIT:**
**Round trip** 17 km (10.5 mi)                   Allow 5.5 hours

**Trails and roads**                             **Good all year**

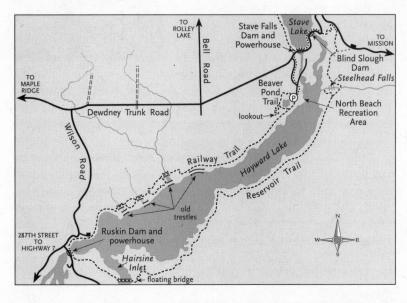

THE ONE-TIME RAILWAY track between Stave Falls and Ruskin gave us a walk along the west side of Hayward Lake, one of the stretches of water created by the Western Canada Power Company but now operated by B.C. Hydro, its successor. More recently, in the forest along the lake's east side, B.C. Hydro has built Reservoir Trail, which, combined with the Railway Trail, makes possible a circumambulation full of interest and variety.

A good place to start this outing is from Hayward Lake Recreation Area, reached by driving east from Maple Ridge on the Dewdney Trunk Road and turning south on the approach road just west of Stave Falls Dam. Here, additional to the long circuit, is a short nature loop, Beaver Pond Trail, which gives you a chance to see the work of beavers, their skill in dam building rivalling that of their human counterparts.

As you walk south on Railway Trail, you must deviate from the right-

Reflections in Hairsine Inlet.

of-way where the railway line was carried over small bays and creek mouths on trestles, two detours in particular taking you up and over, footbridges and walkways supplying the crossings in lieu of the derelict railway bridges. As well, alternative trails diverging from the shoreline path enliven your walk before you arrive at a parking area off Wilson Road. A few minutes more and your trail emerges at Ruskin Dam, some 6 km (3.7 mi) from the start and a possible turnaround, the more arduous part of the circuit being still ahead.

If you decide to continue, cross on the dam and go left to the trailhead information board beyond which you enter the trees, shortly arriving at a viewpoint over the lake. Then, you descend to traverse a floating bridge across the long Hairsine Inlet and proceed to regain the height you just lost, surrounded by tall second-growth forest and a healthy understorey of ferns and moss. Thus, you pursue your upsy-downsy route, down to a canoe landing and up again, into Mission Municipal Forest and out again, over countless creeks, eventually to arrive at a junction with a track dropping left to a vantage point for Steelhead Falls.

After this interlude, your trail crosses Steelhead Creek itself and traverses a long walkway over Brown Creek just before another fork, right going this time to a parking lot on the Dewdney Trunk Road. But you stay left with the Reservoir Trail, ascending a little to cross a power line and come out on the road shortly after. Fortunately, you soon leave the busy thoroughfare and descend on a steep zigzagging track through the forest to meet the road once more, not far east of a dam. This time there's no escape. To complete the circuit, you must walk west (left) on the road, crossing two dams, the Blind Slough and Stave Falls Dams, en route to the access road into the recreation area and thus back to your vehicle.

# BEAR MOUNTAIN TRAILS

**Round trip** 4.6 km (2.9 mi)          **Allow** 2 hours

**Old logging roads**          **Good most of the year**

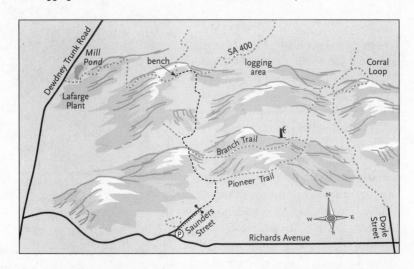

PART OF THE Mission Municipal Forest, Bear Mountain has been the site of logging under a municipal tree-farm licence agreement since 1958. The network of old logging roads is now used by hikers and mountain bikers who connect these tracks with a mixture of trails ranging from gentle to steep.

To reach the forest, drive east on Highway 7 (Lougheed Highway) over the Pitt River Bridge and continue for a further 5 km (3.1 mi), until you see the new overpass for Golden Ears Bridge. Turn left at Dewdney Trunk Road and follow it to Mission, passing over Stave Dam and continuing as the road turns south. Just past the Lafarge plant, turn left onto Richards Avenue, then immediately after house number 32966, turn left on Saunders Street and park in the small lot on the right side.

From here you walk up the narrow and shady road to a yellow gate. Pass the gate and continue up this gravel logging road, where soon you will enter an area with widely spaced, tall trees. This stand of Douglas-firs was thinned 35 years ago to make the trees healthier for their own eventual harvest in 20 to 30 years. To the right, Pioneer Trail leads up to the Corral Trail and from there down to Doyle Road. However, you continue up the logging road to the junction with another logging road and a yellow sign labelled

The summit inukshuk.

"SUT 2." Right is the Branch Trail, which climbs steeply to a communications tower. Your route is straight ahead, following the road uphill through a forest of cedar and maples, whose colours enliven the area in the fall.

Twenty minutes later, you meet another logging road, labelled SA400, but ignore this branch, instead taking the left fork and continuing to climb. At the next logging road, where a regenerating area (SU1) is interspersed with tall unlogged trees, keep left and climb the short distance to the crest of the hill. From the turning circle a trail leads downhill to Mill Pond on Dewdney Trunk Road, but you have reached your destination. Head for the old bike ramp for glimpses of the valley below or rest on the nearby bench dedicated to the memory of Todd Arthur Carter, a young cyclist. This is a fine spot for a snack or a cup of tea as you savour the peace and beauty of the woods. Before you leave, admire the inukshuk that looks like a raven, then retrace your steps back to the car.

# MISSION TRAIL

**Round trip** 5 km (3.1 mi)

**Elevation gain** 150 m (490 ft)

**Trails and paths**

**Allow** 2.5 hours

**High point** 198 m (650 ft)

**Good all year**

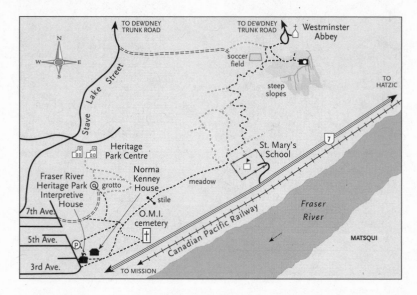

GIVEN THAT THE steep central portion of this trail connects the former St. Mary's Mission and Residential School with Westminster Abbey, the Benedictine Order's edifice on the ridge above, you might consider "Pilgrim's Way" a suitable name for this walk at the east end of the District of Mission, even though it does have flat sections at its beginning and end. In fact, the whole walk has an ecclesiastical flavour, starting as it does in the Fraser River Heritage Park located near the few remaining relics of the original mission and residential school, operated by the Oblates of Mary Immaculate.

Travelling through Mission from east or west on Highway 7 (Lougheed Highway), turn north onto Stave Lake Street, then east on 5th Avenue to park near the restored Norma Kenney House, the first of a series of reconstructions that includes the Grotto of Our Lady of Lourdes. Your first point of reference is the northeast corner of the belt of trees below the ridge that runs east-west, but to start your walk in a suitably chastened frame of mind, you might walk due east to the pioneer cemetery.

Westminster Abbey.

Thereafter, traverse the foundation stones of the former school to pick up your proper trail over to the north, pass into the belt of trees on the right and continue across the meadow beyond, with the present school buildings in view ahead. Just before the school fence, turn left through the bushes into the trees and, ignoring all minor tracks to the left, stay with the main trail to a major fork. Here, going right would take you into the school grounds, so keep left, then left again almost at once as you begin to rise steeply on your *via dolorosa,* the abbey bells perhaps ringing out as you climb, great maples on either side, a splendid sight in the fall. Ignoring all left forks as you head up to the ridge, you emerge finally in the open at the east end of a wide field, crowned not with crosses but with soccer goalposts.

Next, you join a gravel road going right, the abbey tower visible a short distance left. Very shortly comes your reward: a bluff view over the Fraser Valley to Sumas Mountain in the foreground with mighty Mount Baker rearing its snow-clad head aloft to the right, while over to your left the Cheam peaks vie for your attention.

Your best return is by the same route, but before you descend you should stay right on the surfaced path to visit the abbey and seminary, the hilltop location worthy of a religious order whose members have traditionally sought the high places. Mount St. Benedict, a Fraser Valley peak, commemorates their love of the mountains.

Back at the eastern verge of the park, you may turn half right onto a wide gravel track that you soon desert for a footpath signed "To the Grotto" and, rising to a meadow crowned by that picturesque shrine, a fitting finale to this outing.

# KILLARNEY LAKE

**Round trip** 8 km (5 mi)

**Trails**

**Allow** 2.5 hours

**Good most of the year**

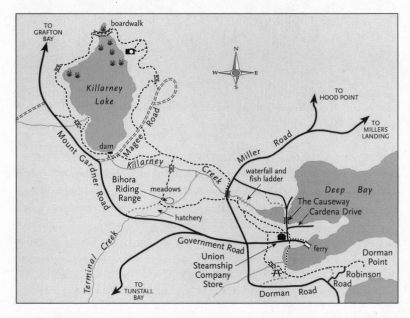

SINCE THIS GEMLIKE stretch of water is on Bowen Island, you must reach it from the mainland by B.C. Ferries from Horseshoe Bay, a short trip but satisfying in itself, with the mountains of Howe Sound for company. Parking near the ferry terminal may be difficult, particularly in summer, so if you have plenty of time you may travel by bus along West Vancouver's scenic Marine Drive or along the highway after having checked the ferry schedule (phone 1-888-223-3779).

On disembarking at Snug Cove, walk towards the one-time Union Steamship Company store (now the library) for information about Crippen Regional Park, in which your walk lies. Go right on Cardena Drive, then left on a wooded trail that passes a memorial garden, which also provides a fine view over Deep Bay to the Howe Sound mountains. Continuing, you pass above a tidy little stream, complete with fish ladders and a viewing platform, and arrive at Miller Road, which you cross onto Hatchery Trail. This leads you through mixed forest to a wide meadow and an intersection, with

Looking across the lagoon from Memorial Garden.

the hatchery to the left. Go right, however, past the Bihora riding range and cross the meadows to meet a major trail, where you proceed left for a short distance to another fork, this time going right to eventually come out on a little country lane, Magee Road.

On this, you go a few metres to the left before turning right onto the Killarney Lake Loop Trail to begin your walk along the lake. Though you are mainly in forest, the ground drops away to the left, giving glimpses of the lake with the Mount Gardner massif behind. Then, finally, after a detour to a viewpoint, you reach marshy ground at the far end of the lake crossed by an attractive boardwalk.

Now on the lake's west side, you turn south, regaled by the sight of water plants and birds. By lake's end, a road and your track are virtually side by side; however, your route soon turns off left towards a picnic area by the dam that reveals the lake's artificiality. On Magee Road again, turn left and cross the outlet, then after a few metres go right on a track that starts up the roadside bank and eventually rejoins the main trail back to Miller Road. Here, you turn right to find your outward trail on the left just beyond the bridge crossing Killarney Creek.

If, as sometimes happens, you have time to put in between ferries, you may, should you still feel energetic, walk south across the picnic area from the ferry terminal and ascend the track on the wooded slope to Dorman Point, with more superb views of the Howe Sound mountains. The round trip is only about 1.5 km (0.9 mi), but the steepness of the last part of the climb suggests that you should allow at least 40 minutes for comfort on your round trip.

# SHANNON FALLS

**TO OLESEN CREEK BRIDGE:**

**Round trip** 2 km (1.2 mi)

**Trails**

**Allow** 1 hour

**Good most of the year**

**TO HIGH BLUFF:**

**Round trip** 5 km (3.1 mi)

**Elevation gain** 473 m (1550 ft)

**Trails**

**Allow** 4 hours

**High point** 510 m (1675 ft)

**Best April to November**

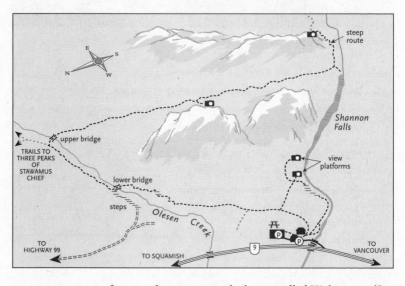

IT IS PRETTY safe to say that everyone who has travelled Highway 99 (Sea to Sky Highway) to Squamish is aware of these falls where Shannon Creek plunges down a nearly vertical cliff before resuming its more placid course to Howe Sound. But what can you do once you have paid your respects to the gods of the waters from the viewing platform? By staying right on leaving the platform, then turning right again on the road that goes north from the picnic area, you find yourself on a trail created by the Federation of Mountain Clubs of B.C. to Olesen Creek, with perhaps a trip to the top of the falls thrown in. At first, your route stays relatively level, as you keep right at one fork and enter the valley of Olesen Creek, but then comes a change as the grade becomes steep indeed, and you mount on steps that might have been designed for giants, gaining altogether some 75 m (245 ft).

Shannon Falls.

At last, relief. A bridge across the creek gives you a breathing space and a view across Howe Sound. Just beyond the screen of trees ahead is the great flight of wooden steps that has replaced the lower Stawamus Chief trail, eroded through overuse. Here, then, you must decide: turn around and retrace your steps or ascend for 185 m (605 ft) on the Chief Trail to a fork that will take you right to recross Olesen Creek on its upper bridge, then travel for some 20 minutes to another viewpoint. Shannon Creek, at the top of the falls, is about 30 minutes beyond that at an elevation of almost 405 m (1330 ft), another possible destination.

If, however, you still have a little energy left, you may proceed, the route now very steep, past the cascades on your right to a bluff with an unobstructed view over Howe Sound and its enclosing mountains as a reward for climbing the extra 100 m (330 ft). This is a satisfying destination at which to linger before returning as you came.

Note that the route you have been following from the top of Shannon Falls was created by the indefatigable Halvor Lunden and beyond this point incorporates stretches of logging roads to link the Chief Trail with Petgill Lake to the south. Farther on, therefore, it may prove a little hard to follow the various connections unless you are experienced in backcountry hiking. As well, it is considerably more demanding in length and altitude gain, requiring as much time again as you have already invested, so you should be properly equipped, with a full day at your disposal, if you decide to push on. Remember, too, that parking fees are in effect here, so purchase your permit in advance.

# SQUAMISH ESTUARY

**Round trip** 7 km (4.3 mi)

**Trails, railway track and roads**

**Allow** 2.5 hours

**Good all year**

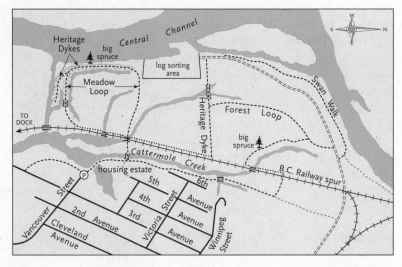

HOW MANY OF us speeding up Highway 99 (Sea to Sky Highway) on our way to the more obvious attractions of Cheakamus Canyon and Whistler ever consider a visit to the Squamish estuary? Yet here, though beleaguered by industrial development, is a destination in whose estuarine sloughs, meadows and woodland are resources to sustain myriad wild creatures and delight the naturalist.

Each of the network of trails may be walked individually, but you may easily combine several to obtain a more comprehensive overview of the whole area. A good place to start on one such combination is at the end of Vancouver Street, which you reach by leaving Highway 99 at the main entry to Squamish and following Cleveland Avenue to its junction with Vancouver Street, where you go right to a parking spot at the end of the street.

On foot, you are faced immediately with a decision: left is a short walk by a slough ending abruptly on 3rd Avenue; so, go right and upstream along the slough, which you soon cross, going left at the bridge and continuing across a railway, a B.C. Rail spur to the docks. Straight ahead, you embark on Meadow Loop, though until the South Bridge is replaced, it must only be a there-and-back walk. Most of the route is on dykes dating as far back as the end of the nineteenth century, when Chinese workers drained the area

The common and poisonous *Amanita muscaria* toadstool.

to grow hay. The dykes now show their age, with bushes and trees growing on them. Today, a dryland log-sorting area is the one obtrusive human activity you notice before you turn south along the Central Channel. Here, you may spot a heron waiting patiently in the shallows or, depending on the season, ducks and other water birds; and as you proceed, you may also note a large old spruce before you swing away eastwards towards the railway once more.

Now, turn north along the spur for some minutes to a faint trail leading left onto another heritage dyke. This starts you west on the Forest Loop, on which you may soon turn right on a route through the heart of the woodland or remain on the dyke, which ends at a gravel road. If you choose the dyke, for a longer circuit, go right along the road for about 200 m, then left into the trees alongside the Central Channel, this trail named the Swan Walk for the numerous viewpoints where in season you may observe trumpeters on their wintering grounds.

To complete your circuit and return to the Forest Loop, leave the waterway at the firepit, head for the road and then backtrack about 20 m to the south, where your route goes left into the trees. Soon there comes a fork, where the two prongs of the Forest Loop meet. Go left again, heading for another three-hundred-year-old spruce tree en route to the rail spur. A left turn north along the tracks takes you to a trail on the east side that veers south onto a grassy dyke top, running behind the residential streets of Squamish all the way back to the new housing estate and your return route to your car.

# FOUR LAKES TRAIL

**Round trip** 6 km (3.7 mi)　　　　　**Allow** 2 hours

**Trails and roads**　　　　　　　　　**Best April to November**

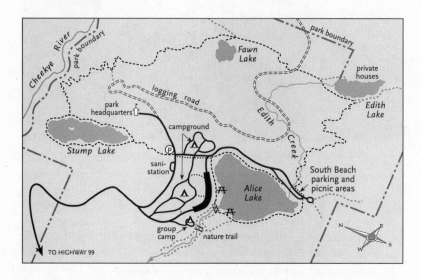

AS IN OTHER areas administered by B.C. Parks, Alice Lake Provincial Park has a well-developed system of hiking trails. There are short ones like those round Alice Lake and Stump Lake and the longer Four Lakes Trail, which includes the paths already mentioned and adds to them the connecting links of a circuit involving Fawn Lake and Edith Lake, even though Edith Lake is not, strictly speaking, in the park.

So well known is Alice Lake park that it is scarcely necessary to say that you reach it by leaving Highway 99 (Sea to Sky Highway) some 12 km (7.5 mi) north of the turnoff for Squamish town centre. At the park entrance, keep left and drive uphill to the small parking area just east of the sani-station instead of making straight for the lake. Here, north of the road and opposite the turnoff for South Beach and the eastern campgrounds, you have on your left the sign for Stump Lake Trail, the start of your walk. Park here, remembering to purchase your parking permit.

At first you are in thick bush, but this thins out when you reach the fork where the arms of the Stump Lake circuit separate, leaving you free to choose whichever you wish. The right branch gives views over DeBeck Hill and towards the Tantalus Range; from the left, you see Mount Garibaldi

View across Stump Lake to Mount Garibaldi.

and Alice Ridge; each gives glimpses of the lake and its clusters of water lilies. At the far end, beyond a little island, the trails join, and here you turn away from the lake.

Back in deep forest, you become aware of the increased rush of water and soon you find yourself just above the Cheekye River, which flows down from Mount Garibaldi, its valley separating Brohm Ridge and Alice Ridge. On this stretch, the influence of the stream is manifest in the type of vegetation: lush skunk cabbage and other moisture-loving plants, quite a bit different from elsewhere—the difference soon obvious as you begin to climb eastwards, passing an escape route back to Alice Lake on the right, then rising to the trail's high point as you near Fawn Lake. Surrounded by young forest, Fawn Lake is a little off the trail to the right; where the spur road goes off to it, the foot trail you have been on develops into a gravel road, a status it maintains until you reach lake number three, Edith Lake.

On the way, you come to a major intersection, your route crossing the main approach to Alice (Cheekye) Ridge, an approach that antedated creation of the park and remains to give access to the forest lands above. Then, at a fork just preceding the lake, you go right along its west side until you come to a signposted junction. Straight ahead, the route leads to Thunderbird Ridge in the Garibaldi Highlands subdivision, but you go right and uphill as a prelude to your descent to Alice Lake, trail and watercourse arriving together at its south end by a picnic and swimming area. From here, you may use either shore to return to your transport. Each is pleasant, but perhaps the one on the east side is the prettier, having views of DeBeck Hill across the water; it is also a little shorter. However, if you choose the longer west and north sides, you may add a little nature study as well by walking down one side of the outlet creek and up the other on the Swamp Lantern Interpretive Trail at the northwest corner of the lake.

At the northeast corner, you must return to pavement again, but only for a short distance as you walk up through the campsites to the intersection with the park headquarters road where your car is parked.

# DEBECK HILL

**Round trip** 4 km (2.5 mi)

**Elevation gain** 270 m (885 ft

**Roads**

**Allow** 2 hours

**High point** 460 m (1510 ft)

**Best April to November**

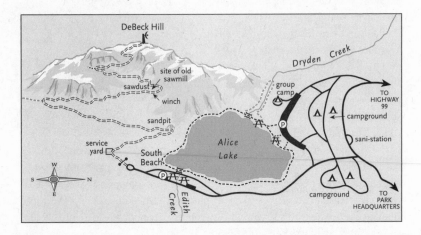

THOUGH THE UPPER part of the route to this miniature mountain has
suffered from the construction of television repeater towers, this trip is still
very much worthwhile, if only for the tremendous panorama from its summit. And not all is lost along the way, either; the lower part of the original
logging road you use is very much as it always was, even to the mellowing
signs of past activity: rusted cable, an old power winch abandoned and forlorn, and what is left of a sawdust pile.

Having paid your parking fee, you can start your hike at the South Beach
parking lot in Alice Lake Provincial Park (Walk 101), from which you walk
south via the turnaround for cars and make your way over, under or around
the barrier at the end. Just beyond and on your right, the one-time logging
road angles back uphill to an old quarry and a change of direction to the
southwest, the route nicely shaded by the regrowth of mixed deciduous and
coniferous trees.

After some 20 minutes and another elbow bend, you find yourself travelling below some impressive bluffs above on your left. It is on this stretch
that you come on signs of bygone logging and pass the old donkey engine
near the site of an old sawmill. Beyond here, you swing back left and

View northeast from the summit: Mount Garibaldi (right) and Brohm Ridge (left).

continue in a southerly direction to the next sharp turn, which takes you back right again. From here, a walk of another 200 m or so takes you to the summit, where, having tuned out the TV monstrosities, you can forget the works of man and enjoy the beauties of nature: the great peaks and glaciers of the Tantalus Range on the west side of the Squamish River valley and the impressive summit of Mount Garibaldi above you on the east. And the humbler scene has its charms as well: the park, densely treed, below you on the right; Cheakamus Valley stretching north, with Cloudburst Mountain to the left of it; and, in the southwest, the flat delta lands around Squamish at the head of Howe Sound, with the sound itself and its enclosing mountains receding into the distance beyond.

Should you wish a longer walk or the road access to South Beach be closed, as is usual in the off-season, you may start from the main day-use area and add a walk round the lake to your outing, allowing yourself an extra hour for the pleasure.

# EVANS LAKE FOREST

**TO HUT LAKES: Round trip** 13 km (8 mi)          **Allow** 5 hours

**Elevation gain** 395 m (1295 ft)          **High point** 610 m (2000 ft)

**Roads**

**RIDGE CIRCUIT: Round trip** 8 km (5 mi)          **Allow** 4 hours

**Elevation gain** 290 m (950 ft)          **High point** 445 m (1460 ft)

**Trails and roads**          **Good April to November**

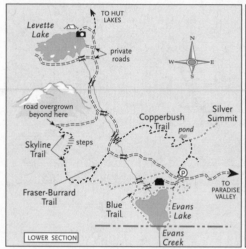

AN OLD LOGGING road gives you access to Levette Lake and Hut (Hud) Lakes, though the last named do involve a longish walk with considerable change in elevation. You may, therefore, consider concentrating on the circular trail system in the south part of the area, given that all of these outings begin at the same spot, the fork where the gated road to the left goes into the private Evans Lake Forest Education Centre.

On your approach, having gone west from Highway 99 (Sea to Sky Highway) for Cheekye opposite the Alice Lake turnoff, drive to the crossing of the Cheakamus River, go right at once on the Paradise Valley road for 2.1 km (1.3 mi), then, at a crossroads, turn left on the Evans Lake road. This road rises steeply for 1.3 km (0.8 mi) to the fork, where there is parking for a few cars, with the old road going on and the start of the loop trail on your right.

Tantalus Range.

With one or all of the lakes as your objective, continue on the old road, by now quite steep and rough in places. After about 45 minutes, you come to two successive private roads to the left, then a third providing a viewpoint over Levette Lake, with the majestic peaks of the Tantalus Range as a background. To reach Hut Lakes, stay right at the third fork, rising steadily on the very eroded, but well-shaded old road. Once over the col, you pass a reedy little pond on your left, then your trail swings west before descending to the lakes' basin, losing height you must regain on your return.

Your interesting alternative, the trail system over the ridges on either side of the road, is mainly in sparse forest, thin enough to allow you views over the Cheakamus Valley south to Sky Pilot Mountain as well as to the Tantalus across the valley of the Squamish. For this, take the Copperbush Trail uphill to the right from your parking by the fork, the orange triangles a tribute to the forest camp staff and students. You may omit the detour to Silver Summit if you intend to do the complete circuit, but having gone left at that junction, you may want to stop briefly at an interesting pool before continuing up over a bluff top with nearly panoramic views, descending the sometimes rocky, bushy trail and crossing a bridge to meet the Levette Lake road, with the option of returning along it if you do not wish to carry on with the loop.

To continue, go right, cross the creek again and walk uphill to where the road recrosses once more. Immediately beyond on the left, Skyline Trail cuts back sharply, using an old logging road at first but leaving it for a trail on the left after about 15 minutes. This heads along a ridge crest with a succession of mountain views until it drops, partway on a log stairway, into a little valley before rising again to the next ridge, then descending again to join another old road now called the Fraser-Burrard Trail. Stay with this when you come to a fork, a former trail to the right being closed to public use. Your present route now makes its way uneventfully to meet the Levette Lake road, where a right turn and a quick march soon return you to your vehicle.

# BROHM LAKE
# INTERPRETIVE FOREST

**Round trip** 8 km (5 mi) or less

**Elevation gain** 150 m (490 ft)

**Trails**

**Allow** 2.5 hours

**High point** 350 m (1150 ft)

**Best** May to October

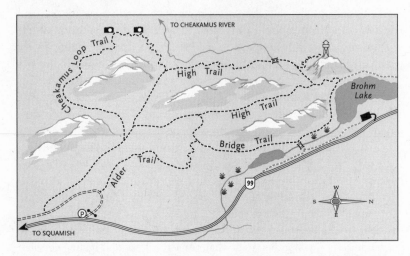

IN RECENT YEARS, the Squamish Forest District has been developing an interpretive trail system for hikers and bikers in the wooded area south of Brohm Lake, and now the pattern of loops, connectors and viewpoints is complete for us to enjoy. With maps and distances indicated at major intersections, nothing remains but to choose the variant with most appeal.

To find the trailhead, drive Highway 99 (Sea to Sky Highway) north of Squamish for just over 2 km (1.2 mi) beyond the Alice Lake turnoff, then move into the left lane and watch for a small parking area with a yellow gate prominent behind. Since you cannot make a left turn here, continue to the Brohm Lake parking lot, 2.2 km (1.4 mi) farther on, where you can turn around and drive back to the parking area at the gate. Just past the gate is an information kiosk with a map and directions to help you fully appreciate your walk.

A few minutes farther along this old road (the original Highway 99), you come to the Alder Trail, forking off to the right and rising gently to meet Bridge Trail, so called because going right on it takes you down to Brohm

Lake, where the narrows have been bridged. If you head that way, an undulating trail along the southwest side of the lake brings you in short order to a connector climbing back to the main system. The subsequent junction with High Trail could also be reached with rather less effort by going left from Alder on Bridge Trail, then right on High as it continues past a small pond, over a boardwalk, through a rocky stretch and down to the fork. Now the route swings abruptly to the left and crosses more bridging before another option presents itself: a steep trail, assisted by even steeper steps, to a "fire lookout" complete with a little shelter. From here, on a fine day the majestic peaks of the Tantalus Range make an unforgettable spectacle.

Back on High Trail, you work round the knoll and emerge on a south-facing slope with another splendid view of the Tantalus peaks seen over a tree-thinning demonstration plot, then you begin the steady zigzag descent into the valley, where your trail merges with an old forest road. Again, you are faced with a decision: whether to take the direct route to the parking lot, passing on the way the other ends of High Trail and Cheakamus Loop before rejoining and turning left on the old Highway 99 in a hollow below the present thoroughfare; or whether to follow the Cheakamus Loop, which climbs first to viewpoints looking northwest towards Cloudburst Mountain and south to the Tantalus before eventually levelling off and merging into an old logging road that winds its way down through the gap between two hillocks to join the main forest road, where a right turn sends you homeward bound.

# BROHM LAKE

**BROHM LAKE AND POWERLINE TRAILS:**
**Round trip** 5.7 km (3.5 mi)          **Allow** 2.5 hours

**Trails**          **Best May to November**

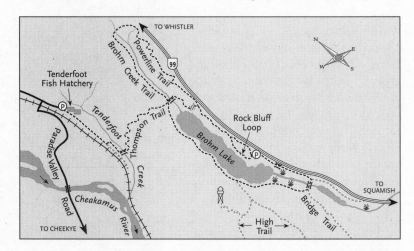

IF EVER A walk revealed the folly of using distance alone as a guide, it is this one on a B.C. Forest Service trail. The apparent discrepancy between distance and time soon disappears, however, as you rise and descend, roller-coaster fashion, the thrill increased on the east side of the lake by the steep drop to the water below.

The usual start for the walk is from the parking lot on the west side of Highway 99 (Sea to Sky Highway), about 4.5 km (2.8 mi) north of the Alice Lake turnoff. From this spot, you may ease into the walk by going south on a gentle trail paralleling the highway, crossing the bridge over the reedy narrows and turning north again at the fork where Bridge Trail (Walk 104) goes left. Now, you begin your upsy-downsy way along the lake, passing en route a second trail into the interpretive forest before arriving at a junction with the Thompson Trail, which leads down to the Tenderfoot Fish Hatchery. Leaving that for later consideration, continue 100 m to another fork. Here, you must decide whether to opt for the short return by the lake, which, however, involves ascending a long flight of steps to a dizzying height above the water, or to choose the longer route starting up Brohm Creek on the left.

Going left, the trail, at first a peaceful, shady, mossy old logging road, follows the creek north for a pleasant kilometre or so before swinging right

Diving rock on Brohm Lake.

across the creek and towards the highway. Just before the road, the route turns south on Powerline Trail, again rising and falling over a series of little ridges with splendid views of the Tantalus Range over to the right front and the Sky Pilot group farther off down the valley to the left. Finally, descending a little, you come to the top of that long stairway where the Lake Trail joins from the right. Here, you turn left on the roller coaster to a final fork, where you may choose either arm of the Rock Bluff Loop, left dropping directly to the parking lot, right taking a more circuitous route by the lake's edge.

And the Thompson Trail? It provides a somewhat more challenging start to either circuit and, combined with their ups and downs, will supply you with a real workout.

To reach its trailhead, you leave Highway 99 at the Alice Lake turnoff and go left to Cheekye, where you cross the Cheakamus River and immediately turn right on the Paradise Valley Road. Stay with this road for 4.2 km (2.6 mi), recrossing the river and coming to a T-junction just across the railway at Midnight Way. Here, you go right for about 200 m to park at the Tenderfoot Fish Hatchery.

On foot, make your way along the track beside the railway, then about 350 m beyond the hatchery premises, go left towards the creek, then right to a bridge. The trail is not long, only 1.7 km (1 mi), but it climbs 230 m (755 ft), working over and round mossy rocks and up steps to crest finally at a gentle divide only a few minutes from Brohm Lake.

# BRANDYWINE / CAL-CHEAK

**Round trip** 8 km (5 mi)

**Allow** 3 hours

**Trails**

**Best May to October**

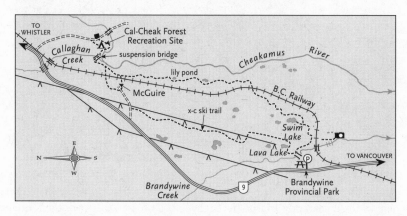

BRANDYWINE FALLS PROVINCIAL PARK exists primarily to provide a viewpoint for the falls on the creek of that name; it has, however, much more to offer: Lava Lake and Swim Lake among them. Even so, the most striking trail, one that leaves the park and takes you north to the confluence of Callaghan Creek and the Cheakamus River (hence the name) was the creation of the B.C. Forest Service; in fact, its northern end is a recreation area for which that ministry is responsible. Construction on Highway 99 (Sea to Sky Highway) has altered the entrance to the park: the former campground is now part of an enlarged day-use area and parking fees are in effect.

From the parking lot about 37 km (23 mi) north of Squamish on Highway 99, you cross Brandywine Creek on the main falls trail, ignoring the track going uphill left just beyond the bridge. That leads to Lava Lake and a wide cross-country ski trail, interesting for its lava surface, broken into cobblestonelike shapes. You, however, continue towards the B.C. Rail tracks, noting the Swim Lake/Cal-Cheak sign just before you cross the line for the falls viewpoint. Enjoy the falls, then go on another 100 m for a view down the valley, including beautiful Daisy Lake.

For the Cal-Cheak walk, return to the sign, and follow the trail to a junction near to Swim Lake, where your trail goes right. Now you head north, rising to a ridge from which you look down on the lake, with, farther on, other smaller bodies of water right and left. Much of your route consists of

Suspension bridge over Callaghan Creek.

lava underfoot, with a healthy growth of forest covering the ridges of shattered columnar basalt, over and between which the trail winds. Then, having crossed the railway tracks some time earlier, you emerge briefly from trees again at the whistle stop of McGuire, its name on a post now the only visible sign of the one-time station.

Back in the forest, you soon hear the river, and from now on your way is along the Cheakamus River to the pedestrian suspension bridge that takes you over its tributary, Callaghan Creek, to the simple recreation site just beyond. This can be reached from Highway 99 if you are coming from the south, by going right a short distance past McGuire and 4 km (2.5 mi) north of the Brandywine Falls park turnoff and driving 1.6 km (1 mi) on an old logging road.

Your return is by the same route all the way, unless you wish to take the road right and uphill at McGuire for a walk back along the route that doubles as a cross-country ski trail in winter. This trail starts on the power line but soon seeks the shade of the trees, lodgepole pine forest mostly, with the occasional marshy area around the numerous little ponds along the way. Your route this time is wholly to the west of the railway, bringing you back to Brandywine Creek just north of the parking lot.

# CRATER RIM LOOP

**Round trip** 8 km (5 mi)   **Allow** 4 hours

**Elevation gain** 325 m (1065 ft)   **High point** 870 m (2855 ft)

**Trails and roads**   **Best June to October**

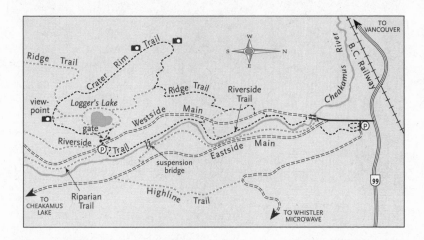

THIS WALK IS in the Whistler Interpretive Forest, the second of three demonstration forests in the Squamish Forest District, created in a previously logged-over area to introduce outdoor recreationists to a young regenerating forest being managed for multiple resource use. Here, for the walker, there are many possibilities—some exclusive to pedestrians, others to be shared with bikers—the guide to the forest presenting a daunting array of choices, far more than suffice for one day's outing. The following description, therefore, samples only part of the forest's potential: a bit of riverside, a lake, the rim of an extinct volcano and a forested ridge to whet the appetite for further explorations on your own.

The approach road (signposted) turns off Highway 99 (Sea to Sky Highway) just north of the railway crossing at Function Junction, 48 km (30 mi) north of Squamish and 7.7 km (4.8 mi) south of Village Gate Boulevard in Whistler. Immediately on your left is the main entrance to the forest, with a parking area and the start of the first of your trails, the Riverside Trail, at its east end.

Enhanced by nature information along the way, the trail rises almost right away over a minor ridge, descends again to cross Eastside Main (Cheakamus Lake Road), and traverses another strip of forest before briefly

joining the Westside Main to pass over the turbulent Cheakamus River. Thereafter, the trail winds up and down along the riverbank, approaching the road from time to time to facilitate kayak "put-ins," until, just over 2 km (1.2 mi) from the start, it comes to a junction, with left crossing high above the torrent on Suspension Bridge 2000 and linking with the east-side trails.

Going straight ahead, you begin to climb to meet the mainline again at the Logger's Lake trailhead and parking place. (If you drive to this spot, you may concentrate on the shorter 2-hour circuit of Crater Rim and Logger's Lake, or continue on Riverside Trail south to connect with other trails, such as the Basalt Valley or Riparian Trails.)

From here, you cross the road, pass a yellow gate and walk up an old logging road for a few minutes to the beginning of the Crater Rim Trail with its sign and statistics, indicating a 100-m (328-ft) rise in the 3.2-km (2-mi) round trip, and you go left, gaining much of that altitude in the short ascent to the rim. Then, the trail undulates along through sparse forest with glimpses inward to the lake and outward to the Cheakamus Valley until you reach a fork where Ridge Trail goes left to join Basalt Valley Spur. You keep right, however, and just beyond the high point you come to an opening with a splendid view of Black Tusk, a good place to pause. Shortly thereafter, as the trail curves round with the rim, you reach another viewpoint, this time westwards towards Mounts Fee and Cayley, before you proceed to lose height quickly on a steep little track down to a rock slide, across which a path has been partially smoothed. Beyond here, the route runs through some alder to join first one old road then another, on which you go left to where the Ridge Trail heads off north into the trees (right goes back to Logger's Lake). As you work along this combined hiking and biking trail, do not be seduced by an attractive-looking pedestrian route going off left to dead-end above a quarry, but instead descend to the next junction. There, for the shorter route back to your transportation, keep left and descend to the mainline, along which a few metres brings you back to Riverside Trail and a retracing of your outward steps.

# CHEAKAMUS LAKE

**TO WEST END: Round trip** 6 km (3.7 mi)     **Allow** 3 hours

Trails                                        **Best late June to October**

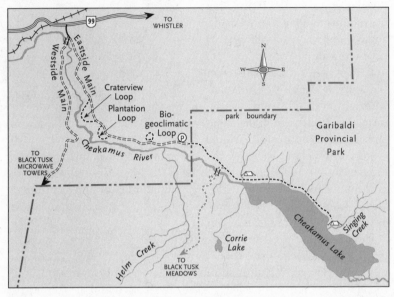

THIS FINE BODY of water, just 3 km (1.9 mi) inside the western boundary of Garibaldi Provincial Park, provides a variety of picturesque spots along its north shore, with views across the lake to the McBride Range and the glaciers of the park's high country.

The approach is as for the Whistler Interpretive Forest, through which it travels (Walk 107). This time, however, pass the parking area at the entrance and go left at the next fork on what is variously called Eastside Main or Cheakamus Lake Road and climb steadily towards the road's end at a parking area 8.5 km (5.3 mi) from the highway.

From here, the trail heads east, crossing two small creeks before bringing you to the park boundary. Now you continue in tall timber, an indication of what this whole area must have been like before so much of it was logged. Progress is easy, for the trail remains virtually level as it gradually converges with the Cheakamus River. After about 30 minutes, you come to a sign pointing right for Helm Lake Trail, one of the routes into the high country to the south.

View south towards Cheakamus Glacier.

Beyond here, your trail continues through the forest with its healthy growth of devil's club, especially where the route is close to the riverbank. Gradually, you notice the current slackening, the water becomes a deeper green, and vistas of the lake begin to open out ahead until you find yourself at its western end.

Though any spot along the lakeshore may serve as a destination, the wilderness campsite at the mouth of Singing Creek provides a point of reference. In any case, the alternation of treed areas with avalanche-created open spaces gives nice contrasts along the trail, the clear forest floor being interspersed with stretches of lush grass and flowers where the sun exerts its influence. In some places, however, a rocky face should be negotiated with care. Wherever you do stop, you are rewarded with views; in addition, fishing is a possibility if you have come prepared. It is peaceful, too, since powerboats are not permitted, though thoughtless bikers may be somewhat intrusive on occasion.

The return poses no problems either. It is pleasant to wander along the trail through the forest until the trees thin out at the park boundary, when, across the river, an interesting lava flow and other volcanic rubble begin to show themselves. Now might be the time to investigate some of the intriguing loops you noted en route to the trailhead. On the west side of the road, viewpoints of interest on the Plantation and Craterview Loops may be reached comfortably by car, as can the Valleyview and Crater Lookouts. Thus, on one outing you may combine a walking trip into a provincial park with an educational foray through a demonstration forest.

# SHADOW LAKE
# INTERPRETIVE FOREST

**Round trip** 6.5 km (4 mi)          **Allow** 2 hours

**Trails and roads**          **Best June to October**

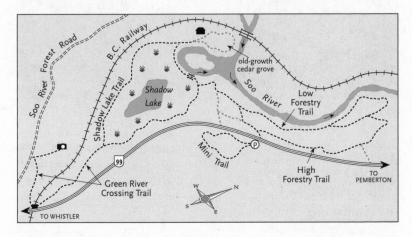

THE MOST DISTANT from Vancouver, this, the third of Squamish Forest District's three demonstration forests, lies some 17 km (10.5 mi) north of Whistler Village. As you drive north, Highway 99 (Sea to Sky Highway) crosses the railway 10 km (6.2 mi) beyond the end of Green Lake and less than 500 m thereafter is a parking lot on the right. Park here by the large information board.

Immediately south of the parking area is a bijou forestry loop of 400 m for those who simply want to stretch their legs and break the tedium of a long drive; those who want more substance must carefully cross the highway to the main trailhead. From here, you may choose any one of several routes varying in length and focus, or you may roll them all into one to experience everything this forest has to offer.

For a longer forest walk, you may start by going north from the main trailhead, following the signs for the High Forestry Trail, which passes through an area planted in 1970 after being clear-cut earlier, so you may study the effects of the various management prescriptions practised as you go along. Shortly after an exit to the highway on the right and gradually descending, the trail changes direction from north to south, then comes

Reflections in Shadow Lake.

to a fork. Here you may continue straight ahead or double back briefly through an area regenerating naturally after selective cutting, before turning south again along the Soo River flats to join the direct route. Now you are travelling on the Lower Forestry Trail, an old logging road maturing nicely to trail status.

Continue straight ahead towards Shadow Lake at the next fork and ignore a second track coming in on the left from the highway. Then, when the lake loop splits, go left, clockwise, along the east side through some fairly tall conifers, natural regeneration after a forest fire in the 1920s. At the south end of the lake, left again will start you on the Green River Crossing Trail, which takes you out in reverse direction to traverse the railway, beyond which a trail leads up a bank across the way and onwards to a parking spot by the Soo River Forest Service Road. From here, a short walk brings you to the top of a mossy rock bluff with limited views of the forest and the valley to the north. However, since you must return by the same route to resume the lake circuit, you may opt to forgo this 1.6-km (1-mi) round trip to the viewpoint and continue northwest along the water's edge to the next junction, where a short loop trail following an oxbow bend of the river winds through a grove of old-growth Western red cedar and past a one-time trapper's cabin.

Back on the lake trail, you cross the outlet creek and soon come to the end of the circuit, going left to retrace your route along the old logging road, the second trail to the right thereafter returning you to highway and transportation.

## USEFUL BOOKS

Armstrong, John E. *Vancouver Geology.* Vancouver: Geological Association of Canada, 1990.

Bovey, Robin, and Wayne Campbell. *Birds of Vancouver and the Lower Mainland.* 2nd ed. Edmonton: Lone Pine Publishing, 2001.

Bryceland, Jack, and Mary and David Macaree. 103 *Hikes in Southwestern British Columbia.* 6th ed. Vancouver: Greystone Books, 2008.

Cannings, Richard, and Sydney Cannings. *British Columbia: A Natural History.* Vancouver: Greystone Books, 2000.

Cousins, Jean. *Nature Walks around Vancouver.* Vancouver: Greystone Books, 1997.

Lyons, Chester P., and Bill Merilees. *Trees, Shrubs, and Flowers to Know in British Columbia and Washington.* Edmonton: Lone Pine Publishing, 1996.

Parish, Roberta, and Sandra Thomson. *Tree Book: Learning to Recognize Trees of British Columbia.* 2nd ed. Victoria: Ministry of Forests, 1994.

Pojar, Jim, and Andy MacKinnon, eds. *Plants of Coastal British Columbia including Washington, Oregon & Alaska.* Vancouver: Lone Pine Publishing, 2005.

Stoltmann, Randy. *Hiking Guide to the Big Trees of Southwestern British Columbia.* 2nd ed. Vancouver: Western Canada Wilderness Committee, 1991.

Vancouver Natural History Society. *Nature West Coast: As Seen in Lighthouse Park.* 2nd ed. Vancouver: Sono Nis Press, 1987.

——. *A Birder's Guide to Vancouver and the Lower Mainland.* Edited by Catherine J. Aitchison. Vancouver: Whitecap Books, 2001.

## WEB SITES

B.C. Hydro recreation site at Buntzen Lake *www.bchydro.com/community/ recreation_areas/buntzen_lake_ trails.html*

British Columbia Provincial Parks *www.env.gov.bc.ca/bcparks*

Burnaby Parks, Recreation and Cultural Services Department *www.city.burnaby.bc.ca/cityhall/ departments/departments_parks/ rcrtn.html*

Coquitlam Parks and Recreation *www.city.port-coquitlam.bc.ca/Citizen_ Services/Parks_and__Recreation.htm*

Cypress Provincial Park (pdfs of brochure and map) *www.env.gov.bc.ca/bcparks/explore/ parkpgs/cypress/#Map*

District of North Vancouver links to trails and parks *www.geoweb.dnv.org/website/ parksonline/viewer.htm*

Federation of Mountain Clubs of B.C. *www.mountainclubs.org*

Fraser Valley Regional District Parks *www.fvrd.bc.ca/Services/Parks and Trails/ExploreourParks/Pages/ default.aspx*

Metro Vancouver Regional Parks *www.metrovancouver.org/services/ parks_lscr/regionalparks/Pages/ default.aspx*

South Coast British Columbia Transportation Authority *www.translink.bc.ca*

Squamish Forest District Interpretive Forests *www.for.gov.bc.ca/dsq/interp Forests/interpretive.htm*

Surrey Parks and Recreation, City of
*www.surrey.ca/Living+in+Surrey/*
*Parks+and+RecreationParks+and+*
*EnvironmentPark+Locations+and+*
*Amenities/default.htm*

Trans Canada Trail official Web site
*www.tctrail.ca*

Vancouver Board of Parks and Recreation
*www.vancouver.bc.ca/parks*

West Vancouver Parks and Environment
*www.westvancouver.net/Visitors/*
*Level3.aspx?id=2130*

## WALKING TIMES

| TIME (HRS) | # | WALK NAME |
|---|---|---|
| 1 | 4 | Chancellor Woods (short circuit) |
| 1 | 46 | Cypress Falls Park |
| 1 | 78 | South Surrey Urban Forests (Sunnyside Ac) |
| 1 | 78 | South Surrey Urban Forests (Crescent Pk) |
| 1 | 83 | Aldergrove Lake (short circuit) |
| 1 | 87 | Chatham Reach (from Harris Rd) |
| 1 | 94 | Kanaka Creek (Riverfront Tr) |
| 1 | 99 | Shannon Falls (to Olesen Cr) |
| 1+ | 62 | Maplewood Flats |
| 1.5 | 1 | UBC Gardens (North) |
| 1.5 | 17 | Barnet Trails (Barnet & Cougar Cr) |
| 1.5 | 22 | Deer Lake Park West |
| 1.5 | 52 | Ballantree |
| 1.5 | 57 | Mahon Park |
| 1.5 | 58 | Lynn Headwaters Loop (Lynn Loop Tr) |
| 1.5 | 59 | Rice Lake (from LSCR) |
| 1.5 | 68 | Mystery Lake (to lake) |
| 1.5 | 70 | Indian Arm Parks (short circuit) |
| 1.5 | 73 | Richmond Nature Park |
| 1.5 | 74 | Deas Island |
| 1.5 | 75 | Boundary Bay (south section) |
| 1.5 | 77 | Redwood Park |
| 1.5 | 85 | Seven Sisters Trail (low level) |

| TIME (HRS) | # | WALK NAME |
|---|---|---|
| 1.5 | 89 | Grant Narrows (southern loop) |
| 1.5 | 94 | Kanaka Creek (Canyon Loop) |
| 2 | 4 | Chancellor Woods (long circuit) |
| 2 | 7 | Jericho Park/Spanish Banks |
| 2 | 10 | Stanley Park |
| 2 | 11 | Renfrew Triangle |
| 2 | 12 | Champlain Heights |
| 2 | 13 | Burnaby Heights/TCT |
| 2 | 15 | Burnaby Mountain West/SFU (short circuit) |
| 2 | 18 | Burnaby Mountainside Trails (short loop) |
| 2 | 23 | Deer Lake |
| 2 | 25 | Molson Way (South) |
| 2 | 28 | Shoreline Trail |
| 2 | 31 | Belcarra Regional Park (to Burns Pt) |
| 2 | 33 | Colony Farm |
| 2 | 34 | Ridge Park Loop |
| 2 | 39 | Whytecliff |
| 2 | 42 | Lighthouse Park (short circuit) |
| 2 | 53 | Capilano Canyon (from park road) |
| 2 | 55 | Baden-Powell Trail (Grouse Mtn: current) |
| 2 | 64 | Historic Mushroom Loop |
| 2 | 79 | Green Timbers Urban Forest (Walk 1) |
| 2 | 79 | Green Timbers Urban Forest (Walk 2) |

| TIME (HRS) | # | WALK NAME |
|---|---|---|
| 2 | 80 | Tynehead Regional Park |
| 2 | 83 | Aldergrove Lake (long circuit) |
| 2 | 86 | Teapot Hill |
| 2 | 91 | Mike Lake |
| 2 | 96 | Bear Mountain Trails |
| 2 | 101 | Four Lakes Trail |
| 2 | 102 | DeBeck Hill |
| 2 | 109 | Shadow Lake Interpretive Forest |
| 2+ | 2 | UBC Botanical Garden |
| 2.5 | 3 | Pacific Spirit Regional Park (east to west) |
| 2.5 | 14 | Capitol Hill |
| 2.5 | 26 | Burnaby Fraser Foreshore Park |
| 2.5 | 27 | Mundy Lake |
| 2.5 | 31 | Belcarra Regional Park (to Jug Island) |
| 2.5 | 38 | Minnekhada Regional Park |
| 2.5 | 40 | Seaview/Larsen Bay |
| 2.5 | 43 | Sahalee/Caulfeild Loop |
| 2.5 | 49 | McDonald/Lawson Creek Loop |
| 2.5 | 56 | Mosquito Creek |
| 2.5 | 59 | Rice Lake (from Lynn Headwaters) |
| 2.5 | 66 | Goldie Lake |
| 2.5 | 67 | Dog Mountain (direct) |
| 2.5 | 68 | Mystery Lake (to peak) |
| 2.5 | 69 | Baden-Powell Trail (Deep Cove) |
| 2.5 | 81 | Derby Reach Regional Park |

| TIME (HRS) | # | WALK NAME | TIME (HRS) | # | WALK NAME |
|---|---|---|---|---|---|
| 2.5 | 89 | Grant Narrows (Katzie Marsh) | 3 | 58 | Lynn Headwaters Loop (to debris chute) |
| 2.5 | 92 | Alouette Nature Loop | 3 | 60 | Two-Canyon Loop |
| 2.5 | 97 | Mission Trail | 3 | 67 | Dog Mountain (via Dinkey Peak) |
| 2.5 | 98 | Killarney Lake | | | |
| 2.5 | 100 | Squamish Estuary | 3 | 70 | Indian Arm Parks (long circuit) |
| 2.5 | 104 | Brohm Lake Interpretive Forest | 3 | 71 | Lulu Island Dykes (Middle Arm & Terra Nova) |
| 2.5 | 105 | Brohm Lake | 3 | 72 | Richmond South Dyke Trail |
| 2.5* | 84 | Matsqui Trail | 3 | 75 | Boundary Bay (north section) |
| 2.5+ | 76 | Elgin Heritage Park | | | |
| 3 | 3 | Pacific Spirit Regional Park (north to south) | 3 | 87 | Chatham Reach (from Alouette Br) |
| 3 | 6 | Musqueam/Fraser River | 3 | 106 | Brandywine/Cal-Cheak |
| 3 | 9 | False Creek | 3 | 108 | Cheakamus Lake |
| 3 | 16 | Burnaby Mountain | 3.5 | 15 | Burnaby Mountain West/SFU (long circuit) |
| 3 | 19 | SFU/Stoney Creek | | | |
| 3 | 20 | Burnaby Lake | 3.5 | 17 | Barnet Trails (with Inlet Trail) |
| 3 | 21 | Brunette River | 3.5 | 18 | Burnaby Mountainside Trails (long loop) |
| 3 | 24 | Molson Way (Central) | | | |
| 3 | 29 | Sasamat Lake/ Woodhaven Swamp | 3.5 | 30 | Buntzen Ridge |
| | | | 3.5 | 41 | TCT/Nelson Creek Loop |
| 3 | 35 | Coquitlam River/ Town Centre Park | 3.5 | 42 | Lighthouse Park (long circuit) |
| 3 | 36 | PoCo Trail (along the Pitt R) | 3.5 | 45 | Whyte Lake Loop |
| 3 | 37 | Woodland Walk | 3.5 | 51 | Hollyburn Heritage Trails |
| 3 | 44 | Caulfeild Trail/ Klootchman Park | 3.5 | 71 | Lulu Island Dykes (West Dyke) |
| 3 | 47 | Hollyburn Mountain | 3.5 | 90 | UBC Malcolm Knapp Research Forest |
| 3 | 53 | Capilano Canyon (from Keith Road) | | | |
| 3 | 54 | Bowser Trail | 3.5 | 93 | Gold Creek Trails (Gold Cr Lookout) |
| 3 | 55 | Baden-Powell Trail (Grouse Mtn: original) | 3.5 | 93 | Gold Creek Trails (Viewpoint Beach) |

| TIME (HRS) | # | WALK NAME |
|---|---|---|
| 3.5 | 95 | Hayward Lake (Railway Tr) |
| 3.5* | 71 | Lulu Island Dykes (Middle Arm & W. Dyke) |
| 4 | 8 | English Bay |
| 4 | 32 | Buntzen Lake (short loop) |
| 4 | 36 | PoCo Trail (along the Coquitlam R) |
| 4 | 50 | Brothers Creek Trails |
| 4 | 53 | Capilano Canyon (from Ambleside Pk) |
| 4 | 61 | Fisherman's Trail |
| 4 | 65 | Three Chop/Old Buck Loop (short loop) |
| 4 | 82 | Campbell Valley |
| 4 | 85 | Seven Sisters Trail (high level) |
| 4 | 89 | Grant Narrows (long loop) |
| 4 | 99 | Shannon Falls (to high bluff) |
| 4 | 103 | Evans Lake Forest (ridge circuit) |
| 4 | 107 | Crater Rim Loop |
| 4* | 36 | PoCo Trail (from Red Bridge to Dominion) |
| 4.5 | 5 | Point Grey |
| 4.5 | 48 | Lower Hollyburn |
| 4.5 | 63 | Northlands Bridle Path |
| 4.5 | 88 | Alouette River Dykes |
| 5 | 17 | Barnet Trails (with Burnaby Mtn) |
| 5 | 32 | Buntzen Lake (long loop) |
| 5 | 37 | Woodland Walks (Coquitlam L viewpt) |
| 5 | 65 | Three Chop/Old Buck Loop (long loop) |

| TIME (HRS) | # | WALK NAME |
|---|---|---|
| 5 | 103 | Evans Lake Forest (to Hut Lakes) |
| 5.5 | 95 | Hayward Lake (Hayward Reservoir circuit) |

\* one-way

\+ or longer

## ROUND-TRIP DISTANCES

| DISTANCE (KM) | # | WALK NAME |
|---|---|---|
| 2 | 99 | Shannon Falls (to Olesen Cr) |
| 3 | 52 | Ballantree |
| 3 | 59 | Rice Lake (from LSCR) |
| 3 | 68 | Mystery Lake (to lake) |
| 3 | 94 | Kanaka Creek (Riverfront Tr) |
| 3+ | 46 | Cypress Falls Park |
| 3.2 | 73 | Richmond Nature Park |
| 3.3 | 62 | Maplewood Flats |
| 3.5 | 94 | Kanaka Creek (Canyon Loop) |
| 3.9 | 4 | Chancellor Woods (short circuit) |
| 4 | 1 | UBC Gardens (North) |
| 4 | 2 | UBC Botanical Garden |
| 4 | 17 | Barnet Trails (Barnet & Cougar Cr) |
| 4 | 75 | Boundary Bay (south section) |
| 4 | 78 | South Surrey Urban Forests (Sunnyside Ac) |
| 4 | 78 | South Surrey Urban Forests (Crescent Pk) |

| DISTANCE (KM) | # | WALK NAME | DISTANCE (KM) | # | WALK NAME |
|---|---|---|---|---|---|
| 4 | 83 | Aldergrove Lake (short circuit) | 5.1 | 58 | Lynn Headwaters Loop (Lynn Loop Tr) |
| 4 | 87 | Chatham Reach (from Harris Rd) | 5.2 | 31 | Belcarra Regional Park (to Burns Pt) |
| 4 | 89 | Grant Narrows (southern loop) | 5.3 | 69 | Baden-Powell Trail (Deep Cove) |
| 4 | 102 | DeBeck Hill | 5.5 | 3 | Pacific Spirit Regional Park (east to west) |
| 4.4 | 74 | Deas Island | 5.5 | 18 | Burnaby Mountainside Trails (short loop) |
| 4.5 | 53 | Capilano Canyon (from park road) | 5.5 | 23 | Deer Lake |
| 4.5 | 68 | Mystery Lake (to peak) | 5.5 | 25 | Molson Way (South) |
| 4.5 | 70 | Indian Arm Parks (short circuit) | 5.5 | 31 | Belcarra Regional Park (to Jug Island) |
| 4.6 | 96 | Bear Mountain Trails | 5.5 | 49 | McDonald/Lawson Creek Loop |
| 4.8 | 80 | Tynehead Regional Park | | | |
| 4.8 | 85 | Seven Sisters Trail (low level) | 5.5 | 79 | Green Timbers Urban Forest (Walk 2) |
| 5- | 39 | Whytecliff | 5.6 | 91 | Mike Lake |
| 5 | 11 | Renfrew Triangle | 5.7 | 105 | Brohm Lake |
| 5 | 13 | Burnaby Heights/TCT | 6 | 4 | Chancellor Woods (long circuit) |
| 5 | 15 | Burnaby Mountain West/SFU (short circuit) | 6 | 7 | Jericho Park/Spanish Banks |
| 5 | 22 | Deer Lake Park West | 6 | 40 | Seaview/Larsen Bay |
| 5 | 28 | Shoreline Trail | 6 | 55 | Baden-Powell Trail (Grouse Mtn: original) |
| 5 | 34 | Ridge Park Loop | | | |
| 5 | 42 | Lighthouse Park (short circuit) | 6 | 57 | Mahon Park |
| 5 | 43 | Sahalee/Caulfeild Loop | 6 | 66 | Goldie Lake |
| 5 | 55 | Baden-Powell Trail (Grouse Mtn: current) | 6 | 67 | Dog Mountain (direct) |
| | | | 6 | 79 | Green Timbers Urban Forest (Walk 1) |
| 5 | 77 | Redwood Park | 6 | 92 | Alouette Nature Loop |
| 5 | 86 | Teapot Hill | 6 | 101 | Four Lakes Trail |
| 5 | 97 | Mission Trail | 6 | 108 | Cheakamus Lake |
| 5 | 99 | Shannon Falls (to high bluff) | | | |

| DISTANCE (KM) | # | WALK NAME | DISTANCE (KM) | # | WALK NAME |
|---|---|---|---|---|---|
| 6.4 | 64 | Historic Mushroom Loop | 8 | 37 | Woodland Walk |
| 6.5 | 14 | Capitol Hill | 8 | 47 | Hollyburn Mountain |
| 6.5 | 38 | Minnekhada Regional Park | 8 | 53 | Capilano Canyon (from Keith Road) |
| 6.5 | 89 | Grant Narrows (Katzie Marsh) | 8 | 59 | Rice Lake (from Lynn Headwaters) |
| 6.5 | 109 | Shadow Lake Interpretive Forest | 8 | 60 | Two-Canyon Loop |
| 6.7 | 51 | Hollyburn Heritage Trails | 8 | 67 | Dog Mountain (via Dinkey Peak) |
| 6.8 | 56 | Mosquito Creek | 8 | 75 | Boundary Bay (north section) |
| 7 | 10 | Stanley Park | 8 | 76 | Elgin Heritage Park |
| 7 | 27 | Mundy Lake | 8 | 81 | Derby Reach Regional Park |
| 7 | 45 | Whyte Lake Loop | 8 | 90 | UBC Malcolm Knapp Research Forest |
| 7 | 83 | Aldergrove Lake (long circuit) | 8 | 93 | Gold Creek Trails (Gold Cr Lookout) |
| 7 | 100 | Squamish Estuary | 8 | 93 | Gold Creek Trails (Viewpoint Beach) |
| 7.2 | 33 | Colony Farm | 8 | 98 | Killarney Lake |
| 7.2 | 44 | Caulfeild Trail/ Klootchman Park | 8 | 103 | Evans Lake Forest (ridge circuit) |
| 7.5+ | 54 | Bowser Trail | 8 | 106 | Brandywine/Cal-Cheak |
| −8 | 26 | Burnaby Fraser Foreshore Park | 8 | 107 | Crater Rim Loop |
| −8 | 104 | Brohm Lake Interpretive Forest | 8.5 | 15 | Burnaby Mountain West/SFU (long circuit) |
| 8 | 3 | Pacific Spirit Regional Park (north to south) | 8.8 | 36 | PoCo Trail (along the Pitt R) |
| 8 | 12 | Champlain Heights | 9 | 6 | Musqueam/Fraser River |
| 8 | 16 | Burnaby Mountain | 9 | 35 | Coquitlam River/ Town Centre Park |
| 8 | 19 | SFU/Stoney Creek | 9 | 41 | TCT/Nelson Creek Loop |
| 8 | 21 | Brunette River | 9 | 42 | Lighthouse Park (long circuit) |
| 8 | 29 | Sasamat Lake/ Woodhaven Swamp | 9 | 70 | Indian Arm Parks (long circuit) |
| 8 | 30 | Buntzen Ridge | | | |
| 8 | 32 | Buntzen Lake (short loop) | | | |

| DISTANCE (KM) | # | WALK NAME | DISTANCE (KM) | # | WALK NAME |
|---|---|---|---|---|---|
| 9 | 71 | Lulu Island Dykes (Middle Arm & Terra Nova) | 12 | 95 | Hayward Lake (Railway Tr) |
| 9.5 | 37 | Woodland Walks (Coquitlam L viewpt) | 12.5 | 36 | PoCo Trail (along the Coquitlam R) |
| 9.5 | 58 | Lynn Headwaters Loop (to debris chute) | 12.5* | 36 | PoCo Trail (from Red Bridge to Dominion) |
| 9.5 | 65 | Three Chop/Old Buck Loop (short loop) | 13- | 8 | English Bay |
| 9.8 | 18 | Burnaby Mountainside Trails (long loop) | 13 | 5 | Point Grey |
| | | | 13 | 65 | Three Chop/Old Buck Loop (long loop) |
| 10- | 32 | Buntzen Lake (long loop) | 13 | 103 | Evans Lake Forest (to Hut Lakes) |
| 10 | 9 | False Creek | | | |
| 10 | 17 | Barnet Trails (with Inlet Trail) | 14 | 17 | Barnet Trails (with Burnaby Mtn) |
| 10 | 24 | Molson Way (Central) | 14.5 | 88 | Alouette River Dykes |
| 10 | 85 | Seven Sisters Trail (high level) | 17 | 95 | Hayward Lake (Hayward Reservoir circuit) |
| 10 | 87 | Chatham Reach (from Alouette Br) | | | |
| 10* | 71 | Lulu Island Dykes (Middle Arm & W. Dyke) | | | * one-way distance |
| 10.4* | 84 | Matsqui Trail | | | + or longer |
| 11 | 20 | Burnaby Lake | | | – or shorter |
| 11 | 50 | Brothers Creek Trails | | | |
| 11 | 63 | Northlands Bridle Path | | | |
| 11.5 | 61 | Fisherman's Trail | | | |
| 12- | 82 | Campbell Valley | | | |
| 12- | 48 | Lower Hollyburn | | | |
| 12 | 53 | Capilano Canyon (from Ambleside Pk) | | | |
| 12 | 71 | Lulu Island Dykes (West Dyke) | | | |
| 12 | 72 | Richmond South Dyke Trail | | | |
| 12 | 89 | Grant Narrows (long loop) | | | |

## ACKNOWLEDGEMENTS

"A book such as this could not have come into being had not we received the assistance of many others, friends and casual informants, as well as representatives of numerous official bodies," wrote Mary Macaree in her introduction to the fifth edition. "To all of these we must express our sincere thanks for their patience and the hope that the resulting product will give them the sense that their time was not ill-spent."

This sixth edition is a clear expression of how much Mary and David's friends and the hiking community as a whole valued their camaraderie, their knowledge and their books. When Mary passed away in July 2008, she had updated nearly two thirds of the walks in this book. Members of the Wednesday and Sunday walking groups, who had accompanied her on many of these hikes, continued to check the trails and the veracity of the instructions even without Mary or David to lead the way. Many family members and friends gave unstintingly of their time and energy to ferret out files and photographs, review and amend text and maps, make corrections and assist in bringing this edition to publication. Without their help, their enthusiasm and curiosity about the publishing process and their unswerving commitment to this book, a sixth edition of *109 Walks* would not have been possible.

Our wish, like Mary and David's, is that their labour of love continue to provide pleasure to all who use it.

# INDEX

Aldergrove Lake Regional Park, 170
Alice Lake Provincial Park, 206
Alouette Nature Loop, 188
Alouette River, 178, 180, 185
Annand/Rowlatt Farmstead, 169
Avalon Pond, 29

B.C.: Bearing Plaza, 55; Native Garden,
    9; Parkway, 2, 26, 52, 54
Baden-Powell Trail, 2, 99, 108, 109,
    124, 131, 132; Deep Cove, 142; Grouse
    Mountain, 114. *See also* Skyline Trail
Ballantree, 108
Barnet Trails, 38
Bates Park, 30
Beaconsfield Park, 27
Bear Mountain Trails, 196
Beaver Creek, 50
Beaver Lake, 25
Belcarra Regional Park, 66
Bell-Irving Fish Hatchery, 192
Blue Gentian Lake, 101, 105
Blue Mountain, 192
Booming Grounds Rock, 17
Boundary Bay Regional Park, 154
Bowen Island, 200
Bowser Trail, 112
Brandywine/Cal-Cheak, 216
British Columbia. *See* B.C.
Brohm Lake, 214
Brohm Lake Interpretive Forest, 212
Brothers Creek, 104, 107, 111
Brothers Creek Trails, 104
Brown Creek, 195
Brunette River, 45, 46
Buntzen Lake, 68
Buntzen Ridge, 64

Burnaby: Fraser Foreshore Park,
    56; Heights/Trans Canada Trail,
    30; Lake, 44; Lake Regional Park,
    46; Scenic Trail, 31, 32
Burnaby Mountain, 36, 38, 42;
    Conservation Area, 34, 35, 39;
    -side Trails, 40; West/SFU, 34
Burrard Inlet, 60, 88
Butterfly Garden, 127
Byrne Creek, 52, 53, 55, 57

Cal-Cheak/Brandywine, 216
Callaghan Creek, 216
Campbell Valley, 168
Candelabra tree, 107
Canyon Creek, 131
Capilano Canyon, 110
Capitol Hill, 32
Captain Cook Park, 29
Cardiac Hill (Burnaby), 35, 42
Cardiac Hill (North Vancouver), 131
Cates Park, 144
Caulfeild Trail/Klootchman Park, 92
Cedars Mill, 121
Celtic Island, 17
Centennial Park, 36
Centennial Trail, 42, 172
Central Park, 52
Century Park, 51
Champlain Heights, 28
Chancellor Woods, 12
Charleson Park, 22
Chatham Reach, 178
Cheakamus Lake, 220
Cheakamus River, 210, 216, 217, 219, 220
Cheekye River, 207
Cliff Falls, 192

Colony Farm Regional Park, 70
Community Gardens, 70
Confederation Park, 31, 33
Cooper's Park, 23
Coquitlam Lake View Trail, 79
Coquitlam River, 70, 76; Park, 74, 77;
    and Town Centre Park, 74
Crater Rim Loop, 218
Crescent Park, 160
Crippen Regional Park, 200
Cultus Lake, 174
Cultus Lake Provincial Park, 176
Cypress Falls Park, 96
Cypress Provincial Park, 98

Daisy Lake, 216
David C. Lam Asian Garden, 8
David Lam Park, 23
Deas Island, 152
DeBeck Hill, 208
De Boville Slough, 77
Deep Cove: Baden-Powell Trail, 142;
    Lookout, 135; Park, 144
Deer Lake, 50; Brook, 45; Park West, 48
Deering Island, 17
Delta Centennial Beach, 155
Derby Reach Regional Park, 166
Dinkey Peak, 139
Dog Mountain, 138
Dorman Point, 201
Douglas Taylor Park, 173
Dutch Mile (garden), 53

Eagle Harbour, 84
Eagle Mountain, 72
East Point, 21
Edgewater Bar, 166
E.H. Lohbrunner Alpine Garden, 9
Elgin Heritage Park, 156
English Bay, 18, 20, 24
Evans Lake Forest, 210
Everett Crowley Park, 28, 29

False Creek, 22
Fawn Lake, 206, 207
Finnie's garden, 71
Finn Slough, 148
Fisherman's Trail, 124, 126

Fish Fence, 193
Flower Lake, 137
Forest Ecology Loop Trail, 123
Forest Glen Park, 49
Fort Langley (original), 166
Fort-to-Fort Trail, 167
Four Lakes Trail, 206
Francis Creek, 134
Fraser River, 54, 56, 152, 172, 192;
    Heritage Park, 198; Middle Arm,
    146; Musqueam, 16; North Arm, 11,
    14, 16; South Arm, 148; Trail, 166
Fraser Valley Regional Trail, 173

Garibaldi Provincial Park, 220
Garry Point Park, 147, 149
Gates Park, 77
George Wainborn Park, 23
Gladstone Park, 57
Gold Creek Trails, 190
Golden Ears Provincial Park, 186, 188, 190
Goldie Lake, 136
Grant Narrows Regional Park, 182
Granville Island, 20, 21, 22, 23
Gravesend Reach, 152
Green Timbers Urban Forest, 162
Grimston Park, 55
Grotto of Our Lady of Lourdes, 198
Grouse Mountain (Baden-Powell Trail), 114

Habitat Island, 23
Hadden Park, 21
Hairsine Inlet, 195
Harbourview Park, 33
Hayward Lake, 194
Heritage Harbour, 21
Heritage Park, 157
Heywood Park, 113
Historic Mushroom Loop, 132
Hollyburn: Douglas-fir, 107; Heritage
    Trails, 106; Mountain, 98, 100, 108
Horseshoe Slough, 148
Hoy Creek, 73
Hume Park, 46
Hut (Hud) Lakes, 210
Hyde Creek, 77

Indian Arm Parks, 144

Jericho Beach, 18
Jericho Park/Spanish Banks, 16
John Hendry Park, 26
John Molson Way. *See* Molson Way
Jug Island Beach, 66

Kanaka Creek, 192
Kensington Park, 32
Keswick Park, 43
Killarney Lake, 200
King Creek, 163
Kitsilano Park, 21
Klootchman Park/Caulfeild Trail, 92

Lafarge Lake, 75
Lake Beautiful, 69
Larsen Bay Beach, 85
Larsen Bay/Seaview, 84
Lava Lake, 216
Lawson Creek Loop/McDonald Creek, 102
Levette Lake, 210
Lighthouse Park, 88, 93
Lions Park, 77
Locarno Beach, 19
Logger's Lake, 219
Lookout Hill, 21, 23
Lost Lagoon, 25
Lost Lake, 59
Lower Burke Ridge (Woodland Walks), 78
Lower Hollyburn, 100
Lower Seymour Conservation
    Reserve (LSCR), 122, 124
Lulu Island Dykes, 146
Lynn Creek: Canyon Park, 124;
    Headwaters Loop, 120;
    Headwaters Regional Park, 123

Mackay Creek, 113, 115
Mahon Park, 118
Malcolm Knapp Research Forest (UBC), 184
Maplewood Flats Wildlife Sanctuary, 128
Matsqui Trail, 172
McDonald Canyon, 107
McDonald Creek/Lawson Creek Loop, 102
Mike Lake, 186
Minnekhada Regional Park, 80
Mission: Creek, 119; Municipal
    Forest, 195, 196; Trail, 198

Molson Way, 2, 26; Central, 52; South, 54
Mosquito Creek, 116
Mount Everett, 29
Mount Seymour, 134
Mount Seymour Provincial Park,
    132, 136, 138, 140
Mundy Lake, 59
Mundy Park, 58
Musqueam/Fraser River, 16
Mystery Creek, 131
Mystery Lake and Peak, 140

Naheeno Park, 37
Nelson Creek Loop/Trans Canada Trail, 86
Nicomekl River, 156
Nitobe Memorial Garden, 7
Noons Creek, 61
North Alouette River, 185
Northlands Bridle Path, 130
North Shore Mountains, 86

Old Buck/Three Chop Loop, 134
Old Buck Trail, 132
Old Orchard Park, 60
Olesen Creek, 202
Olympic Village, 23

Pacific Spirit Regional Park, 10, 12, 15
Page Lake, 173
Panorama Park, 142, 144
Paramount Pond, 149
Physic Garden, 9
Pioneer Park, 18, 19
Pitt Lake, 183
Pitt River, 76, 77, 178
Plaza of Nations, 23
PoCo Trail, 71, 76
Point Atkinson, 88
Point Grey, 14, 18

Rainbow Bridge, 193
Redwood Park, 158
Renfrew Ravine Park, 26, 27
Renfrew Triangle, 26
Rhododendron Garden, 53
Rice Lake, 122
Richmond Nature Park, 150
Richmond South Dyke Trail, 148

Ridge Park Loop, 72
Rocky Point Park, 60
Ron McLean Park, 52, 55

Sahalee/Caulfeild Loop, 90
St. Mary's Mission, 198
Sasamat Lake/Woodhaven Swamp, 62
Schara Tzedeck Cemetery, 54
Scott-Goldie Creek, 137
Sears Garden, 53
Seaview/Larsen Bay, 84
Second Beach, 24
Serpentine River, 164
Seven Sisters Trail, 174
Seymour River, 126, 131, 138
Shadow Lake Interpretive Forest, 222
Shaggy Mane Trail, 168
Shannon Falls, 202
Shoreline Trail (Port Moody), 60
Silver Summit, 211
Simon Fraser University (SFU),
    34, 36; Burnaby Mountain West,
    34; Stoney Creek, 42
Singing Creek, 221
Siwash Rock, 25
Skyline Trail, 100, 105, 107, 109, 211
SkyTrain stations: Edmonds, 52, 53, 54,
    55; Metrotown, 52; Nanaimo, 26;
    New Westminster, 54; Patterson, 52;
    22nd Street, 54; 29th Avenue, 26
Slaughterhouse Creek, 60
Snug Cove, 200
Soo River, 223
South Surrey Urban Forests, 160
Spanish Banks/Jericho Park, 16
Squamish Estuary, 204
Stamp's Landing, 23
Stanley Park, 20, 24
Stave Falls, 194
Steelhead Creek and Falls, 195
Steveston Park, 149
Stewart Farm, 157
Still Creek, 27, 45
Stoney Creek, 42, 47
Stump Lake, 206
Sturgeon Bank, 146, 147
Sugar Mountain Trail, 64
Suicide Bluffs, 139

Suspension Bridge 2000, 219
Swamp Lantern Interpretive Trail, 207
Swan Falls, 69
Swim Lake, 216

Teapot Hill, 176
Tenderfoot Fish Hatchery, 215
Terminus Park, 57
Terra Nova Rural Park, 147
Three Chop/Old Buck Loop, 134
Town Centre Park/Coquitlam River, 74
Trans Canada Trail (TCT), 34, 39, 74, 77, 94,
    101, 108, 173, 180; Burnaby Heights, 30;
    Burnaby Scenic, 30, 32; Joe's, 36; Nelson
    Creek Loop, 86; Skyline, 100, 105, 107
Trout Lake (Coquitlam), 69
Trout Lake (Vancouver), 26, 27
Two-Canyon Loop, 124
Tynehead Regional Park, 164
Tynehead Salmon Hatchery, 164

University of British Columbia (UBC):
    Botanical Garden, 8; Chancellor
    Woods, 12; Gardens, 6; Malcolm Knapp
    Research Forest, 184; Pacific Spirit
    Regional Park, 10; Point Grey, 14

Vanier Park, 21
Variety Park, 53
Viewpoint Beach, 191

Wagg Creek, 118
Waterfront Park, 57
Westminster Abbey, 198
Westwood Plateau, 72
wheelchair accessible walks, 122, 160
Whistler Interpretive Forest, 218
Whyte: Creek, 94; Islet, 82; Lake Loop, 94
Whytecliff, 82
Wickenden Park, 144
William Griffin Park, 116
Windermere Creek, 63
Windfall Creek, 174
Woodhaven Swamp/Sasamat Lake, 62
Woodland Walks (Lower Burke Ridge), 78
Woodward Park, 102
Woodward Slough, 149
Wreck Beach, 15